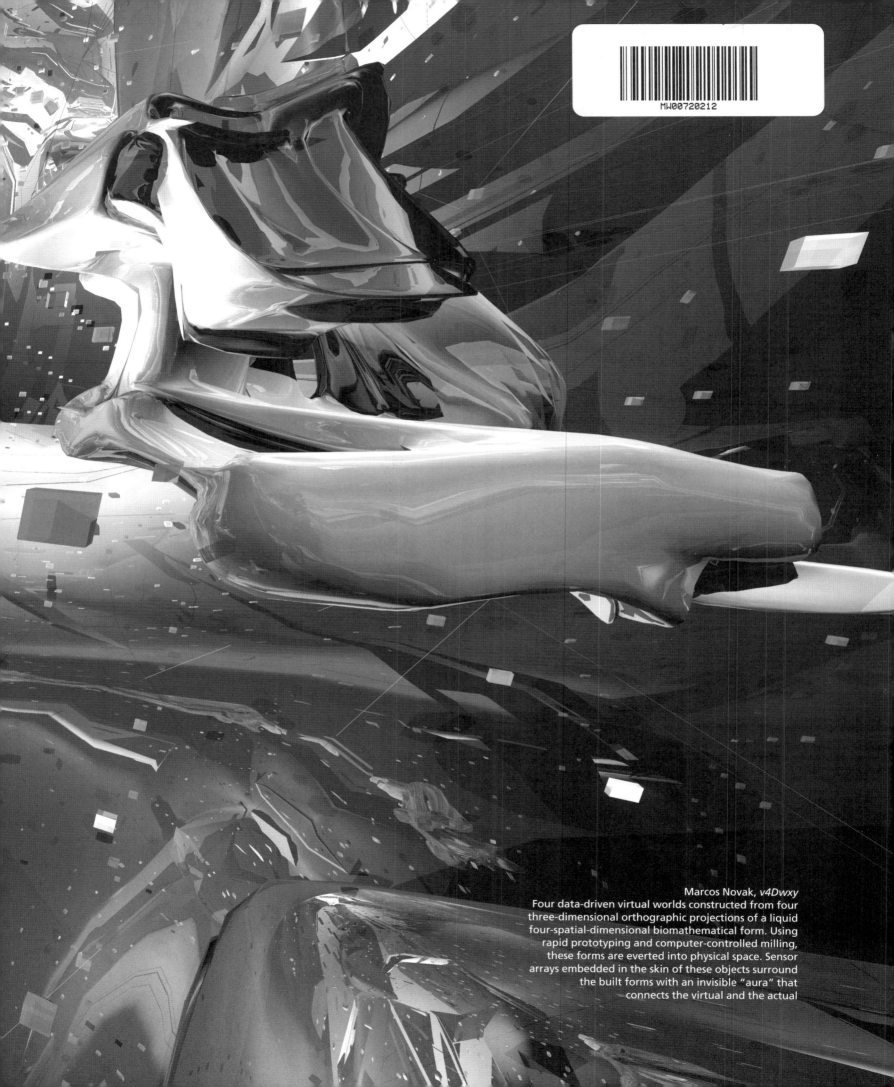

Marcos Novak, *v4Dwxy*
Four data-driven virtual worlds constructed from four
three-dimensional orthographic projections of a liquid
four-spatial-dimensional biomathematical form. Using
rapid prototyping and computer-controlled milling,
these forms are everted into physical space. Sensor
arrays embedded in the skin of these objects surround
the built forms with an invisible "aura" that
connects the virtual and the actual

innovation

Future Systems, Selfridges Birmingham, detail of façade

A glass wind-tunnel corridor bridging a snow-covered wasteland: that was the bleak techno-meets-nature setting for Alexander McQueen's fall show in Paris

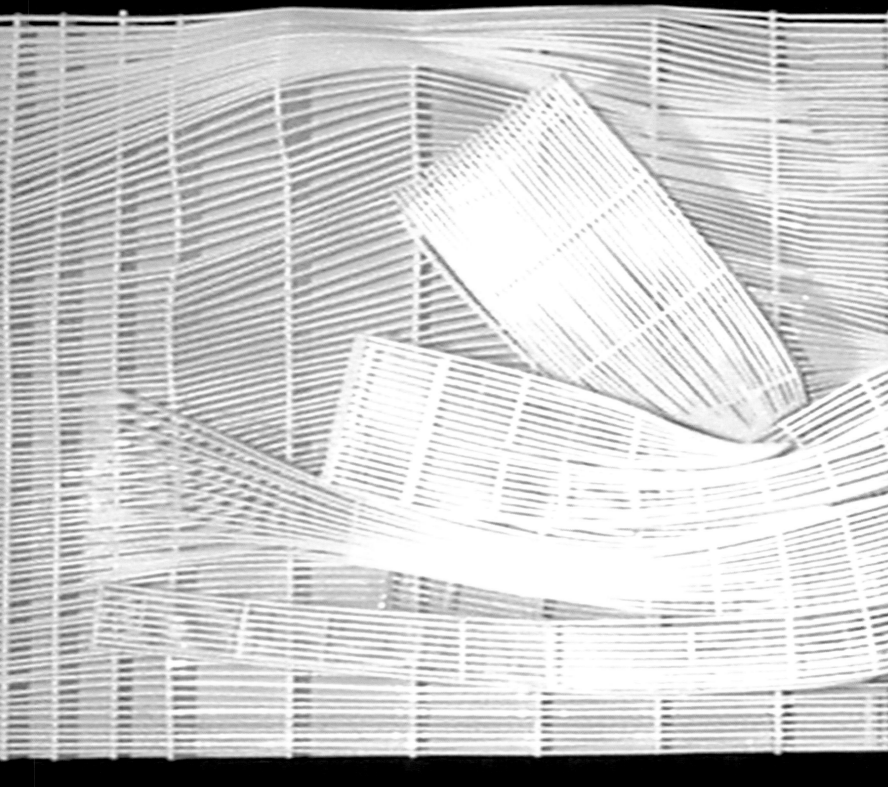

ALEXANDRA & ANDREAS PAPADAKIS

innovation

from experimentation
to realisation

Reiser + Umemoto, Sagaponac House, plan view of model

NEW**ARCH** • 07

Head Office New Architecture Group Ltd
16 Grosvenor Place
London SW1X 7HH
United Kingdom

Tel. +44 (0)20 7823 2323
Fax +44 (0)20 7823 2322
email info@newarchitecture.net

Editor-in-Chief Dr Andreas C Papadakis

Editor Alexandra Papadakis

Assistant Editor Xenia Adjoubei

Design Director Aldo Sampieri

Editorial Board Tadao Ando • Mario Botta •
Peter Eisenman • Dimitri
Fatouros • Colin Fournier •
Kenneth Frampton • Jorge
Glusberg • Michael Graves •
Allan Greenberg • Hans
Hollein • Josef Paul Kleihues
• Léon Krier • Kisho
Kurokawa • Daniel Libeskind
• Richard Meier • Marcos
Novak • Cesar Pelli • Paolo
Portoghesi • Peter Pran •
Hani Rashid • Jacquelin
Robertson • Robert A.M.
Stern • Bernard Tschumi

Subscriptions to New Architecture Magazine
are available for four consecutive numbers

Institutions: £100 / $150
Individuals: £75 / $115
Students: £50 / $75

prices inclusive of postage & packaging

Printed and bound in Singapore

EDITORIAL

THEORY

Marcos Novak, *v4Dwxy*

FEATURED PROJECTS

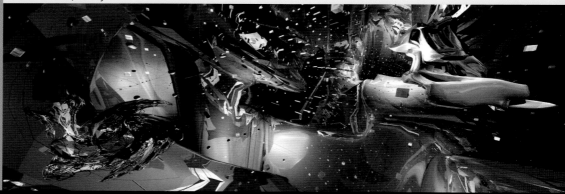

COVER ILLUSTRATIONS:

PHOTOGRAPH: **Nicole Tran Ba Vang**
Collection Printemps/été 2001, Sans Titre 06
DRAWING: **Uli Blum, Dillon Lin, Jon Ritter**
ConEx Space (Contractive-Expansive Space),
sought to address the highly dynamic nature
of corporate organisations. A topographical
secondary infrastructure is grafted to existing
office blocks and through its fluid and folding
surfaces, allows for extended and continuous
corporate territories to interweave. These
territories have the flexibility to appropriate,

ACKNOWLEDGMENTS

We are pleased to welcome two new members of our
editorial board: **Colin Fournier** and **Marcos Novak**. We
are grateful to all who have made this volume possible,
especially the members of the board and the many
architects, artists and designers who have generously
contributed material for publication. We wish to thank
Richard P. Taylor, **Marcos Novak** and **Lars Spuybroek** for
their articles and **Continuum Press** for permission to
reproduce substantial extracts from *Art and Fear* by
Paul Virilio; **Marcos Lutyens** for his illuminating performances of *Second Skin* in London and Birmingham.

Juda for allowing us to publish images from *Painting
on Paper*, to **Jenny Holzer** and to **Peter Pran** and **Siri
Blakstad** for drawing these works to our attention.
Nicole Tran Ba Vang for her generous hospitality and
for lending material for reproduction. The art and
design section is highly enriched by contributions from
exhibitions at **Tate Modern London, Guggenheim New
York, Graz 2003 Cultural Capital of Europe;** and **The
Venice Biennale** for **Arata Isosaki's** *City of Girls* and
much more. We owe a great debt to **Alexander
McQueen, Nick Knight** and **SHOWstudio** whose work
greatly enriched the fashion section; and special thanks
to **Mary McCartney Donald** for her exciting hand-

C O N T E N T S

ARCHITECTURE · ART · DESIGN · MEDIA · FASHION

SHOWstudio + Nick Knight design for Massive Attack's *100th Window*

Innovation and Beyond

Andreas & Alexandra Papadakis

Innovation (inõvei∫en)
the alteration of what is established
or, more forcefully,
revolution, rebellion or insurrection

New technologies and new philosophical concepts have converted what was once wishful thinking and referred to disparagingly as 'paper ideas' into a world suddenly full of exciting architectural forms. Today, in the words of Wolf Prix, 'You can only succeed in architecture if you are doing visionary buildings in terms of programme, shape and structure.' These new ideas, inspired also by science and the space industry, have filtered through to the worlds of business, sport, shopping and entertainment. This is not innovation for the sake of innovation but art and architecture based on carefully considered ideas that enhance and add visually to our experience of life today.

It used to be said that artists have the uncanny ability to see what is wrong with the world, and then turn it into art. The artist was regarded as an agent provocateur. Nowadays the situation is a little more complex. With the lowering of the boundaries between the disciplines, architects and leaders in the design world are joining an elite group of thinkers who can influence changes in society outside their traditional territories.

Indeed, Baudrillard predicts that "there still exists beyond all illusion or disillusion a future for architecture… even if that future is not necessarily architectural." By extension, entire disciplines will need to search for new territories.

But Paul Virilio's vision of both art and science today is pessimistic and the advent of terrorism came as no surprise to him in a world where we are in danger of becoming 'the negationists of art'.

But as Marcos Novak explains, with the advent of nanotechnology we stand at the threshold of a major new technological advance. "the control of the construction of the world from the grains up. As the shift to the digital fades into ordinariness, computation and its corollaries become the given upon which a transition to an ever stranger, *alien* reality is being built."

Paul Virilio

Art and Fear

Paul Virilio, *Art and Fear*
Continuum, London and New York,2003
ISBN 0 8264 6080 1

In the recent book entitled "Art and Fear" Paul Virilio presents his pessimistic vision of a world where art and science vie to destroy the human form. He reveals with brutal logic the inevitable progression, from the beginning of the twentieth century to today, from the tortured human form of the avant-garde and its disappearance in abstraction to the trenches of the Great War; from the portraits of the damned by the German Expressionists to the 'medical' experiments of the Nazi eugenicists; from sensationalist advertising and experiments such as Dr von Hagen's corpses to terrorism.
The first extracts are from the essay entitled "A Pitiless Art".

If so-called old-master art remained *demonstrative* right up until the nineteenth century with Impressionism, the art of the twentieth century became '*monstrative*' in the sense that it is contemporary with the *shattering effect* of mass societies, subject as they are to the conditioning of opinion and MASS MEDIA propaganda – and this, with the same *mounting extremism* evident in terrorism or total war.

At the end of the millennium, what abstraction once tried to pull off is in fact being accomplished before our very eyes: the end of REPRESENTATIVE art and and the substitution of a counter-culture, of a PRESENTATIVE art. A situation that reinforces the dreadful decline of *representative democracy* in favour of a democracy based on the rule of opinion, in anticipation of the imminent arrival of *virtual democracy*, some kind of 'direct democracy' or, more precisely, a *presentative* multi-media democracy based on automatic polling.

In the end, 'modern art' was able to glean what communications and telecommunications tools now accomplish on a daily basis: the *mise en abyme* of the body, of the figure, with the major attendant risk of *systematic* hyperviolence and a boom in pornographic high-frequency that has nothing to do with sexuality: *We must put out the excess rather than the fire*, as Heraclitus warned.

Today, with excess heaped on excess, desensitization to the shock of images and the meaninglessness of words has shattered the world stage. PITILESS, contemporary art is no longer improper. But it shows all the impropriety of profaners and torturers, all the arrogance of the executioner.

The intelligence of REPRESENTATION then gives way to the stunned mullet effect of a 'presence' that is not only weird, as in the days of Surrealism, but insulting to the mind. The whole process, moreover, implies that the 'image' suffices to give art its meaning and significance. At one extreme the artist, like the journalist, is redundant in the face-off between performer and viewer.

'Such a conception of information leads to a disturbing fascination with images *filmed live*, with scenes of violence and gruesome human interest stories', Ignacio Ramonet writes on the impact of television on the print media. 'This demand encourages the supply of fake documents, sundry reconstructions and conjuring tricks.'[2]

But surely we could say the same today of art when it comes down to it. Take the example of the NEW NEUROTIC REALISM of adman and collector, Charles Saatchi, as revealed in the London (and New York) exhibition, '*Sensation*', with its fusion/confusion of the TABLOID and some sort of would-be avant-garde art. Yet the conformism of abjection is never more than a habit the twentieth century has enjoyed spreading round the globe.

Here, the brutality is no longer so much aimed at warning as at destroying, paving the way for the actual torturing of the viewer, the listener, which will not be long coming thanks to that cybernetic artefact: *the interactive feed-back of virtual reality.*

If the contemporary author is redundant – see Picasso on *Guernica*[3] – and if the suicide rate has only kept accelerating in cultural circles to the point where it will soon be necessary to set up a WALL OF THE FEDERATED COMMUNE OF SUICIDES in museums (to match the wall of the federated communards of the Paris Commune in Père Lachaise cemetery), then make no mistake: the art lover's days are numbered!

This is how Rothko put it: 'I studied the figure. Only reluctantly did I realize it didn't correspond to my needs. Using human representation, for me, meant mutilating it'. Shot of all moral or emotional compromise, the painter seeks to move '*towards the elimination of all obstacles between the painter and the idea, between the idea and the onlooker*'.

This is the radiographic triumph of transparence, the way radiation of the real in architecture today goes hand in glove with the extermination of all intermediaries, of all that still resists revelation, pure and simple.

But this sudden OVEREXPOSURE of the work, as of those who look upon it, is accompanied by a violence that is not only 'symbolic', as before, but practical, since it affects the very intentionality of the painter.

...

Thirty years on, how can we fail to feel the concentration of accumulated hate in every square metre of the 'uncivil cities' of this fin de siècle?

...

Ethics or aesthetics? That is indeed the question at the dawn of the millennium. If freedom of SCIENTIFIC expression now actually has no more limits than freedom of ARTISTIC expression, where will *inhumanity* end in future?

After all the great periods of art, after the great schools such as the classical and the baroque, after contemporary expressionism, are we not now heading for that *great transgenic art* in which every pharmacy, every laboratory will launch its own 'lifestyles', its own transhuman fashions? A chimerical explosion worthy of featuring in some future *Salon of New Realities* — if not in a *Museum of Eugenic Art.*

As one critic recently put it: '*Artists have their bit to say about the laws of nature at this fin de siècle.*' What is urgently required is '*to define a new relationship between species, one that is not conceived in the loaded terms of bestiality*'.[4]

...

Already, more or less everywhere you turn, you hear the words that precede that fatal habituation to the banalization of excess. For certain philosophers the body is already no more than a phenomenon of memory, the remnants of an archaic body; and the human being, a mere biped, fragile of flesh and so slow to grow up and defend itself that the species should not have survived ...

To make up for this lack, this 'native infirmity' as they call it, echoing a phrase used by Leroi-Gourhan: man invented tools, prostheses and a whole technological corpus without which he would not have survived ... But this is a retrospective vision incapable of coming to terms with the outrageousness of the time that is approaching. Géricault, Picasso

and Dali, Galton and Mengele ... Who comes next?

Where will it end, this impiety of art, of the arts and crafts of this 'transfiguration' that not only fulfils the dreams of the German Expressionists but also those of the Futurists, those 'hate-makers' whose destructiveness Hans Magnus Enzensberger has dissected.

Remember Mayakovsky's war cry, that blast of poetic premonition: 'Let your axes dance on the bald skulls of the well-heeled egoists and grocers. Kill! Kill! Kill! One good thing: their skulls will make perfect ashtrays.'[5]

The following are extracts from the second essay entitled "Silence on Trial".

In a decidedly fin de siècle world, where the automobile questions its driver about the functioning of the handbrake or whether the seatbelt is buckled, where the refrigerator is gearing itself up to place the order at the supermarket, where your computer greets you of a morning with a hearty 'hello', surely we have to ask ourselves whether the silence of art can be sustained for much longer.

This goes even for the mobile phone craze that is part and parcel of the same thing, since it is now necessary to *impose silence* – in restaurants and places of worship or concert halls. One day, following the example of the campaign to combat nicotine addiction, it may well be necessary to put up signs of the 'Silence – Hospital' variety at the entrance to museums and exhibition halls to get all those 'communication machines' to shut up and put an end to the all too numerous cultural exercises in SOUND and LIGHT.

Machine for *seeing*, machine for *hearing*, once upon a time; machine for *thinking* very shortly with the boom in all things *digital* and the programmed abandonment of the *analogue*. How will *the silence of the infinite spaces of art* subsist, this silence that seems to terrify the makers of motors of any kind, from the logical inference motor of the computer to the research engine of the network of networks? All these questions that today remain unanswered make ENIGMAS of contemporary ethics and aesthetics.

With architecture, alas, the jig is already up. Architectonics has become an audio-visual art, the only question now being whether it will shortly go on to become a VIRTUAL ART. For sculpture, ever since Jean Tinguely and his 'Bachelor Machines', this has been merely a risk to be run. As for painting and the graphic arts, from the moment VIDEO ART hit the scene with the notion of the installation, it has been impossible to mention CONCEPTUAL ART without picking up the background noise of the mass media behind the words and objects of the art market.

Like TINNITUS, where a ringing in the ears perceived in the absence of external noise soon becomes unbearable, contemporary art's prosecution of silence is in the process of lastingly polluting our representations.

Having digested the critical impact of Marcel Duchamp's retinal art, let's hear what French critic, Patrick Vauday, had to say a little more recently:

"The passage from image to photography and then to cinema and, more recently still, to video and digital computer graphics, has surely had the effect of rendering painting magnificently *célibataire*. Painting has finally been released from the image-making function that till then more or less concealed its true essence. Notwithstanding the 'new' figurative art, it is not too far-fetched to see in the modern avatar of painting a *mise à nu* of its essence that is resolutely ICONOCLASTIC."[6]

At those words, you could be forgiven for fearing that the waxing twenty-first century was about to reproduce the first years of the twentieth, albeit unwittingly!

Under the guise of 'new technologies', surely what is really at work here is the actual CLONING, over and over, of some SUPER-, no, HYPER-ABSTRACTION that will be to virtual reality what HYPER-REALISM was to the photographic shot. This is happening at a time when someone like Kouichirou Eto, for instance, is gearing up to launch SOUND CREATURES on the Internet along with his own meta-musical ambient music!

What this means is a style of painting no only *without figures* but also *without images, a music of the spheres without sound*, presenting the symptoms of a *blinding* that would be the exact counterpart of the *silence of the lambs*. Speaking of the painter Turner, certain nineteenth-century aesthetes such as Hazlitt denounced the advent of '*pictures of nothing, and very like*'.[7] You can bet that soon, thanks to digital technology, *electro-acoustic* music will generate new forms of visual art. *Electro-optic* computer graphics will similarly erase the demarcation lines between the different art forms.

Once again, we will speak of a TOTAL ART – one no longer indebted to the cinematograph, that art which supposedly contained all the rest. Thanks to electronics, we will invent a GLOBAL ART, a 'single art', like the thinking that subtends the new information and communications technologies.

...

And so, after the SACRED ART of the age of divine right *monarchy* and after the contemporary PROFANE ART of the age of *democracy*, we will look on helplessly, or just about, as a PROFANED ART emerges in the image of the annihilated corpses of *tyranny*, anticipating the imminent cultural accident – the imposition of some multimedia 'official art'.

Art breakdown, contemporary with the damage done by technoscientific progress. If 'modern art' has been synonymous with the INDUSTRIAL revolution, 'postmodern art' is in effect contemporary with the INFORMATION revolution – that is, with the replacement of analogue languages by digital: the computation of sensations, whether visual, auditory, tactile or olfactory, *by software*. In other words: through a computer filter.

After the like, the ANALOGOUS, the age of the 'likely' – CLONE or AVATAR – has arrived, the industrial *standardization* of products manufactured in series combining with the standardization of sensations and emotions as a prelude to the development of cybernetics, with its attendant computer *synchronization*, the end product of which will be the virtual CYBERWORLD.[8]

Notes:

1 Paul Virilio, *Art and Fear*, translation by Julie Rose, Continuum, London and New York,2003.

2 Ignacio Ramonet, *La Tyrannie de la communication* (Paris: Galilée, 1999), pp. 190-91.

3 When a German interrogated Picasso in 1937 about his masterwork GUERNICA, he said: '*That's your doing, not mine!*'

4 Axel Kahn, "L'Acharnement procréatif', *Le Monde*, 16 March 1999.

5 *Ouest-France*, 12-14 March 1999.

6 Patrick Vauday, '*Y a-t-il une peinture sans image?*', a paper given at a seminar held by the Collège International de Philosophie, Paris.

7 Norbert Lynton, *The Story of Modern Art* (London/New York: Phaidon, 2001), p. 14, from Chapter I, 'The New Barbarians' (originally published 1980).

8 'Quite apart from the suppression of definitely heretical words, reduction of vocabulary was regarded as an end in itself, and no word that could be dispensed with was allowed to survive. Newspeak was designed not to extend but to diminish the range of thought, and this purpose was indirectly assisted by cutting the choice of words down to a minimum,' George Orwell, *Nineteen-Eighty-Four* (London: Penguin, 1989), p. 313 (first published 1949).

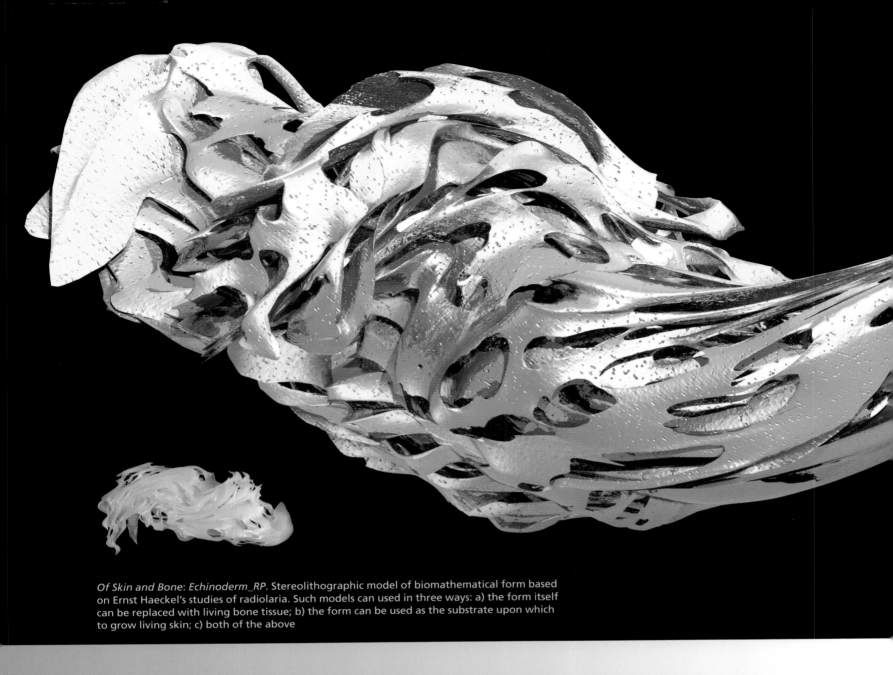

Of Skin and Bone: Echinoderm_RP. Stereolithographic model of biomathematical form based on Ernst Haeckel's studies of radiolaria. Such models can used in three ways: a) the form itself can be replaced with living bone tissue; b) the form can be used as the substrate upon which to grow living skin; c) both of the above

"I would like to describe a field, in which little has been done, but in which an enormous amount could be done in principle."

Richard Feynman, December 29, 1959

THE VERY SMALL

"There is plenty of room at the bottom." These were the words with which physicist Richard Feynman ignited what was to become the nanotechnology revolution. In his 1959 talk at the California Institute of Technology, Feynman demonstrated the vastness of the unexplored frontier of the very small. Forty years later, armed with computational devices that already take advantage of high miniaturization, we stand at the beginning of another major

technological advancement: the control of the construction of the world from the grains up. In many places around the world, nanotechnology research centres have begun to build the research foundation for a wave of new industries. As the shift to the digital fades into ordinariness, computation and its corollaries become the given upon which a transition to an ever stranger, alien reality is being built.

Nanometers measure the world at the scale of a billionth of a meter, the scale of atoms and molecules, and this brings us into direct contact with a level of control over matter that approximates that of animate nature itself in many regards. Feynman himself realized this in his talk, and drew

several of his examples from the biological. Nanotechnology tends to biotechnology. We cannot separate or overestimate the relation between nanotechnology and biotechnology, or that between the construction of new materials, molecule by molecule and atom by atom, and that of the mapping and inevitable alteration of the human genome, chromosome by chromosome, gene by gene, nucleotide by nucleotide, base by base.

The shift to this level of control of the world brings with it a paradoxical loss of control. As we reach into the world of the very small, the numbers of what we want to control swell beyond our capacity to dictate order from above. The world of the

Marcos Novak

Neuro~, Nano~, Bio~:

New Atomism And Living Nanotectonics

"Of all the species of the invisible, the most remote is the alien; and of all the species of the alien, the most ineffable is the alien within."

MN

very small is that world of the very many, and it requires strategies of distributed processing, assembly, and control. Like every other major technological shift, the shift to the very small requires an entirely different intellectual mode. This is a mode in which one must relinquish control in order to gain it, a mode in which, even more than in the case of the algorithmic, one lets go of the submicroscopic particular – that which consists of particles – in order to gain access to the scope of the macroscopic.

ABUNDANT COMPUTING

The question of the control of large numbers is not new to us – it is integral to our use of the digital. But the encounter with the very many brings up another issue: the pervasiveness of computation in nature: in quite a serious way, every particle of every grain of sand is a computer, and nature assembles itself by a computation that is ubiquitous and massively parallel. We are entering this arena of abundant computing as innocents to the lions. This is not to say that we must not enter – it is inevitable that we will; nor to say that we must be fearful – though we surely must be careful. It is simply to indicate how unprepared we are to think in this way, even though, in fact we do literally think this way: our consciousness itself depends on a similarly massive parallelism, constructed as it is neuron by neuron, synapse by synapse, neurotransmission by neurotransmission.

Nobel-prize laureate Gerald Edelman's theory of "neuronal group selection" shows how the genetic algorithm – Darwinism – is present in the formation of the brain, of memory, and even in the living moment of consciousness. This is the manner of operation we must capture and harness.

GROWING ARCHITECTURE

And what of Architecture? As always, there are numerous ways to draw impressionistic inspiration from the sciences of the very small, but the final challenge must surely be to once again reconceive Architecture, this time not as the built environment, but as

Invisible Architectures installation at the Venice Biennale. Rapid-prototyped three-dimensional orthographic projections of a liquid four-spatial-dimensional bio-mathematical form. Interspersed between the forms are invisible architectures created using infrared sensors that sensitize specific regions of space into distinct, interactivated shape. These precursors to the *AlloBio* project demonstrate the parallel exploration of virtual, actual, and invisible space, and anticipate that combination of a bio~ and nanoscale degree of control over form and its development with that concurrent

AlloBio: A new language for a living architecture, based in the premise of nanotechtonic control over form. Living physical presence is combined with full participation in information space and virtuality

▼

the grown environment. New materials have always implied new architecture; nanotechnology is combining with biotechnology to create materials that are not only new, but that stand at the border of the animate and the inanimate, tending toward the living. A corresponding architecture will surely follow. These materials must be seeded, grown, and nurtured; so must the buildings that are formed by the same processes.

But there can be no mistake: as living as these buildings may be, they will also participate in the worlds that we have built before them, and specifically, in the informational matrix of cyberspace that has already escaped from the confines of computers and screens and has spilled, wirelessly, into every crevice of our cities. These living architectures will be wirelessly wired, aware as much of themselves as to every aspect of knowledge and information we choose to put on the Internet, and every inference that can be drawn from that knowledge.

ATOMIC MUSIC, ATOMIC ARCHITECTURE

Implicit in the world view of the Greek Atomists – Leucippus, Democritus, Epicurus, and in the writings of the Roman Epicurean poet Lucretius, formalized in the calculus of Newton and Leibniz, and operationalized in contemporary media by techniques such as sampling, quantization, and digital signal processing is an epistemology of the assembly of the world from the very small. Even though the limit by which we judge the very small changes, and at each new scale a different apparatus must be brought to bear on the materials we wish to organize, the fundamental insight persists and remains at the core of what we mean by knowing something about the world.

Music has already undergone the transition that architecture now faces: in going from the scale of staffs and notes to the scale of sampled bits, its entire theoretical, compositional, and performative logic had to be revised. Composers needed the conceptual and technological tools with which to order decisions at the scale of microseconds. Even before this, there was a long debate about whether sound was a wavelike or "corpuscular." Following Einstein's prediction of phonons, quasi-particles consisting of wave-packets that have some of the properties of particles, Dennis Gabor described sound quanta, and composers such as Iannis Xenakis experimented with "sound clouds." Like the story of the struggle trying to resolve the unresolvable nature of light as wave or particle, the story of this question in sound is fascinating, and is told in detail by composer/researcher Curtis Roads in his book microsound, where he also outlines his own efforts in granular synthesis. The advent of technologies such as rapid prototyping – stereolithography, fused-material deposition, laminated object manufacturing – allows form to be assembled particle by particle, in much the same way as digital sound is now assembled sample by sample. Many of the techniques of digital sound can be brought to bear upon from controlled grain by grain but understood simultaneously as wave pattern.

N-DIMENSIONAL MODULATIONS

It is possible to organize music, image, moving image, solid, space, interaction, and liquid architectures as phenomena of increasing dimensionality. Broadly, music is one-dimensional; images are two-dimensional; solids are three-dimensional, interactive spaces are three-plus-one-dimensional (three spatial and one temporal, as opposed to four spatial), and so one. Surely this is a partial and limited schematization, and is not meant to deny the many additional dimensions that each of these modalities carries with their many and varied attributes. Still, if we allow ourselves to consider them in this way, as instances in a continuum of modulation of ever-increasing dimensionality, we can then transpose the operations of one onto another, either by extrusion up to higher dimensions, or by projection or section down to lower dimensions.

This conception of the sound, still image, moving image, still form, moving forms, still space, moving space, all as modulations of n-dimensional modalities permits us to carry the algorithmic theories and techniques of computer music into the realm of architecture. Some of this has already been done. What has not been done, and what therefore limits the transposition of compositional strategies from one to the other, is the shift in underlying representation – we have not developed a representation of architecture as streams, sheets, or clouds of bits. The techniques exist – volume rendering in scientific visualization, for instance – but they have not been adopted into the conception or execution of architecture. We understand what it means to compress a sound: but what does it mean to compress a building, when that building is composed as three or more dimensional wave and built granule by granule? In music, granular synthesis is an active topic, both as research and as avant-garde compositional practice. What would it mean to compose and synthesize a building grain by grain?

LIVING MUSIC, LIVING ARCHITECTURE

So far we are still in the realm of the digital. The nano~ and the bio~, to be followed by the pico~ (and, in time, the femto~, atto~, zepto~, yocto~), the quanto~, lead both architecture and music, and all the other modalities, into unexplored territories. What is nanomusic, biomusic, nanoarchitecture, bioarchitecture? The question does not seek an answer in the form of a conventionally built building that is inspired by nanotechnology or biotechnology – it seeks an answer that embodies these into its true fabric. Perhaps a nanomusical composition is a resonant nanoengineered material that, when activated, sounds a sarabande; perhaps a biomusical composition is a quasi-living sound producing organism that, when engaged, sings a symphony.

Architecture and music are synonyms for space and time; between them they address nearly everything – what remains is transactivity: mutable behaviour, evolution, life, consciousness. This is where we are headed – into a world in concord with nature but of our own making, a world within which we are transacting with artificially living, artificially conscious n-dimensional modulations of sensory and informational modalities, only vestigially, and perhaps nostalgically, named architecture or music.

PERIPHERAL EVIDENCE

The work shown here is the anticipation of these other architectures. These projects draw upon the biological and the mathematical, the generative and the generated, the algorithmic, the genetic, and the transgenic. Various directions are being explored here: perhaps the most intriguing is that of creating nanoscale architectures and sculptures by using fragments of RNA as building modules.

The very small, the very large, the very fast, the very slow, the observable at the limit of observation bring the empiricism upon which science depends to the edge of epistemology. What we might have known all along is made plain: what we describe as reality is a construct based in peripheral evidence. In Leibniz's Monadology, reality is simply the agreement between elementary monads, a structure of coincidences exhibiting certain patterns and invariances we come to recognize and trust. If the nanoscale architecture project succeeds, how will we even know there is anything there? The architectures and sculptures produced will fit 10,000 times in the width of a human hair. A virtual reality setup will be required to design them; an algorithmic engine will be required to sequence them; a molecular wet lab will be required to assemble the requisite molecules and the resultant RNA architecture; and rapid prototyping, interactive installations, and a host of other translations will be needed to manifest them in human scales.

Each of these steps leaves conventional architecture far behind. It is, no doubt, speculative work, work whose benefit is the formative act of constructive anticipation itself. In growing this architecture, we grow the bridge to the future.

And so, to paraphrase Feynman, I would like to describe a transvergent, living, alien architecture, in which little has been done, but in which an enormous amount could be done in principle.

This work is made possible by my affiliation with CNSI (the California NanoSystems Institute), MAT (Media Arts and Technology), and Art Studio, at UCSB (the University of California, Santa Barbara): and is done in collaboration with my colleagues Luc Jaeger (molecular biochemistry) and Lisa Jevbratt (systems/network art).
Marcos Novak: www. centrifuge.org

Second Nature

Fractured Magic from Pollock to Gehry

by Richard P. Taylor

Frank Gehry's proposal for
Guggenheim Manhattan 2001
Photo Courtesy Guggenheim Foundation

We are all familiar with the Manhattan skyline, with its many skyscrapers reaching high into the clouds. Imagine a skyscraper shaped like the clouds surrounding it. Three years ago, the Guggenheim Museum unveiled a design by Frank Gehry for a 'cloud-like' building to house its modern art collection. With its swirling layers of curved surfaces spanning three piers, the proposed forty-five storey structure was predicted to re-shape New York's waterfront. If it goes ahead, how will people respond to this unusual architecture? My recent studies of human reaction to fractal patterns indicate a bright future for buildings that incorporate Nature's shapes into their design.

From the first moment I saw one of Frank Gehry's buildings, his architectural style reminded me of the creations of another radical visionary – the abstract painter Jackson Pollock (1912-1956). Pollock rolled vast canvases across the floor of his studio and then dripped paint directly onto them, building majestic swirling patterns. Over the last fifty years, Pollock's paintings have frequently been described as 'organic,' suggesting his imagery alludes to Nature. 'Organic' seems an equally appropriate description for Gehry's creations. Lacking the cleanliness of artificial order, their imagery stands in sharp contrast to the straight lines, the triangles, the squares and the wide range of other 'man-made' shapes known in mathematics as Euclidean geometry. But if Pollock and Gehry's creations celebrate Nature's organic shapes, what shapes would these be? Do organic objects, such as trees and clouds, have an underlying geometry, or are they 'patternless' – a disordered mess of randomness?

Whereas mathematicians have pursued the study of Euclidean geometry with remarkable success since its introduction in 300BC, the complexities and apparent irregularities of Nature's organic patterns in our every day lives have proven more difficult to define. One approach, doomed to failure, was to model Nature's imagery using Euclidean shapes. "In retrospect," noted the mathematician Benoit Mandelbrot, "clouds are not spheres, mountains are not cones, coastlines are not circles, and bark is not smooth, nor does lightning travel in straight lines." The correct approach arrived in the 1970s, when Mandelbrot identified a subtle form of order lurking within the apparent disorder of Nature's scenery. Natural objects were shown to consist of patterns that recur at increasingly fine magnifications. Mandelbrot christened this repetition a 'fractal' (a term derived from the Latin 'fractus', meaning fractured) to emphasise their irregular appearance when compared to the smoothness of Euclidean shapes. Catalogued in his epic work *The Fractal Geometry of Nature* (1977), a range of natural objects were shown to be fractal, including mountains, clouds, rivers and trees. Natural fractals, such as the tree shown opposite left are referred to as statistical fractals. Although the patterns observed at different magnifications are not identical, they have the same statistical qualities such as pattern density, degree of roughness, etc. This type of fractal pattern stands in contrast to exact fractals, shown opposite right, where the patterns repeat exactly at different magnifications.

Given the prevalence of fractal objects in Nature, is it possible to construct fractal buildings? The challenge lies in the ability to repeat the construction process at different scales. Exact fractals are the simpler proposal because the same shape is employed at each

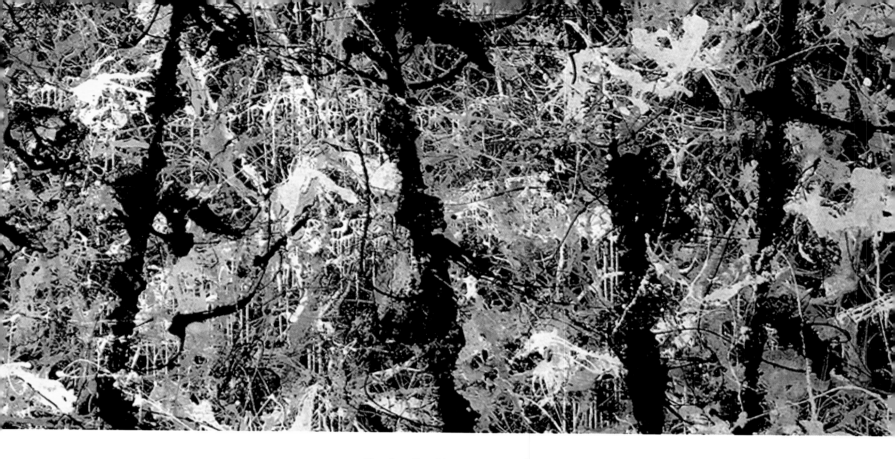

▲

Jackson Pollock, *Blue Poles: Number 11*.
Courtesy National Gallery of Australia,
Canberra

left: natural fractals in the form of trees
(known as statistical fractals)
right: exact fractals, where the patterns
repeat exactly at different magnifications
▼

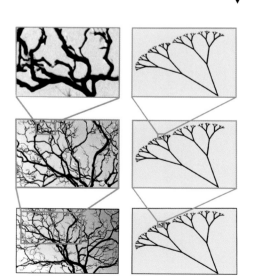

magnification. For this reason, exact fractals have appeared regularly throughout the history of art, dating back to Islamic and Celtic patterns. This exact repetition can be extended to three dimensions. An obvious example is that of Russian dolls, where a large doll hides an identical but smaller doll inside, which then hides an even smaller doll. In terms of architecture, the Castel del Monte, designed and built by the Holy Roman Emperor Frederick II (1194-1250), has a basic shape of a regular octagon fortified by eight smaller octagonal towers at each corner. A more recent example is Gustave Eiffel's tower in Paris, where the repetition of a triangle generates a shape known amongst fractal geometrists as a Sierpinski Gasket. The Eiffel Tower serves as a demonstration of the practical implications of fractal architecture. If, instead of its spidery construction, the tower had been designed as a solid pyramid, it would have consumed a large amount of iron, without much added strength. Instead Eiffel exploited the structural rigidity of a triangle at many different size scales. The result is a sturdy and cost-effective design. Gothic cathedrals also exploit fractal repetition

in order to deliver maximum strength with minimum mass. The fractal character also dominates the visual aesthetics of the building. A Gothic cathedral's repetition of different shapes (arches, windows and spires) on different scales yields an appealing combination of complexity and order. In contrast to the 'filled-in' appearance of the Romanesque structures that pre-dated it, the carved out character of the Gothic buildings delivers a distinctive skeletal appearance that results in their remarkable luminosity. More recently, the visual appeal of Frank Lloyd Wright's Palmer House in Ann Arbor (USA) of 1950-51 has been analysed in terms of Lloyd's use of triangular shapes at different scales.

In contrast to the exact fractals discussed above, statistical fractals represent a far greater challenge to both artists and architects. M.C. Escher is known within the art world for his mathematical dexterity and his ability to manipulate repeating patterns at different scales. However, even Escher restricted himself to drawing exact fractals and did not attempt to capture the intricacy of statistical fractals. Similarly, Leonardo da Vinci is renowned for his scientific illustrations

  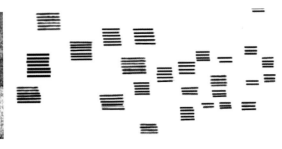

of turbulent water dating back to 1500, yet his representations of swirling water fail to capture the statistical fractal quality generated by turbulence. In 1999 I showed that the drip process developed by Jackson Pollock generated statistical fractals similar to those found in Nature's patterns. Pollock's astonishing achievement has been called 'fractal expressionism,' to distinguish it from the statistical fractals that appeared with the advent of computer art in the 1980s. Pollock's method was not one of 'number crunching' and intellectual deliberation but an intuitive process in which the fractal character was established after two minutes of intense activity. Lee Krasner (Pollock's wife and a respected artist) believed that his talent lay in an ability to paint three-dimensional patterns in the air and anticipate how the paint would condense on to the two-dimensional surface of the canvas. Pollock's paintings thus demonstrate that it is possible to create statistical fractals in three-dimensional space. However, to design a building based on statistical fractals, an architect would have to create similar three-dimensional statistical fractals but with the added restriction that the design would have to be assembled into a structurally-sound object.

What are the possible motivations for creating a building based on statistical fractals? Such fractals have a large surface area to volume ratio. For example, trees are built from statistical fractals in order to maximise exposure to the sunlight. Similarly, bronchial trees in our lungs maximise oxygen absorption into the blood vessels. Possible advantages of this large surface area for buildings therefore include solar cells on the rooftops

and windows that deliver a large amount of light to the building's interior. However, the main reason for such a design focuses on the associated aesthetics and the hope of mimicking a natural 'organic' shape. How would an observer react to an artificial object that assumes a natural fractal form? The study of aesthetic judgement of fractal patterns constitutes a relatively new research field within perception psychology. Only recently have researchers started to quantify people's visual preferences for fractal content. The visual appearance of a statistical fractal object is influenced by a parameter called the fractal dimension D. This quantifies the visual complexity of the fractal pattern. Its value lies between 1 and 2 and moves closer to 2 as the visual complexity increases. This is demonstrated opposite for drip paintings (three images on the left) and corresponding natural scenery (three images on the right). Starting top left, the smooth straight line is visually uncomplicated and has a base D value of 1. An equivalent pattern in nature is the horizon. Moving down, the fractal drip painting is a very sparse, simple pattern with a D value of 1.3. Equivalent fractal patterns in nature are clouds. Moving down, the fractal drips are very rich, intricate and complex with a much higher D value of 1.9. Equivalent fractal patterns in nature are trees in the forest.

Since the D value of a fractal pattern has such a profound impact on its visual appearance, a crucial question is whether people prefer patterns characterised by a particular D value. In 1995, Cliff Pickover used a computer to generate fractal patterns with different D values and found that people expressed a preference for fractal patterns with

a high value of 1.8. However, a survey by Deborah Aks and Julien Sprott also used a computer but with a different mathematical method for generating the fractals. This survey reported much lower preferred values of 1.3. The discrepancy between the two surveys would suggest that there is no universally preferred D value but that the aesthetic qualities of fractals depend specifically on how the fractals are generated. To determine if there are any 'universal' aesthetic qualities of fractals, I collaborated with psychologists Branka Spehar, Colin Clifford and Ben Newell. We performed perception studies incorporating the three fundamental categories of fractals: 'natural' (scenery such as trees, mountains, clouds, etc.), 'mathematical' (computer simulations) and 'human' (cropped sections of Pollock's dripped paintings). Participants in the perception study consistently expressed a preference for fractals with D values in the range 1.3 to 1.5, irrespective of the pattern's origin. Significantly, many of the fractal patterns surrounding us in Nature have D values in this mid range.

Recent scientific investigations indicate that the appeal of mid-range fractals extends beyond that of visual aesthetics – these fractals actually reduce the stress of an observer. In a study by James Wise, people were seated facing a 1m by 2m artwork and were asked to perform a sequence of stress-inducing mental tasks such as arithmetic problems, with each task separated by a one-minute recovery period. During this sequence, Wise continuously monitored each person's skin conductance. Skin conductance measurements are a well-established method for quantifying stress – heightened perspiration

►
Frank Gehry's sketch for the
Experience Music Project

◄ left: a realistic rendition of a natural
landscape; middle: an artistic rendition
of a natural landscape; right: a pattern
of painted lines

left: Drip paintings
right: corresponding natural scenery
▼

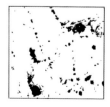

under stress decreases the skin conductance. The amount of stress induced by mental work can therefore be quantified by the increase in skin conductance DG between the rest and work periods – a large DG value indicates high stress. Wise used the three art works shown opposite: a realistic photograph of a forest scene, an artistic rendition of a natural landscape, and a pattern of painted lines, together with a uniform white panel serving as a control. DG was found to depend on which artwork was observed. For the 'artificial' pattern of lines, DG was 13% greater than for the white control panel indicating that this artwork actually increased the observer's stress. In contrast, the DG values for the 'natural' images were 3% (middle) and 44% (left) lower than for the control indicating a reduction in stress. This result confirms an earlier proposal that natural images might be incorporated into artificial environments as a method of stress reduction. Why, though, was the middle image far more effective in reducing stress than the left image? To answer this question I recently teamed up with Wise and performed a fractal analysis of the two images. Significantly, the D value of the middle natural image was found to be 1.4, lying within the category of fractals previously established as being visually appealing. In contrast, the image on the left had a D value of 1.6, lying outside the visually pleasing range. It appears then that the appeal of mid-range fractal patterns (D=1.3 to 1.5) extends beyond simple visual aesthetics and is sufficient to deliver a profound physiological impact on the observer.

This is potentially exciting news for Frank Gehry and his 'cloud-like' design for the Guggenheim Museum: clouds are fractal patterns with a D value of 1.3 that lies within the 'magic' range of preferred visual complexity. But will Gehry's design be capable of mimicking the fractal character of Nature's clouds? The challenge may not be as difficult as it seems. Contrary to popular belief, Nature's fractals do not repeat over many magnifications. Whereas computer-generated fractals repeat from finitely large to infinitesimally small magnifications, typical fractals only repeat over a magnification range of twenty-five. Thus, for a cloud-like building, the largest features would only have to be a factor of twenty-five bigger than the smallest features. This is challenging but not impossible. Furthermore, the low D value of a cloud ensures that the fractal structure will be relatively smooth and sparse (see left). If Gehry had chosen a forest-like fractal structure, the intricacy and complexity of this high D fractal structure would have been significantly more difficult to incorporate into a building.

If this proposal does become reality, it will be fascinating to see if people's fundamental appreciation of fractal clouds will inspire New Yorkers to embrace Frank Gehry's revolutionary building design.

Further reading:

"Order in Pollock's Chaos," R.P. Taylor, *Scientific American*, December 2002

"Fractals and the Birth of Gothic," A.L. Goldberger, *Molecular Psychiatry*, vol 1, pp. 99-104, 1996

"Fractal Geometry in the Late Work of Frank Lloyd Wright: the Palmer House," L.K. Eaton, *Nexus II: Architecture and Mathematics*, edited by K. Williams, 1998.

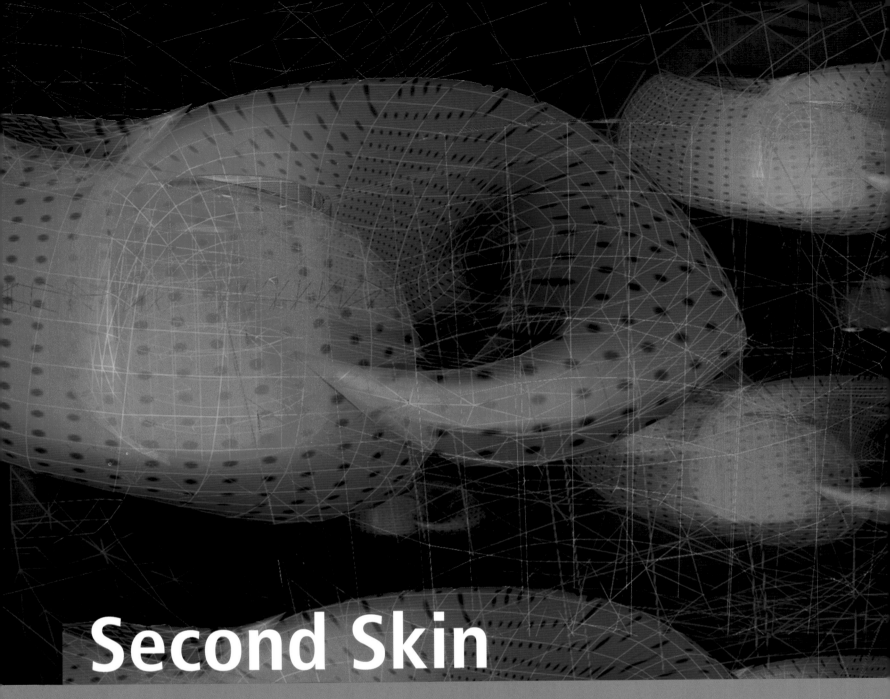

Second Skin

BUILDING FROM THE SPACE OF MIND
MARCOS LUTYENS with Tania Lopez Winkler

Second Skin is a project that explores the structure of mind as mirrored by emergent architecture.

It involves architecture students and professionals from around the globe. It began at the Architectural Association in London, and extended to the Academy of Art, Gdansk, Poland, and the International Festival of Media in Architecture in Florence, Italy. Students at the Instituto Tecnologico y de Estudios Superiores in Monterrey, at the faculty of Queretaro, Mexico collaborated both in architecture and programming to develop Second Skin into a dynamic model of emergent architecture.

Urbanisation and architectural strategies usually follow a vector from macro to micro, from general to specific, from prescribed and mandatory to subjective and personal. Second Skin turns this trajectory around, seeking a process of emergent design. Second Skin starts by examining patterns, qualia and structures within the unconscious that relate to concepts of shelter and dwelling. Following Jung's ideas on unconscious archetypes and Kant's investigation of schemata, what could be termed intratypes are fleshed out. Intratypes may be defined as recurring dynamic patterns of our unconscious interactions and mental programmes that give coherence and structure to our

experience, and manifest as conscious thought, intelligence and actions.

The modules of mental processing are coaxed out through a hypnotic induction technique and projected into the terrain of architecture. Following suggestions of amnesia and agnosia which disengage the subjects from conscious tendencies to apply filtered external conceptions to their thought processes, such as contamination from media or indirect peer pressure, they are asked to extend their consciousness to envelop a *Second Skin*, which is an architec-

tural space that corresponds to an enlarged self and comprises aspects of memory, brain function and deeply-rooted notions of protection and shelter. It uses mind processes as a model for architectural approaches and uses architecture as a metaphor for housing the collective space of the mind.

Each student listens to a trance-inducing audio track designed to evert architecturally-based forms from the unconscious. The students draw their impressions on paper in a trance state, and record a detailed description of them, including

specific qualities relating to size, form, structure, materials, viewpoint, kinaesthetic and proprioceptive experiences related to their own *Second Skin*.

The next stage involves everting this information into a format that can be objectively assessed, mapped, processed and reconfigured. The aim is to build a model of an intratypical dwelling, in short, a structure that emerges and evolves from a morphing and merging of a collective of intratypes. Patterns and correlates that arise from this process are then mapped.

"….(to) that which is about to come into being, of the open sea whether or not there is land that lies beyond…"

– Isaiah Berlin
Russian Thinkers

Eric Owen Moss

Mariinsky Theatre

St Petersburg

▲
Exterior view of theatre

▶
Model of plaster-cast pillows

▶
(far right) Section

I am an advocate of new architecture. What does that signify for architecture and planning in St. Petersburg? Simply that history records no permanent solutions. Ideas rise, gain power, dissipate, and are replaced. What remains is the historic record. And that record in St. Petersburg is powerful and compelling. But historic paradigms are provisional. They move. If not in St. Petersburg then elsewhere…but always somewhere and always moving. So why not in St. Petersburg today, propelled by the initial courage of those who founded the city, and the practitioners from east and west who sustained the momentum and implemented the vision?

It is a stunning view from the north bank of the Nieva River. The ice melts and cracks slightly. Perhaps a new conception is about to appear though St. Petersburg is not an assemblage of discrete buildings. Rather it is a chronology of monumental spaces that sweep us along from plaza and canal to building and monument. The city centre extends from the Winter Palace on the east to New Holland on the west, then south past the Rimsky-Korsakov Conservatory and the Mariinsky Theatre to St. Nicholas Cathedral.

The centre is historically vital because of what it portends. Buildings originated in different eras and were built in various styles but the consistent lessons are scale and power. There is no consigning the asymmetry of those public spaces to a sedate conclusion. To intervene architecturally in the area is to exploit its spatial message. The tradition of long diagonal views and expansive public space is open ended. There is room for more. We are encouraged to continue.

The New Holland and the New Mariinsky sites are not so much locations for new building 'events' in the historic centre of St. Petersburg (though they surely suggest that aspect), but rather extensions of the existing organisation of the historic district.

The New Mariinsky is aligned on axis with the existing theatre. Two opposing forces, the external constraints of the site and the internal programmatic needs of the theatre, give shape to the three modules that define the requisite volumes of the theatre. The surface of these modules is further differentiated in response to the severe climate. The resultant expression is that of an iceberg. The interior surfaces combine to form a grand theatrical space that is conceptually adjustable, moldable, and fluid.

The ensemble of glass and steel will be one of the world's most technically sophisticated performance venues.

ERIC OWEN MOSS

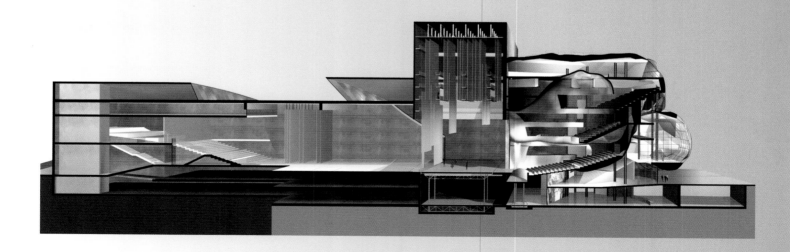

Morphosis

NOAA: Ears of the Building

The NOAA Satellite Operation Facility is a sensory organ ingesting data from hundreds of satellites placed in orbit to survey and map the physical conditions of our planet and thus it functions dually as a purposeful signifier of NOAA's mission to survey and care for our environment.

The facility consists primarily of two forms, a bar and a berm: the first is a slender, faceted three-storey tower that houses the programmme most integral to the control and operation of the satellites. It is the sense organ, the place where trans-missions from the satellites are received and processed; the second form is a large piece of augmented landscape under which workers literally inhabit a strata of the earth.

The bar building hovers above the landscaped berm, which covers a single level of high-tech office space and ancillary programme. The bar's true North-South orientation optimises the performance of the antennae that crown it, while the concentration of dishes on the roof asserts the iconographic character of the project and maximises the open green space on the extended site, thus producing a park-like environment.

The bermed landscape engages the northern edge of the roof structure, merging with the dome's planted surface; the roof plane thus reads as an extension of the surrounding landscape.

The design aims to minimize the building by transforming it and blurring its edges. The piece that surfaces is a didactic piece that holds the antennae – it is the ears of the building – the receiver of information from space. It is an extension of the human sensory device allowing us to expand both our senses and our imagination outwards.

MORPHOSIS

Reiser + Umemoto

Eyebeam Museum of Art and Technology

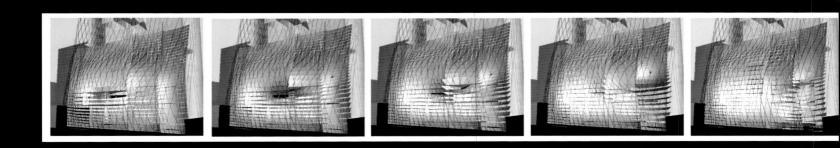

The crucial question facing the design of a Museum of Art and Technology foregrounds paradoxically not the technology *per se* but the physicality of space itself. It is pointless to fix the configuration of a building based on technologies that are both fugitive in their effects and whose software and hardware undergo continuous replacement over time. Further, the spaces of this new type of museum must balance flexibility of use with highly specific environments in terms of their mood and character. It is only recently that such a balance between the generic and the inflected is possible. What is proposed is a series of flexible yet qualitatively vibrant environments for exhibitions. 'Neutral' exhibition spaces can thus be mounted in this museum, but such spaces do not determine the overall architectural effects.

The museum embodies a comprehensive conception of media. Beyond the relatively familiar associations of media with electronic technologies and dematerialisation, there is a more inclusive model founded on the logics of material computation (of which electronic media is a subset). Architecture as building is coextensive with this model and is the motivating concept for the building, which is based on flows: flows of people, of energy, of matter and of technology.

◀

View of lobby

Exterior view ▶

Makoto Sei Watanabe

Iidabashi Subway Station

"…In fact, the plates temporarily making up the surface of the road conceal a huge abyss opening many metres into the depths of the earth: the construction site for a subway line. "

MSW

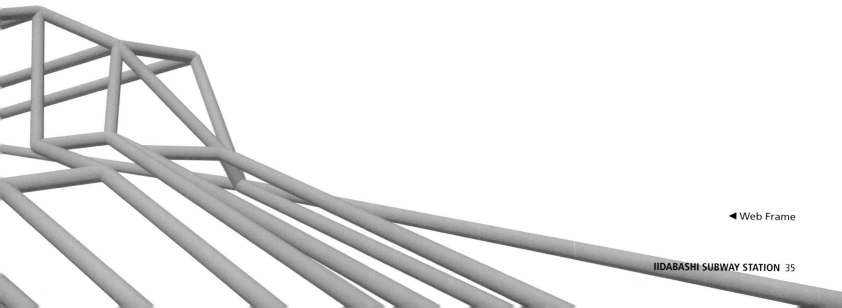

◄ Web Frame

Wind Wings ventilation towers resemble
these natural forms, without imitating
them directly

A car approaches an intersection and hits a bumpy surface. Instead of the usual smooth asphalt pavement, the surface of the road is uneven. The bumpy patch lasts only briefly before the smooth pavement returns. Pedestrians hurriedly crossing the same intersection give little thought to the fact that the road beneath their feet is covered with heavy iron plates, not asphalt. Nor are they aware of the fact that beneath the iron plates a chasm yawns. In fact, the plates temporarily making up the surface of the road conceal a huge abyss descending many metres into the depths of the earth: the construction site for a subway line.

The subway, or underground railway, is a tube extending beneath the surface of the earth. It is a long, intricately winding pipeline which is separate from the networks above the ground.

Under ground, the 'sealed machines' – pride of the construction industry – move about at will. Rotating drill bits eat their way into the rock. In their wake, a finishing material, called 'segment,' is poured into place, and metre after metre of under-ground tubing is created. These machines, though guided by human operators, are virtually robots carving their way through the earth beneath our feet. All subway construction work is done by these machines that tunnel through the earth. No one sees the outer surfaces of the tubes they construct. Or at least, they are not meant to be seen. But in fact there are points at which they come into view.

Thirteen subway lines run beneath the centre of Tokyo. At terminal stations where different lines converge, newly constructed tubes pass beneath those already in place. At such points, sealed construction techniques cannot be em-ployed. Instead, the surface of the earth

▲
Subterranean spaces

must be broken and a cavern opened into the ground. Within this cavern, existing subway tubes are first excavated and supported in mid-air (or mid-earth?). In this way, after spending years or decades buried in the earth, the old tube is for the first time exposed to view, dug up like a fossil of the industrial age.

Descending into the construction site, one discovers a jungle of steel structures. The freshly excavated concrete tubes appear suspended in the light penetrating down from above. This is what lies beneath those iron plates. Neither cars nor pedestrians are aware of this other intersection deep in the ground.

The outer walls of the tubes glisten with dripping water and the reflected light shimmers with the vibration of trains passing through the tube. Passengers on the train are oblivious to the spectacle.

Once the newly built subway station is completed, it becomes one more interconnecting tube, part of an interwoven, criss-crossing space folding back on itself like a topological sample. Soon, the outer walls of the new tubes will be buried in the earth. The inner walls are themselves hidden by the finishing and the panelled surfaces of the interior of the station.

One of the purposes of this project is to make what is hidden into something that is seen, an intention which also underlies the K-Museum project at the Tokyo Bayside city centre. That museum also deals with the themes of invisible, multi-purpose underground channels.

Making visible what is invisible – whether it is the structures of the city or its economy, its beauty, its moods or even its feelings – by means of tangible materials is the meaning and significance of 'making' things, not only in architecture but in the widest sense.

The first thing aim of the project was to make visible the physical fabric of the framework used in the construction of the subway tube, thus enabling the subway station to become a kind of museum of industry. Elimination of the interior finishing of the station would also substantially reduce overall construction costs.

And yet, many obstacles stood in the way of making bare, and thus visible, something which has always been concealed. The obstacles encountered included engineering issues (waterproofing, etc.), but more significantly legal codes, the 'system,' and sheer habit. After a long process of persuading and gradually

winning the cooperation of many parties, what had been hidden for so long has at last been exposed in all its naked beauty.

This was accomplished in part by inserting another kind of tube, the Web Frame, which 'inherits' the DNA of the engineering framework, selecting, transforming and enhancing its features: an interweaving, entangling, expanding, pulsating Web growing towards the light of day, another species of subterranean tubule.

The growth of the Web Frame was facilitated by a computer programme for the automated generation of codes, which was a development and practical realisation of an on-going research project entitled 'Induction Cities.' And this project is the world's first implementation of what is called PGA, Programme Generated Architecture.

The 'Induction Cities' programme does not generate a single, completed solution to a given set of problems. Hence its flexibility. The solutions it generates are not conclusions; they are links in a continually changing process: design which continues to evolve and grow.

Perhaps the same is true of real cities? They mature, and change, like living beings.

MSW

Deformation diagram showing the interior
volumes within exterior forms

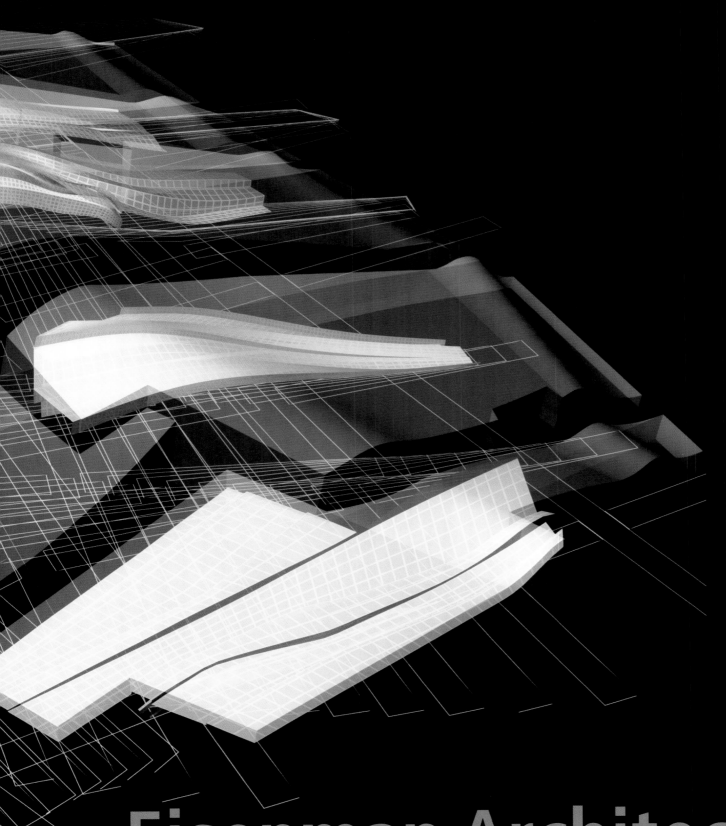

Eisenman Architects

City of Culture of Galicia

More than thirty years after the social revolutions of 1968, we are still facing an unresolved urban condition: an implosive one resulting from a saturation of media and information technology that, no longer able to expand, must contract. If the force of this contraction is almost unintelligible to us, it is because our entire image repertory is based on a logic of expanding systems. Architecture too addresses and approximates the expansionist paradigm, amplifying its gestures as it attempts to hide from itself the futility of its effects.

Given the logic of today's implosive reality, models of randomness are rapidly superseding models of determinacy and classical causality. This change expresses the passage from definite systems of expansion to multidirectional systems of matter – both expanding and contracting – a pulsation of surface, Baudrillard argued over two decades ago, that is "capable of infinite and interstitial saturation."

Architecture has traditionally been a semiotic system expressing a defined expansion of matter. Today, however, due to an oversaturation of media and information technology, we are moving from a time of liberation and release of energy into a phase of implosion and social inversion. This implosion marks a shift from a representation-obsessed semiotic culture – with its overabundance of information – to another sensibility.

Such a post-semiotic sensibility is not dominated by easily consumed imagery of representational signs and their signifieds, but rather is understood as a series of traces, marks that produce an alternative condition of figure and ground. This project evolves from the super-imposition of three sets of traces. First, the plan of the old city centre is placed on the hillside site. Second, a Cartesian grid is laid over these medieval routes. Third, the topography of the hillside is allowed to distort the two flat geometries, thus generating a topological surface that superimposes old and new in a simultaneous matrix.

The original medieval centre of Santiago conforms to a figure/ground urbanism. The buildings are figural and the streets residual. The project is a warped surface that is neither figure nor ground but a figured ground and a figured figure that supersedes the figure-ground urbanism of the old city. In this transformative operation, Santiago's medieval past appears not as a form of representational nostalgia but as an active present found in a tactile, pulsating new form.

The six buildings of the project are conceived as three pairs: the Museum of Galician History and the New Technologies Centre; the Music Theatre and the Central Services building; and the Galician Library and the Periodicals Archive. The experiences of the visitors to any given building will be affected by its relationship to its immediate partner.

As a condition of the implosion of contemporary secular culture, and as a deliberate gesture against obsolete explosive models, the City of Culture generates a powerful new figure/figure urbanism in which the buildings and topography become merged figures. The secular centre thus takes a different form from the religious centre below, yet expresses the trace of the old city as its foundation.

▲

Competition model

Site diagram with layers of information, phases 1-3
▼

The multiple levels in the library supplement the volumetric details worked out in models
▶

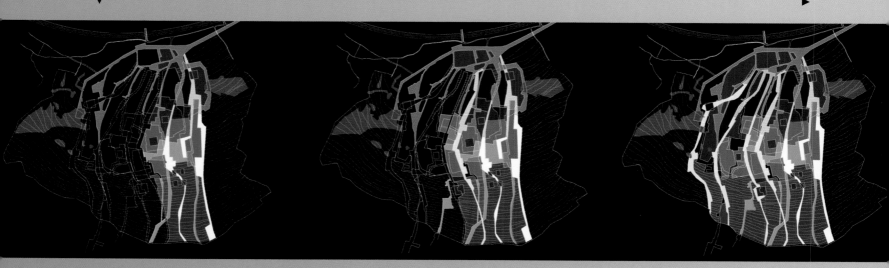

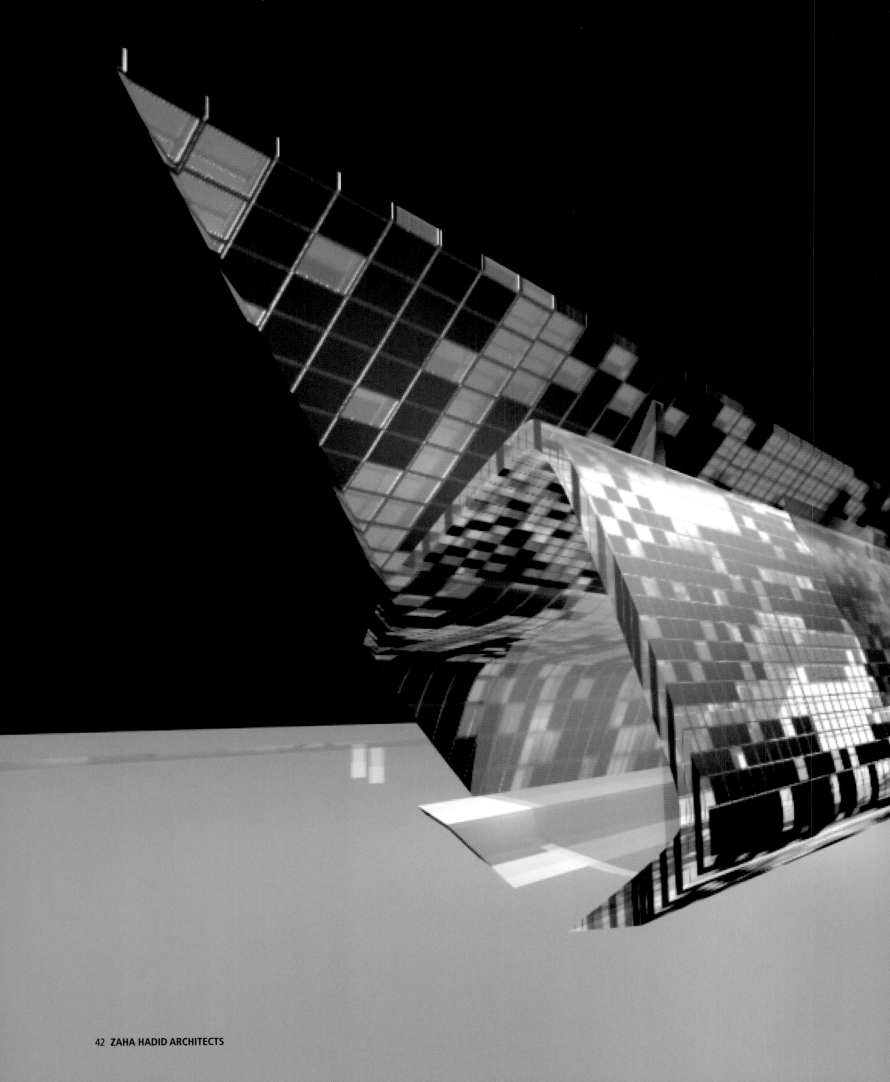

Zaha Hadid Architects

Temporary Guggenheim Museum, Tokyo

"We are proposing a snakeskin-like pixellation that allows the formally coherent integration of various surface performances."

ZHA

animated by the entrepreneurial spirit of rapid development. In this context the ten-year intervention of the temporary Guggenheim will be an instant cultural hotspot and a catalyst for related activities. It will also be a trend setter in terms of the architectural identity of the area.

The architectural iconography should signify the creative employment of state-

object of desire it must at first appear mysterious, an unknown territory waiting to be discovered and explored.

In line with the temporary nature of the structure a light weight envelope has been selected. A strong signature figure is created as two folded planes – like sheets of paper leaning against each other and encapsulating a generous space. This

However, the empty space is itself an attraction. Although the spatial concept is simple – in effect the parallel extrusion of three simple sections – the size, level of abstraction and dynamic profile of the folded planes ensure an exhilarating spatial sensation. The diagonal cleft at the top exerts a dramatic sense of vertigo as the light washes down the tilted plane.

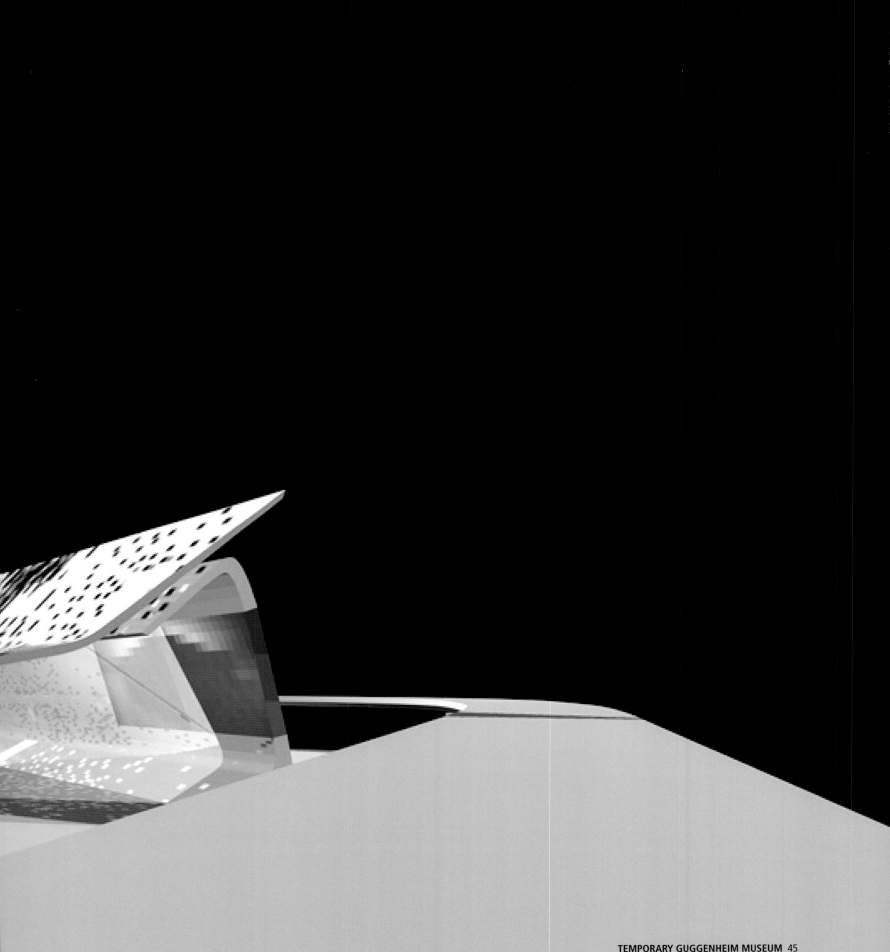

A third extruded section captured between the two folded planes acts as a mezzanine. This plane is inserted like a large table that affords the clean accommodation of all support spaces below and a generous exhibition area above – thus offering the viewing advantages afforded by a raised plateau in the 'garage' space.

At both ends the three extrusions are cut off at different angles. This simple move effectively articulates the ends and emphasises the entrance zone with a dramatic gesture.

Another important aspect to be noted is the quality of the skin. What is proposed is a snakeskin-like pixellation that allows the formally coherent integration of various surface performances.

The primary cladding material is large scale ceramic tiles that offer smooth surfaces and brilliant colours. These would be interspersed by light-boxes to allow further daylight to penetrate the space as well as acting as artificial light sources at night. Further panels would be photovoltaic elements. Finally a large media

screen in the form of honey-comb based 'smart' slabs would be almost camouflaged in the overall animation of the skin.

Internally the skin operates according to the same concept but is aesthetically much more muted. Light, ventilation and heating systems are all incorporated within the pixel logic.

The lighting and climate controls can be adapted to different exhibition requirements and environmental plug-ins can be used to completely change the internal atmosphere of the building.   *ZHA*

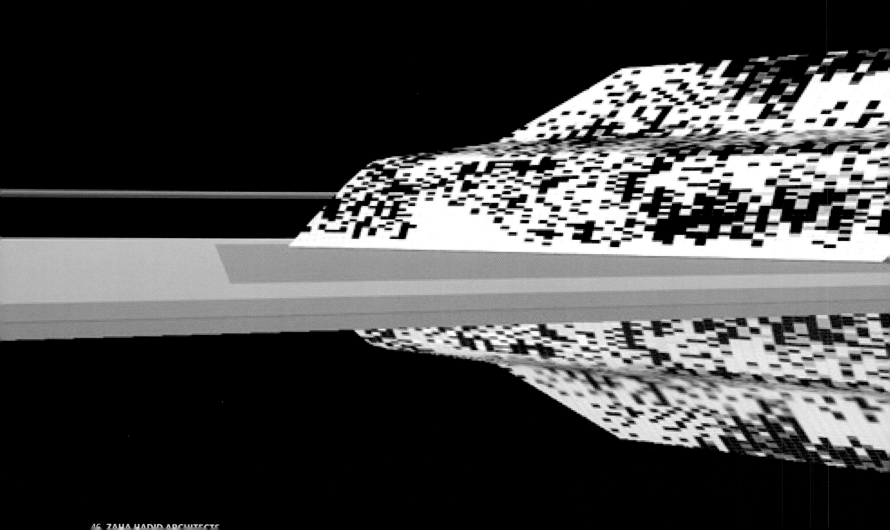

Plaça
Fòrum

Ronda litoral

Esplanada

Depuradora

EN PROYECTO

Pavelló
diversitat

Parc Auditoris

PISCINA DE SUBMARINISME

Zona de banys

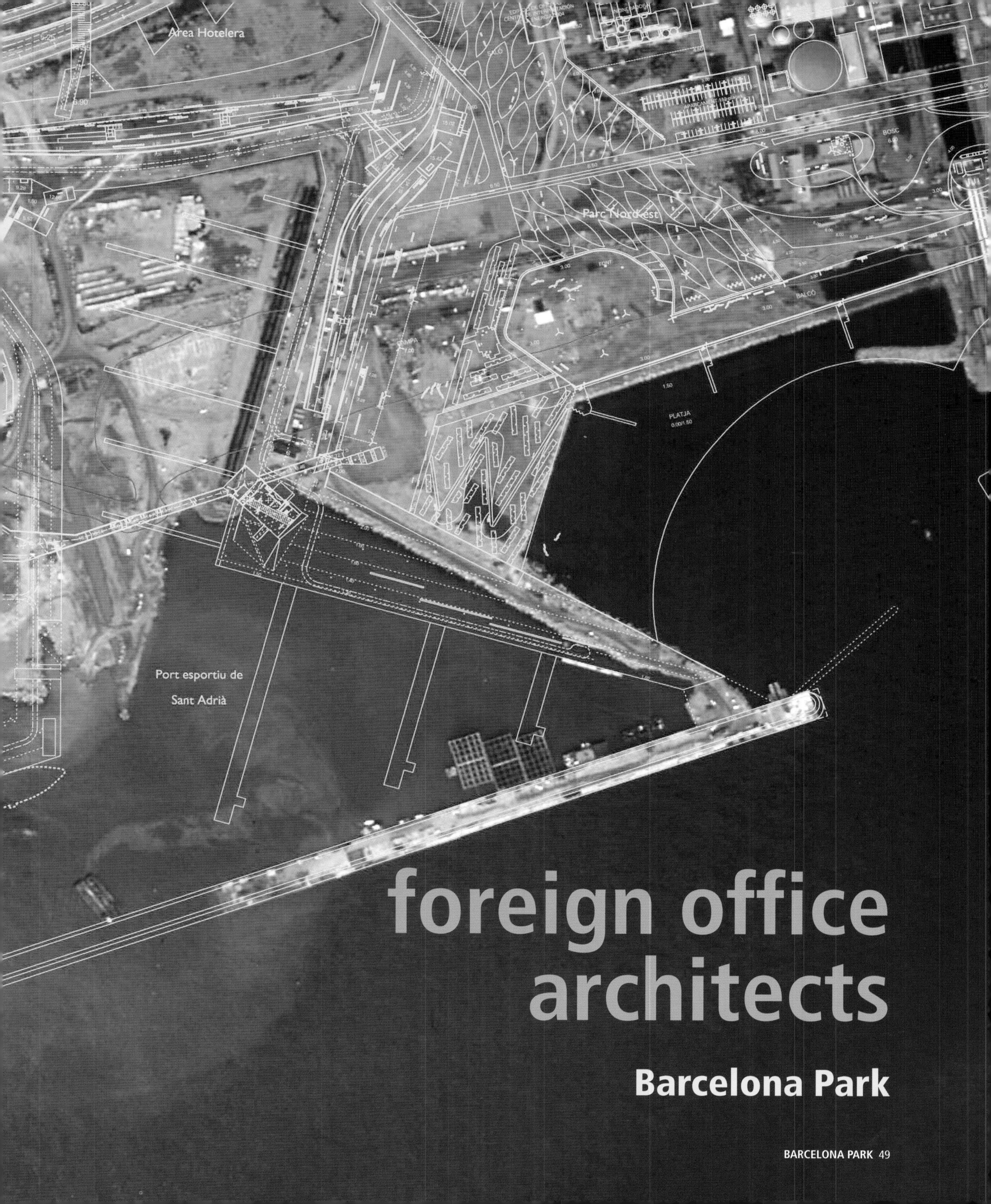

Area Hotelera

Parc Nord(est

PLATJA
0.00/1.50

Port esportiu de
Sant Adrià

foreign office architects

Barcelona Park

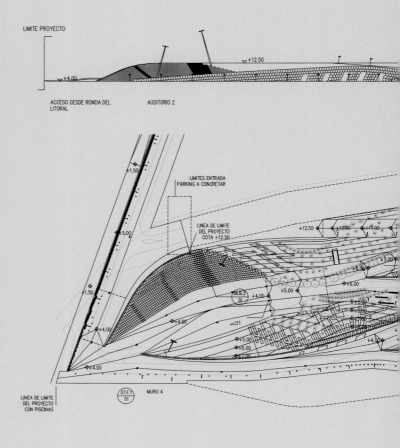

LÍMITE PROYECTO

+12.50

+4.00

ACCESO DESDE RONDA DEL
LITORAL

AUDITORIO 2

LÍNEA DE LÍMITE
DEL PROYECTO
CON PISCINAS

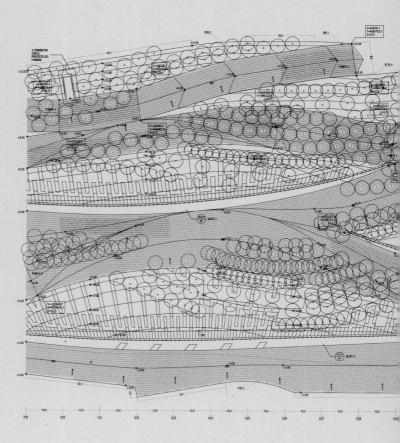

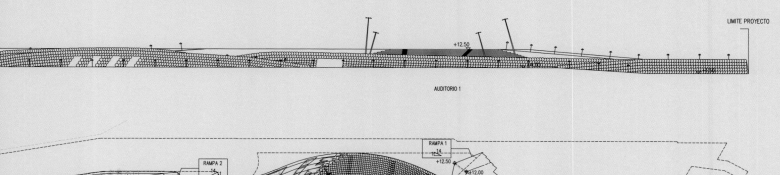

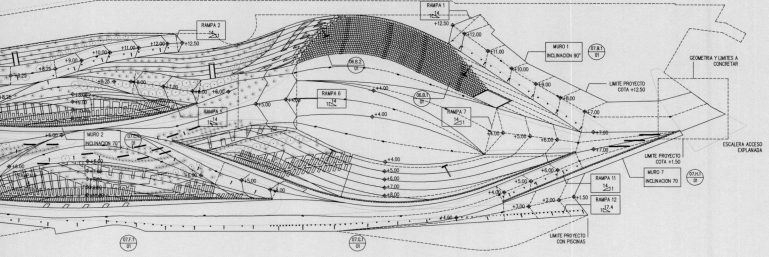

◄ (left) organisation system

(far left) aerial view

▲ (top) elevation from the sea; 1/2,000

(above) general park plan; 1/2,000

The Southwest Coastal Park and Auditoriums project is part of the infrastructure planned by the city of Barcelona as Host City for the International Forum of Cultures to be held in 2004.

This proposal is intended as an alternative to the rational geometry, whether artificial and linear, consistent or contradictory, and the organic geometry approximations that reproduce the picturesque qualities of nature.

It explores strategies that cause complex organizational landscapes to emerge through the creation of topographies artificially generated by a mediated integration of rigorously modeled orders. The organisational prototype for the park is borrowed from a frequent model in coastal areas: the dunes. They are a form of material organizsation with little internal structure, consisting of sand shaped by the wind. The programmatic distribution structure is based on an analysis of the various sport and leisure activities that will take place on the platforms that generate the topographies. These activities are modeled as a network of diverse circuits that will permit a gradation of the different paths or activity zones, from walking to running, biking, skateboarding and a series of performance and relaxing areas.

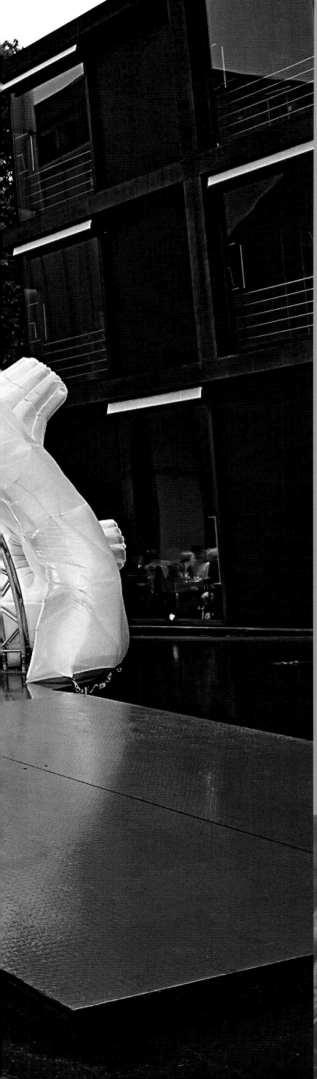

veech.media.
architecture

Mobile Environments

The Sprachpavillon was the central element in a touring exhibition for the European Year of Languages 2001. Its architectural aim was to develop a fluid form of communication and information through an expression of flexibility, transparency, lightness, and elasticity.

The distorted pneumatic form provides a soft interface between interior and exterior spaces which activates the surrounding urban context through subtle natural and dynamic artificial lighting. This provides the framework for the 'interior' human content, language and communication, which is achieved by the use of a 'terminal' located in the centre of the interior volume. The terminal represents an experimental approach to the expression of languages in a visual context by means of architecture/design, film, and typography. The typographical element is a linear band wrapped round a transparent skin with motorised interior cylindrical forms reflecting the superimposition and overlaying of words and sentences in the languages of the European Union.

The architectural, graphic and human entities revolve and interact around this point in space eliminating borders, boundaries, and obstacles.

◀ Sprachpavillon, Mobile Architecture, 2000

UN Studio

In this huge project for the reorganisation and expansion of the station area in the town of Arnhem in the Netherlands, bus terminal and train station are combined to form a new type of complex – an integrated public transportation area, which is organised as a roofed-over, climate-controlled plaza that interconnects and gives access to trains, taxis, buses, bikes, parking, office spaces and the town centre. The existing complex of bus terminals and train station requires drastic revision to permit the expansion plans of the joint owners; the town itself and Dutch Railways. The expansion will generates 80,000 sq.m of office space, 11,000 sq.m of shops, 150 housing units, a new station hall, a fourth railway platform, a railway underpass, a car tunnel, storage for 5,000 bicycles and a garage for 1,000 cars. The parties involved include several project developers, various state ministries and the European Union as well as the town of Arnhem and Dutch Railways.

van Berkel & Bos

Arnhem Central Station

The new identity of the station area acknowledges the regional significance of Arnhem. More than 65,000 people pass through it every day and with its central bus stops for regional and local buses and parking facilities, the station area forms the main gateway to the town. This accentuates the need for good connections to the old centre but equally important is the urban quality of the area itself for the people who work, wait, change buses or trains, meet and shop there daily.

Arnhem Central focuses on finding overlapping areas of shared parameters and common values. Pedestrian movement which concerns everyone involved in the redevelopment, forms that shared element making movement studies the cornerstone of the proposal: the analysis of the types of movement includes the directions of the various trajectories, their prominence in relation to other forms of transportation on the site, duration, links to different programmes, and interconnections.

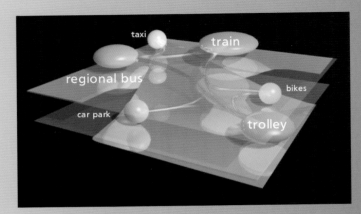

▲ visualisation of traffic organisation

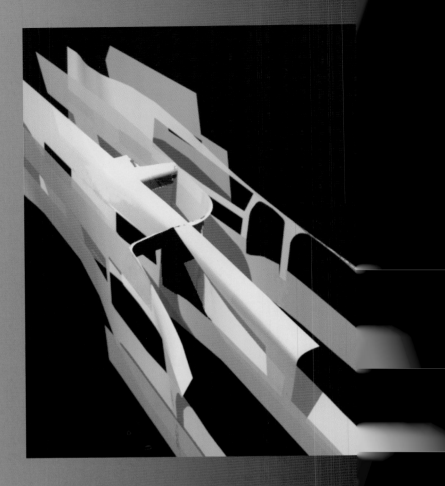

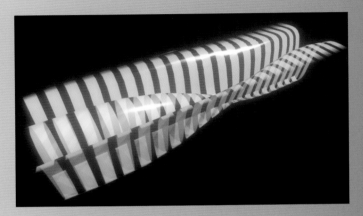

▲ organizsational V - construction

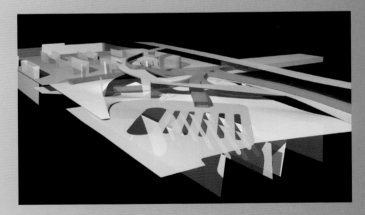

▲ traffic movements and flows

transfer hall and offices ▼

The station area emerges from these motion studies as a landscape of interrelated movements. The existing differences in height on the location are reconstructed to bring all transport systems and facilities together in one terminal. The holes in this landscape create a system of shortcuts between programmes. This movement originates in a concept of circulation that is a hybrid of a centralised system and an exhaustive pattern of all possible connections. Natural differences in height, pedestrian connections, sight lines and density surveys modify the position of the folds in the landscape. Surveys of waiting times and transfer percentages are used to identify spots suitable for the creation of secondary programmes such as fun shopping and run shopping. The intersection of different traffic systems is reduced to a minimum in order to optimise pedestrian accessibility to all facilities.

Light penetrates the lower entrances to the station, garage and offices and creates clear, lengthy vision lines, aiding pedestrian orientation and wayfinding. Work with investors on the development of a 24-hour programme contributes to an active and safe location. Pedestrian movements, transport systems, light, construction and the distribution of the programme are fused in one continuous landscape.

A year into the project, the topology of relations demanded the introduction of a diagram to encapsulate and advance the technical/spatial organisation. The finding of a diagram is never serendipitous; as part of the search for a new way of understanding the station area, a study of mathematical knots was undertaken since a landscape with holes could as readily be seen as a knot of planes. The diagrammatic outcome of this is a Klein bottle, which links the different levels of the station area in a hermetic way. The Klein bottle is as deeply ambiguous as it is comprehensive; it stays continuous throughout the spatial transformation that it undergoes from a surface to a hole and back again. As the ultimate outcome of shared, motion-based relations, the Klein bottle is an infrastructural element both pragmatically and diagrammatically.

Arnhem Central is being realised in stages; this poses the question of how to ensure flexibility while at the same time retaining the one terminal concept. Solutions for the underground car park, which is already under construction, have to take into account future changes in programme. The garage is the foundation for the shunting-yard for trolley buses, the station hall and the bus deck; offices are located at higher levels. Decisions regarding the placement of entrances, lifts and other communal passages to these as yet undesigned higher levels have therefore to be made in advance. A way of integrating aspects of function, construction, installations, lighting and orientation has been found in co-operation with Ove Arup & Partners. 'V-collectors' support the entire construction and form the connections between the garage, plaza and bus station levels. They also enable light and fresh air to reach the deepest levels of the garage.

▲
Willemstunnel (realized 1999)

◄ (left and above) underground parking

◄ (opposite top) structural diagram of underground parking

◄ (opposite bottom) exploded view of parking and transfer hall

Kas Oosterhuis

Cockpit in an Acoustic Wall

THE RULES OF THE GAME

The brief is to combine an acoustic barrier with industrial buildings. We decide to design with a speed of 120 km/h to streamline the concept and to be able to work with a telescopic perspective. Cars, powerboats and planes are streamlined to diminish drag. Along the A2 highway the acoustic barrier and the industrial buildings themselves do not move, but they are placed alongside a continuous stream of passing cars. The car-stream flows along the acoustic barrier at a speed of 120 km/h. The proportions of the built volumes emerging from the acoustic dyke are stretched tenfold along the length of the dyke. The building, which has been fused with the earth body of the dyke is

▶
Long stretched elastic lines define the contours of the cockpit

The cockpit is streamlined into the body of the acoustic barrier
▼

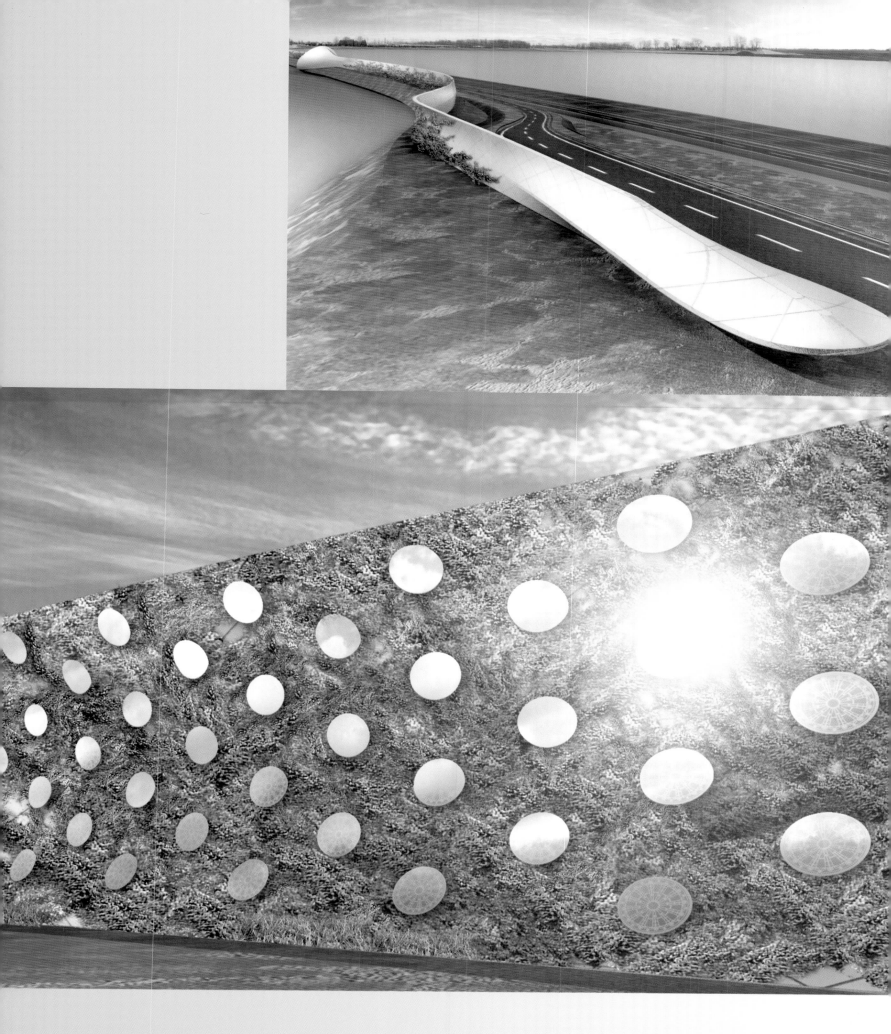

experienced as a streamlined cockpit in the body of the acoustic barrier. Animation studies indicate that a single cockpit in a single continuous stretch of the acoustic barrier provokes the strongest impact. The cockpit functions as a 3D logo for all the industrial facilities hidden behind the acoustic barrier.

LONG ELASTIC LINES

The most striking design principle is the use of long continuous lines, lines which do not have either an explicit beginning or an abrupt end. When they reach the actual volume of the cockpit the lines divide into a top and a bottom line. Within the volume of the cockpit the building is inserted with the precision of a plastic surgeon. The extra barrier at the top of the body of the acoustic barrier – shaped like a standard guard-rail – is pushed up by the volume of the cockpit. At the top of the cockpit the guard-rail sinks slowly into a concealed gutter. To embody a variety of possible clients, the long stretched lines that define the contours of the cockpit are seen as long pieces of elastic that

stretch with the volume of the building programme.

RULES FOR THE ELASTIC LINES

The classic lines, with radii of r1, r2 and r3 respectively, can be stretched from the vertexes a, b, c, d and e according to the indicated vectors.

Vertex a can slide up and down along the 1:3.5 slope of the road next to the acoustic barrier. Vertex b can be positioned higher or lower along the vertical axis. Vertex c can move inwards to the industrial zone behind the barrier. Vertexes d and e can slide horizontally along the top of the dyke. Moreover, the straight sloping façade in front of the highway can become convex and bulge by diminishing radius r4.

Further rules determine that the length of the cockpit must measure at least ten times the height; the width of the building must be at least twice the height. These rules ensure that the cockpit keeps its smooth appearance when passed at a speed of 120 km/h.

Kas Oosterhuis
www.oosterhuis.nl

The cockpit is a 3D logo for the industrial facilities behind

Telescopic perspective from car ▶

The car stream flows at speed along the acoustic barrier

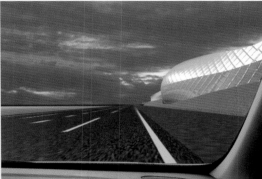

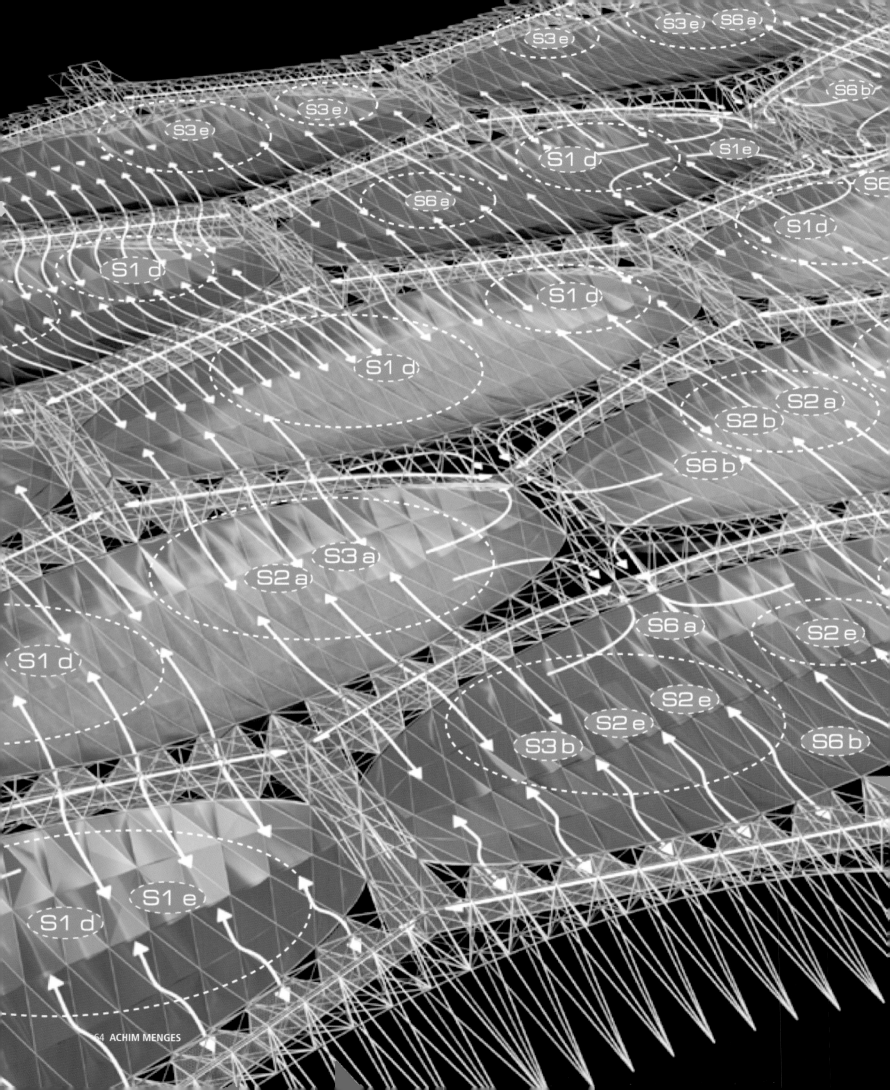

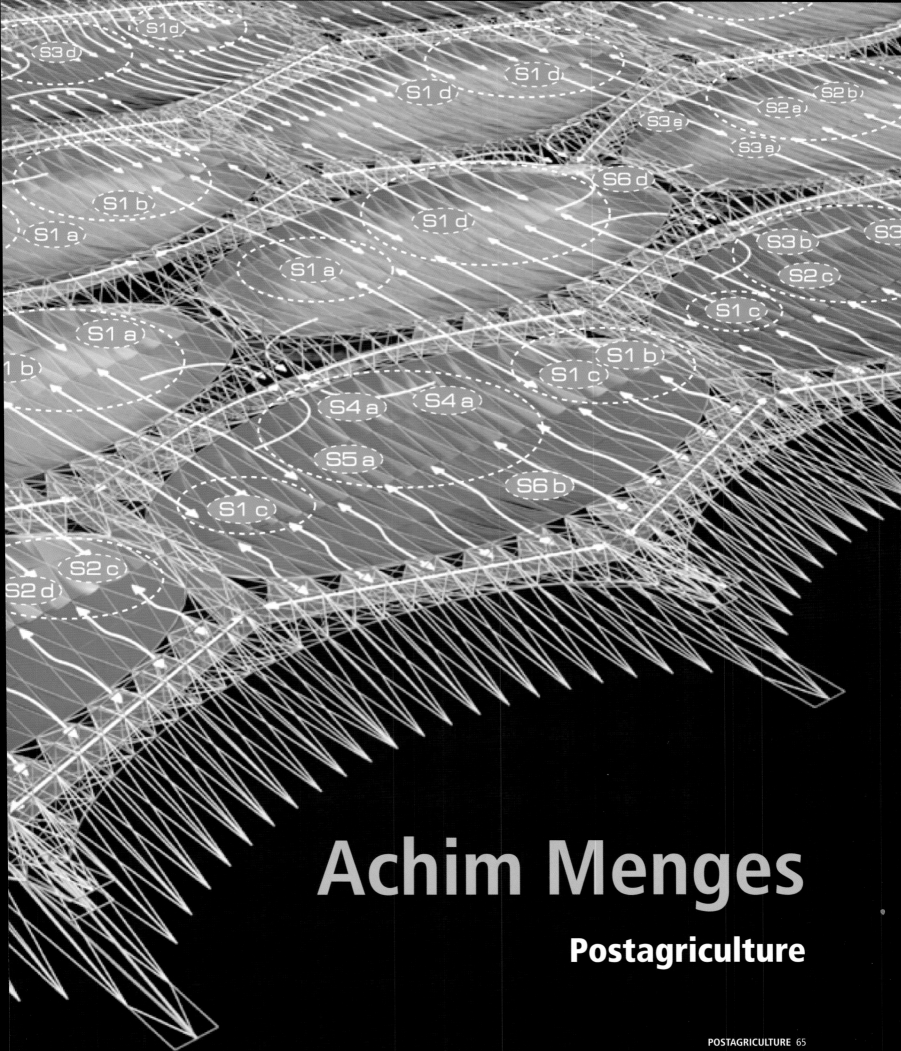

Achim Menges

Postagriculture

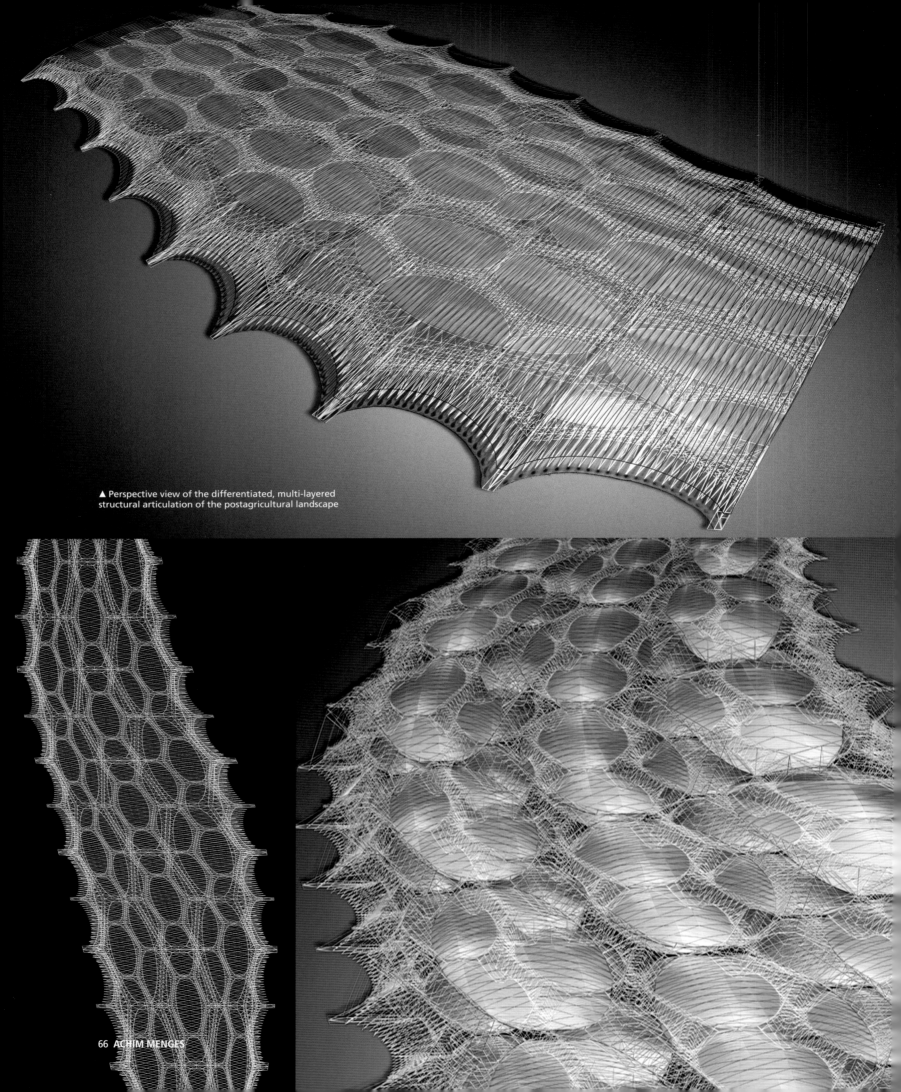

▲ Perspective view of the differentiated, multi-layered structural articulation of the postagricultural landscape

Agriculture has rarely been the site of critical speculation in architecture, although it could be said that it emerges as a critical domain when society undergoes a major technological paradigm shift. In daily life we are immersed in a soporific bath of pastoral images, constructed by the food industry, by politicians and by tourist boards. Such images are constantly reinforced by film and text, where they stand as icons, a shorthand for health, happiness and a wholesome way of life. But behind this image lies something different, a complex organisation of production processes that is powered by an enormous energy consumption, slow to respond to change and dangerously inflexible.

The ambitions of this project stem from the recognition of the critical importance of environmentally and socially sustainable food production. Its aim is to develop an inclusive and responsive strategy that will enable a mode of agriculture that is highly integrated, mutable and a vital urban programme. Intensive farming and industrialised greenhouse growing often coexist in close proximity to high-density urban areas. This intensifies the competition between agricultural use and more profitable recreational use of the land. Agriculture also has a severe impact on the use of infrastructure through increased congestion. The area chosen as the site

◄ Plan projection (far left) and perspective view (left) of the differentiated, multi-layered structural articulation of the postagricultural landscape

Multi-chamber component prototype of a self-supporting pneumatic surface derived from a feedback between digital and physical form finding processes ►

Previous page: Structural articulation organising the service infrastructure and the inter-systemic connectivity crucial to the simultaneous, cyclic processes of agricultural production

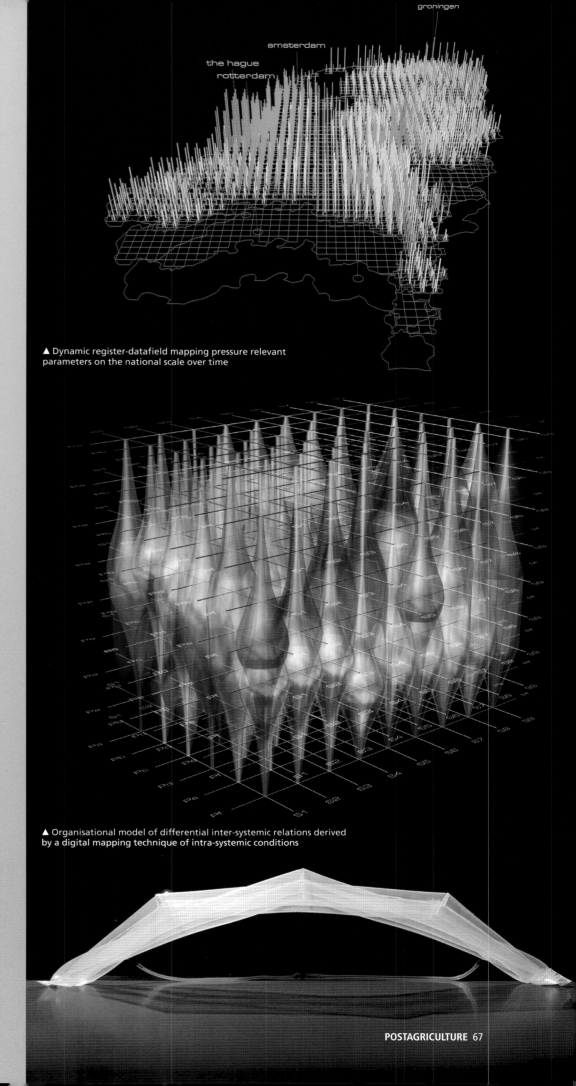

▲ Dynamic register-datafield mapping pressure relevant parameters on the national scale over time

▲ Organisational model of differential inter-systemic relations derived by a digital mapping technique of intra-systemic conditions

for the project is the largest and densest greenhouse growing area in the Netherlands, adjacent to the metropolitan areas of Rotterdam and The Hague. It thus offers the possibility to demonstrate the potential for negotiating opposed development aims. It requires an organisation that promotes the interrelation of open systems of agricultural production and recreation activities, an organisation that yields multiple conditions.

The performative environment necessitates thinking about structure as a condition that generates and differentiates. Rather than a static object, it is helpful to think of structure as a process of structural and material operations. Manipulations

tiation process is based on an investigation of one structural component, which indicates the possibilities and constraints of parametric variations in relation to performance criteria. The component variants can then be proliferated to construct a highly differentiated overall system.

Pneumatic structures were explored, as they have great potential for differentiation, and this was achieved by exploiting their non-linear characteristics and differential states of stability. Starting with a simple inflated cushion and investigating the basic structural principle of the relations between the pressure of the compressed air volume and the pre-stressing of the membranes, a pneumatic component was

the production of a physical model, which has a number of forms and pressure states in which it is stable. The resulting prototype is a self-supporting pneumatic surface, geometrically defined by different surface tensions and with seams that are structural elements. Parametric changes of variables such as the orientation, distribution, density and differential reinforcement of the seams, the depth and the internal pressure of the 'pneus,' and the type and treatment of the surface material were all tested, analysed and catalogued in relation to their structural performance and their capacity to modulate light and climatic conditions. In addition, the specific climatic and light

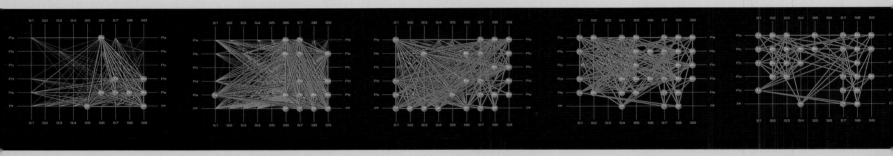

within the organisational logic and constraints of the structural system are intrinsically connected to the modulation of microclimatic conditions. In fact, the structural articulation enables the organisational model of differential light and climatic intensities to become operative. The development and assessment of the structure is not simply limited to its load bearing capacity but to a whole set of other performance criteria. The logic of the structural system is to distribute forces along a material articulation, combined with a capacity to organise light and influence climatic conditions. It is also a tool for spatial differentiation and related programmatic speculations. The differen-

evolved. The working methodology was based on feedback between different modalities – a digital definition of the boundary points and the related cut patterns produced in an engineering software, physical modelling, digital form finding and digital structural analysis. Multiplying the evolved 'single cushion' component a prototype was developed, a multi-chamber surface component. In response to the dynamic relation between structural stability, surface geometry and internal air pressure the boundary definition points were animated and then transferred back into the structural software package. This provided the input for digital form finding processes, and enabled

conditions of the site and the particular urban context had to be addressed. The resulting deep structure is a manifold of local geometries within a global system.

This integral feedback loop between material articulation and the modulation of interior conditions dissolves an understanding of structure as an accumulation of discrete, jointed parts towards an overall yet locally differentiated and performative system.

The site is at the sea front and has specific light and climatic conditions that vary daily as well as in seasonal time cycles. The existing local agriculture and recreational networks and infrastructure are important additional parameters.

Together, these disparate parameters inflect the distribution of macro-environments and the macro-systemic connectivities; they are further modified by ecologies and informatics of advanced agricultural production processes. For example, aeroponic systems of greenhouse production have plants suspended in mid-air, fed by minimal, direct injection of substrates to exposed roots and maintained by robots.

The macro-environmental distribution combined with the differentiated structural system evolves a highly articulated post-agricultural landscape. The top layer of the structure is a wide-spanning pneumatic surface with distributed perforation at the perimeter. Recreation activities are inter-

The livestock and solar gain are the main heat and light sources, conserved and modulated by the thermal mass of the fish basins. A one-year digital simulation run indicated how the structure responded to locally specific load-bearing requirements and evolved micro-climatic differentiation thus enabling the organisational model to become operative. More importantly, the analysis of the structural and environmental performance indicates the gradient transition from the hard-modulated micro-environments to a negotiable field of soft-modulated areas. These areas emerge in between the regulated material and surface manipulations and engender a robust distributed open system over a range of

change, and active key structural elements provide adaptation for divergent criteria.

The structure also organises the service infrastructure and the connections between systems crucial to the simultaneous, cyclic processes of agricultural production. It adapts the ecology by regulating thermal flows and the circulation of biomass. For example, carbon dioxide and heat produced by the livestock are reused for horticultural production. Waste-water from the green-houses is enriched with purified pig urine to grow algae and fish, that in turn become protein feed for livestock. Manure and greenhouse waste is fermented into methane gas or reused as fertiliser. With a footprint of 31 hectares, the project could

Process matrix of digital mapping techniques leading to an alternative organisational model based on differential intersystemic relations

woven with horticultural production on the upper mid surfaces and lower mid surfaces, smoothly blending into the surrounding landscape. The surfaces are organised and supported by the primary structure; the differential reinforcement of structural seams has additional functionality as the service infrastructure. Lower down, the infrastructure is more capillary, the spans are smaller and the seams denser. This provides for the higher imposed loads of livestock farming and processing activities, that can also extend into the climatically more stable residual spaces between the soil-covered, deep anchor points. At the bottom of the structural system are the processing pits and basins for fish farming.

conditions that can trigger and accommodate manifold programmatic mutations.

For example, a relatively stable, warm location within the deep structure of the postagricultural landscape could provide for regular horticultural production processes such as tomato propagation but with changing demands become a flower growing area interwoven with recreational use – perhaps an 'oxygen beach' exploiting the enriched O_2 level of greenhouse production – or it may cater for short public events such as a 'green-house rave.'

The project follows a twofold strategy, one passive, one active. The negotiable field of differentiated microenvironments passively provides for anticipated criteria of

save 600,000 Gig Joules of energy per year, while providing the population of Rotterdam and The Hague with organically produced food with a 25km transport radius.

In conclusion, the project demonstrates how an intensified localisation of agriculture could save future resources by including vital urban programmes in a production landscape. It clarifies the critical agenda of agricultural production, presenting an argument for a paradigmatic shift away from the current practice of hiding industrialised food production. Interweaving agriculture with leisure facilities makes it highly visible, and socially sustainable as part of everyday urban life.

Achim Menges

Future Systems

Selfridges Birmingham

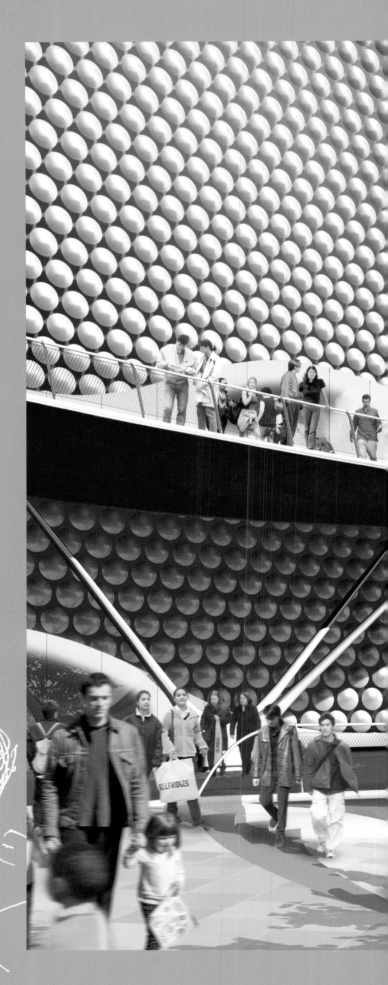

Selfridges' ambition is a state-of-the-art department store that is an architectural landmark and a genuine catalyst for urban regeneration in Birmingham. The store and its shopping mall will revitalise the Bullring and set a standard for future development.

The relationship between the 19th century St. Martin's Church and the new department store is critical to the development as a whole. Two very different buildings must coexist in harmony but a harmony created not by sameness but by contrasts in form, materials, mood, colour. Each must be true to itself, its function and its century.

The form is soft and curvaceous in response to the natural curve of the site, sweeping around the Moor Street/Park Street corner and wrapping over the top to form the roof. Just like the church, it expresses what it is in a way that is aesthetically innovative but also clearly signifies its function as a department store without any need for signage. The expressive plan creates a gentle backdrop to the church and defines the boundary of the new urban plaza.

The cladding is seen as a skin. It uses conventional rain screen techniques, innovation coming through the aesthetic not the technology. A series of anodised aluminium disks clad the building allowing a loose fit for tolerances and wrapping easily over the double curved surfaces. Large abstract glazed areas are carved out of the overall form, which has a dramatic roof terrace that will remain open in the evening.

The fluid form is matched inside by an organically shaped atrium stretching across the floor plan like an urban canyon deep inside.

Plasma Studio

Silversmith's Workshop

In the silversmith's studio, Plasma were presented with a standard live/work shell, and asked to provide a structure within that met the requirements of a Silversmith/Tai Chi instructor. Hence the engagement was between a standardised building and a set of highly individualised needs and activities. Within the orthogonal shell, Plasma produced an ascending spiral that incorporates the functions of vertical movement with a series of platforms that serve the programmatic needs – exhibition, display, practice – of the client. While providing spaces for specific functions, the structure does not segregate these as discrete and isolated activities, nor does it inscribe limitations on use. Rather, a tectonic and visual dialogue unfolds between user and form that enacts a dynamic of functional integration and dispersal, a non-choreographed trajectory of work, play and possibility. Plasma have responded with an innovative, nuanced solution that engages with the complex patterns of contemporary living. The topographical engagements hint at larger social processes in which slippage and interplay increasingly disrupt normative divisions of work, leisure and domesticity, private space and public space.

Douglas Spencer

◄ The upward spiralling surface from industrial grating is guided and structurally supported by a truss structure that also acts as a balustrade

The solution creates a continuous 'landscape' circumscribing a central void beneath the existing roof light ▶

TEN Arquitectos

Brooklyn Public Library

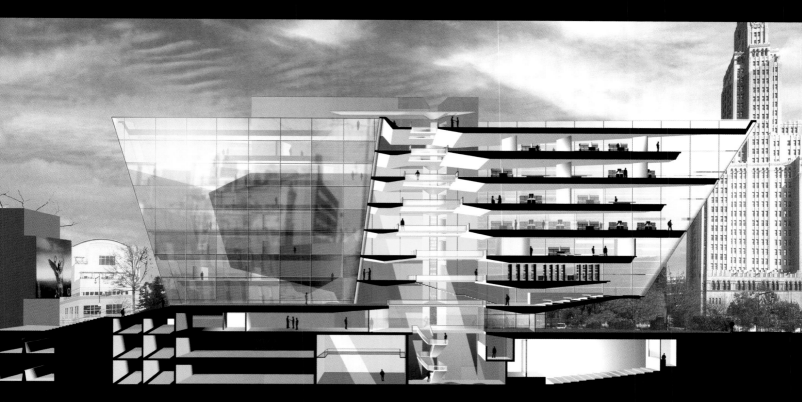

◄ Massing study

Cross section ▲

The V-shaped structure, transparent and permeable, of Brooklyn's new Visual and Performing Arts Library invites use and claims its place in the global media scene as a leader and icon of excellence and innovation.

Its glazy skin changes constantly and spontaneously, allowing views of the activities inside, forming a collage of space, form, people and movement that enlivens its triangular site at the heart of Brooklyn's new mixed-use Cultural District.

Adjacent to other cultural institutions that include the Brooklyn Academy of Music, the Mark Morris Dance Center and a new Performing Arts Theatre the new library responds to both the opportunities and the complexities of its site.

Behind a double wall of glass the building houses a theatre, an auditorium, galleries, media labs, reading rooms and a media lounge. Sandwiched between the window panels, horizontal louvres control the amount of light reaching the interior.

The Flatbush Avenue façade is pulled away, like a curtain, to reveal a plaza that lies within the courtyard formed by the V-shaped plan and frames views of the Brooklyn Academy of Music and beyond. This plaza is approached by a cascade of steps that can serve as an outdoor amphitheatre.

The visual flow between interior and exterior space creates environments that seamlessly weave urban context and building programme.

"It is not that we should change
in order to live in society, but
society has to change so we
can live in it"
Rudi Dutschke said.

"It is not that we should change
in order to live inside architecture,
but architecture has to react to
our movements, feelings, moods,
and emotions so that we want
to love inside it.
We say.

Coop Himmelb(l)au

BMW Welt

The image of the BMW Group will be enhanced by its new centre for brand experience and vehicle delivery located next to the towers of the Group's existing headquarters in Munich.

The main element of Coop Himmelb(l)au's design is a large, permeable hall with a sculptural roof from which emerges a double cone that counterbalances the existing headquarters complex opposite. The upper layer is curved upwards in a cushion shape. The lower layer is shaped by simulated reactions to the areas below. The room bars in between link the two grid layers into a spatial structural entity. The interior topography of the new building is determined by differentiated spatial densities and fluid subspaces.

It will function as a marketplace with many varied uses and will include an area able to hold up to 600 people attending technical presentations, scientific colloquia and artistic events. But its main purpose will be to provide in the heart of the building a striking 'Première' vehicle delivery area where up to 250 cars can be collected daily.

Suspended above this event space are lounges from which customers and visitors can observe the vehicles and activities in the delivery area below and catch glimpses of the BMW headquarters opposite.

The new centre creates a visual bond with the existing architecture of the complex formed by the Olympic site and the towers of the headquarters building.

Once inside, buying a car becomes retail theatre
▼

▲
Elevations

▶
BMW World; interior detail

Perspective with existing BMW Tower by
Karl Schwanzer
▼

Bernard Tschumi

Expo 2004

The theme for the Exposition Internationale 2004 is the 'image' in all its manifestations. The spatial concept is thus constructed like an image and consists of different 'image-situations': moving images versus surface images; the image of the part versus the image of the whole; images that shock versus images that form part of a smooth transition. These 'situations' are created by different 'phenomena of the image', namely, the point, the line, the grid, the frame, and the pixel.

The design concept relies on the interaction between these diverse 'situations' and the role each plays within the exposition itself. This interaction is a result of the organisation of movement (the circulation sequences), the organisation of 'matter' (the mineral versus the vegetal; the global structure versus the exceptional deviation); and of the organisation of the different buildings (the different types of pavilion).

From these proposed multiple situations, the aim of the Exposition is to create one strong image or sense of place,

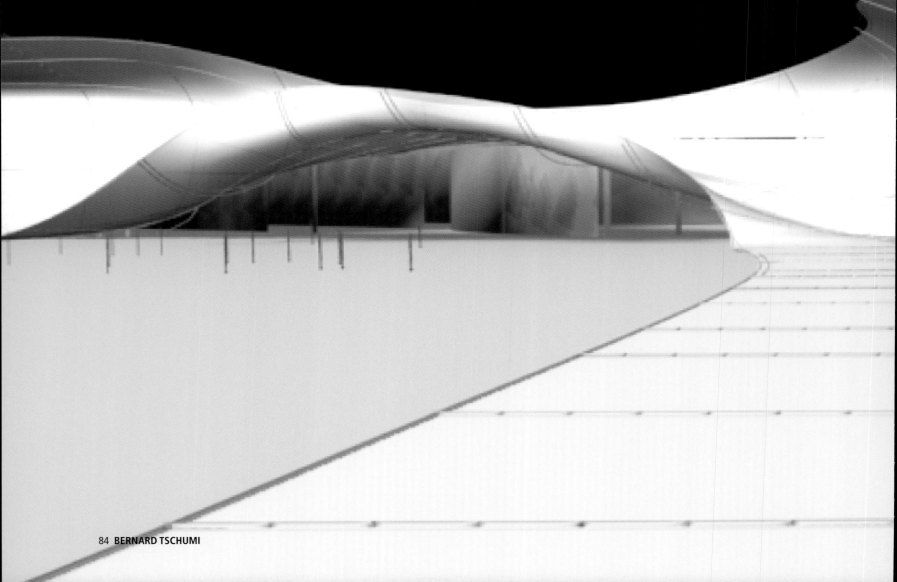

▲ Expo 2004 pavilions

which will be the general plane of reference, and which will be read as the overall structure of the event itself. Within this, the sequence and choices of each visitor will give diversified readings of place. Each person brings his own colour and point of view to this 'image-place' resulting in an infinite number of re-compositions.

The Exposition is arranged along a looping sequence which forms a 'long-court', an animated urban space of encounters, which traverses the site along a longitudinal axis and links the three main sectors of the Exposition (from east to west: the site adjacent to the existing Exposition Park, the 'Aire des Vents' and the natural reserve land adjacent to the Parc de La Courneuve). The long-court also integrates in its structure the bridge over the highway. All the principal activities of the Expo are attached to this long court. There are also several small 'escapes' from the long court which allow for secondary, more secret path sequences. The ground-treatment along the sequence suggests the nature of the activity that will take place there or that will attach to it, for example there are different treatments for crowds in movement, crowds in line, groups, individuals, etc.

Like an image, the project is structured with a decrypting code so that the visitor is not inundated by an overload of signs. It presents itself in the form of a series of filters of equal significance.

▼ Commissariat

Washingtonia
robusta

irrigation pipe
safety bold
prefabicated
planter

drain

illumination

steel mast

West 8

Arroyo Parkway Pasadena

West 8 has transformed the Arroyo Parkway traffic corridor (part of the historic Route 66) into a new, iconic entrance for the city of Pasadena. The plan is based on car use, the California climate and the all-American roadscape.

Domestic Washingtonia palms are planted on 26m high steel, champagne glass-shaped pedestals that provide the boulevard with light and make it visible from the valley. Other elements are a botanic rhythm of mixed vegetation and flowers at every junction, street furniture and a plaza with palms.

◄ View of Arroyo Parkway between Glenarm and California

"Where Object and Subject touch, there is life."

Johan Wolfgang von Goethe

"Time is a boundary condition on phenomena."

Philip Turetzky

Ocean North

Innovation: Feed it Forward

An approach toward Time-based Design and the Architecture of Change

◀ Extraterrain - a programmatically un-prescriptive inhabitable interior landscape

Extraterrain furniture aims at charging a simple material surface with potential for habitation and social formations ▶

When contemplating architecture's agenda of transformation and its implicit relation to innovation the question arises as to why architects promote an agenda of change and yet their design approaches to the stabilising of the built environment fail to satisfy the growing need for changeability, responsiveness and dynamic differentiation of the increasingly dense urban environment. OCEAN NORTH proposes a time-based design paradigm rooted in an understanding of the human environment as a vigorous, performative milieu in continual transformation.

What follows is an outline of an approach to the dynamic formative processes that articulate the human environment over time and an investigation of the implications of instrumentalising such processes and putting them into practice. Understanding the human environment

as inherently dynamic entails the coupling of human behaviour with the articulation of matter in order to derive a dynamic organisational model. The dynamic relationship between subject and environment constitutes a feedback process of reciprocal influences such that the process continuously modifies their relationship. Feedback loops may be negative and have a stabilising or inhibitory effect, or positive and have a disruptive or facilitating effect, depending on their dynamic structure and openness to external influences. For time-based design the notion of facilitating feedback is most interesting: it implies that conditions and processes are fed forward in time and opened up to their intrinsic latent tendencies for change and extrinsic contingencies. This calls for an approach that is concerned with differences, instability, openness and open-ended-ness.

Most architectural designs still proceed through the shaping of finite and discrete objects that prioritise gestalt over formative processes. Moreover, the predominant mode of conceiving gestalt is based on the functionalist fantasy of deterministic control over the object's utilisation, which reduces the relational dynamic between object and subject to a singular and static programmatic alignment. To rework this approach it is necessary to recognize the relationship between object and subject as immediate material for design. A useful inroad to this notion can be found in Umberto Eco's concept of open works. Eco characterises an open work by a deliberate ambiguity in meaning. According to Eco open works must leave the arrangement of some of their constituents to the public or to chance, thus giving these works a field of possible orders rather than a single definite one. The subject moves freely within this field of ambiguity, which serves to avoid conventional forms of expression and prescribed interpretation. At the same time Eco points out that this is not a quest for total laissez-faire and amorphousness, but rather that there must be a guiding directive from the designer that structures the field of possibilities in some way.

Likewise the American urbanist Albert Pope has pointed out that planning and design must concern themselves with a space/time composite manifested in the

mation. It therefore seems odd that most contemporary architects choose to take an exclusive detour via the programming of spaces to make functional provisions, thus acting on the context and the subject from the outside. Such a strategic approach to programming prevents tactical engagement with the dynamics of context and site-specificity. The latter can then only be re-enacted through notions of event-space as a space away-from-control. This notion creates the problem of space that can emerge but not be designed. In consequence there can only be annotated

kunstwerk and its attributes of totality, completion and finitude, designing with dynamics must be based on openness – openness to contingency and open-ended-ness. This design paradigm places relationships over entities, development over structure, and formation over gestalt. It requires careful negotiation between control and cycles of monitoring, assessment and intervention. Methodologically, this implies the revision of common practice in design, which progresses linearly from an initial analysis to the design phase and the finalisation of a project. The

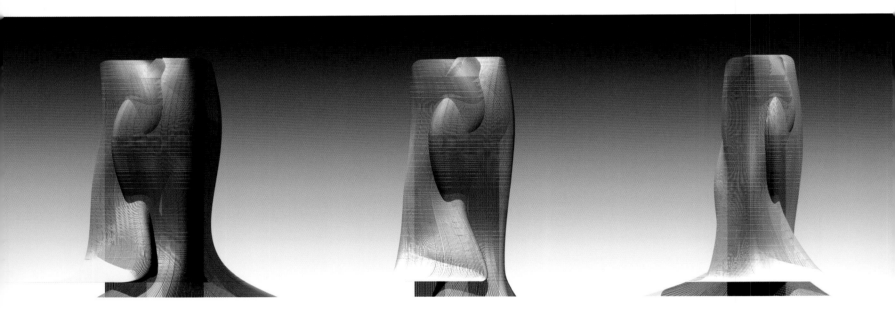

▲ Study for a World Center for Human Concerns (New York, 2001-02)

relationship between space, articulated by material form, and individual and collective patterns of occupying space. Much as in Eco's notion of open works, the subject becomes a generative contingency that acts on space and its articulation through appropriation and adaptation.

According to Robin Evans spatial organisations yield certain types of social arrangements and interaction. Evans pursued an implicit relation between spatial organisation, inhabitation and social for-

or programmed space or spaces that must escape articulation by the designer/planner. This raises the question whether there could be an actively enacted event-space incorporating contingency to such a degree that it can resist the tendency of settling into fixed programmatic alignments. However, an architecture that engages dynamic relations between space and subject must commit itself to formative processes as a continual unfolding. Contrary to the notion of the *Gesamt-*

inclusion of contingency requires that analyses be ongoing as the formative process between subject and milieu continues to unfold.

OCEAN NORTH is pursuing the notion of a relational dynamic between the built environment and the human subject through computational and analogue modulation and articulation of material geometries and effects. Their Extraterrain furniture project (Helsinki, 1996) aimed at charging a simple material surface with potential for habitation and social formations, while at the same time avoiding indications of an object-specific proper use. Various sectional geometries were digitally sampled and lifted into a non-decomposable surface to arrive at an abstract composite geometry free from references to any existing furniture types. Computational modelling enabled the rapid re-assemblage of the sampled geometries with the aim of building ergonomic capacity into the surface geometry. The finished piece was tested in various social events. The hard glass-fibre

Commissioned by the Max Protetch Gallery OCEAN NORTH's study for a World Center for Human Concerns (New York, 2001-02) proposes a space for all peoples and cultures. The 440m tall volume provokes a sensuous image of formation, continuity and multiplicity. It remains intelligible whether one single object folds upon itself or divides, or whether two objects are entwined in conflict or fusion, reflecting the simultaneous diversity and connectedness of human existence. Minoru Yamasaki's Twin Towers are visible as vague figures through the textured and

tiation, proliferation and distribution.

The emergent time-based design paradigm has consequences for architectural thought and practice. The context-specific tactical engagement with vigorous and dynamic environments encompasses three interdependent types of operational feedback relations: the relation between the built environment and its inhabitants where change offers an alternative notion of democratic space via dynamic difference; the involvement and exchange between all actors in the articulation and transformation of the built environment, thus eroding the artificial

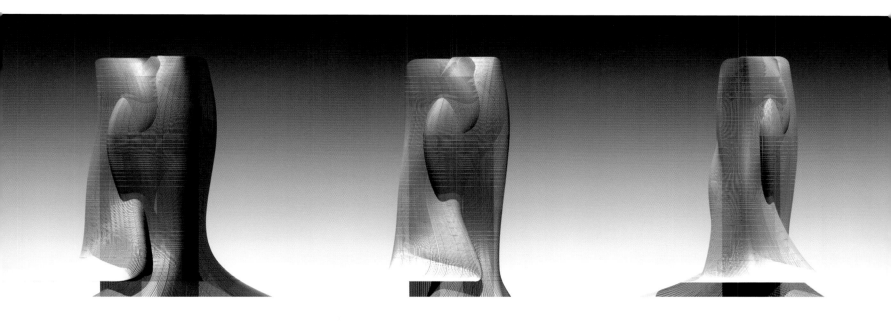

surface implies that the human body needs to adapt to the surface, and the large size of the piece, which enables co-occupation, together with the lack of sub-divisions into individually assigned zones yields a need for ongoing territorial negotiations. Thus, the way the surface is occupied depends on the user's characteristics – age, weight, size, etc. – and readiness to discover ways of occupying the piece. Geometry and positioning trigger incidental individual use.

folded skins of the new building. Its spaces result from the draping and folding of the building skin around the volume of the twin towers and articulate the building volume as a set of interstitial spaces that escape a singular spatial hierarchy and homogeneous relation between the built environment and its inhabitants. The differentiated material geometry of the object enables a spatial politic of temporal experiential formations – both individual and collective – and yields their differen-

dichotomy between urban design and building design; and the relationship between project and designer – if projects are conceived as open-ended a revision of the entire procedural and contractual set-up of architectural services is necessary, implying a change from service-based to time-based.

With more investigation the discipline of architecture can be revised through an emergent time-based design paradigm to become an architecture of change.

MICHAEL HENSEL

Asymptote

Technology Culture Museum, Manhattan

▲
City skyline

◄ Interior view

The end of the twentieth century saw the proliferation and profound impact of information technology, dematerialisation, and simulation on all aspects of culture. Museums and other places of cultural dissemination have been grappling with what constitutes experience, aesthetics, and perhaps most explicitly, reality. The Technology Culture Museum as conceived by Asymptote will house the output of late modernity, the result of a trajectory through the last century and a fluctuating notion of progress and innovation. It articulates and makes explicit the convergence of art, technology, culture, and commodity. It merges convention-centre typology with the utility of a hangar structure, and the public event programming of sports stadia with museum programming. The resulting building is a 300m-long structure off piers 9 and 11 in the East River in lower Manhattan. The vast interior is designed to accommodate large-scale expositions, media events, and public spectacles as well as more intimately scaled activities. Visitors will experience the aesthetic qualities and cultural relevance of technological innovation much as they became accustomed to experiencing art in museum settings during the late twentieth century.

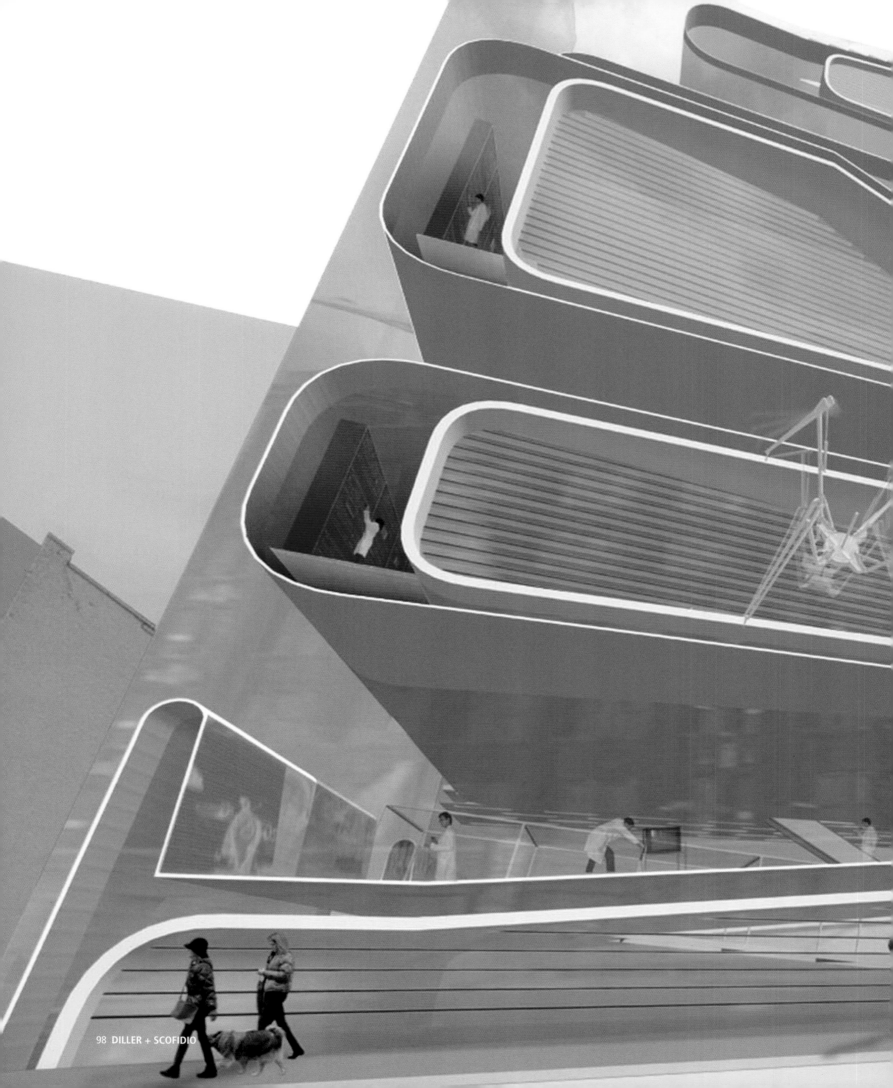

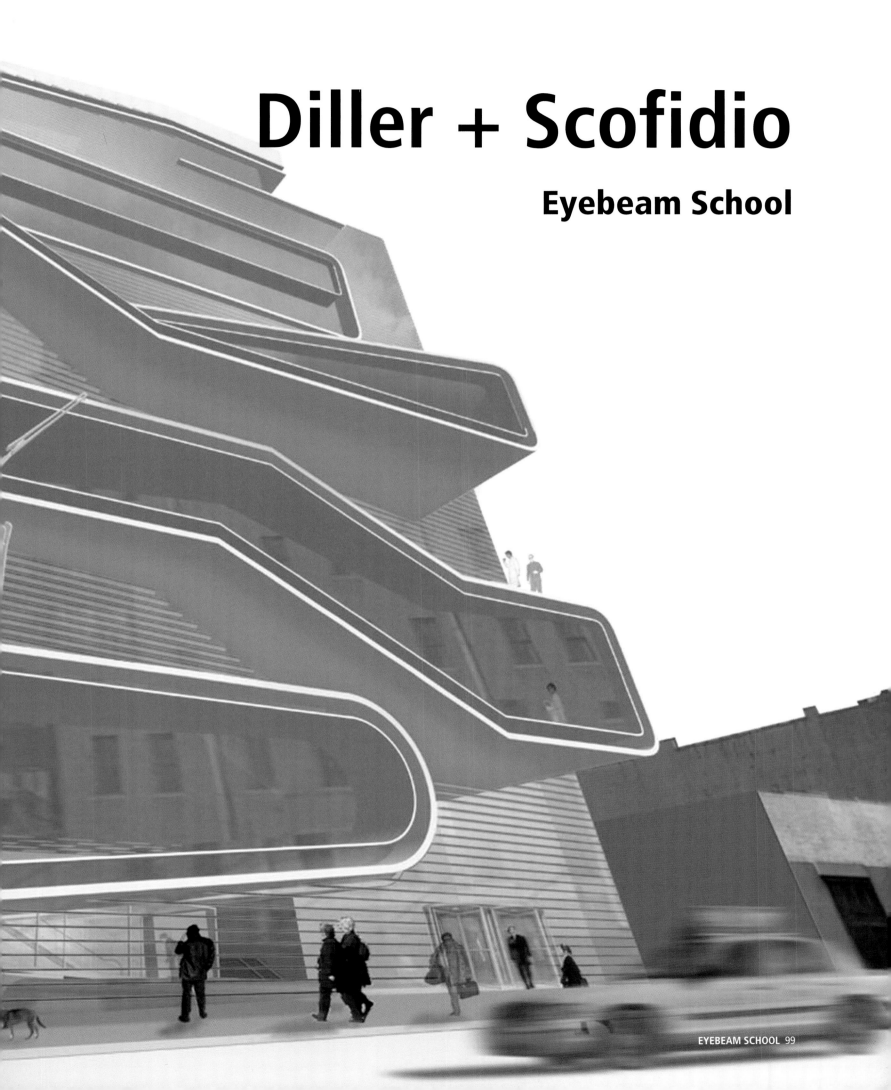

Diller + Scofidio

Eyebeam School

The spatial logic of Diller + Scofidio's design is based on a pliable ribbon that locates production to one side and presentation to the other, dynamically integrating conventionally distinct programmes. The ribbon undulates from side to side as it climbs: floor becomes wall, turns into floor, becomes wall again. With each change of direction the ribbon enfolds a production or a presentation space, alternately. The alternating programmes require the building's two diverse populations – residents and visitors – to pass through the space of the other while moving between successive levels. The relationship becomes more intricate when a loop of ribbon at one level is sheared in half and slipped into alignment with a level above or below, creating a controlled contamination that juxtaposes technical processes with their effects – people at work with people at leisure, the prosaic with the poetic. The ribbon is two-ply: smooth concrete ply facing the exhibition space, modularised panels facing the atelier, with a technical space sandwiched between layers that house the building's nervous system.

The production spaces and exhibition spaces each constitute a discrete building: one filled with light, both natural and artificial, and one that can be darkened. The levels of the buildings appear to be shuffled together like a deck of cards, their qualities put into relief on the façade.

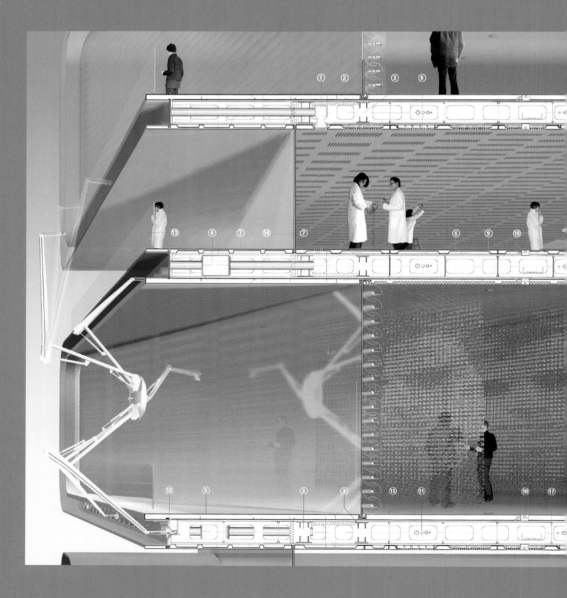

Interior renderings:
(left) exhibition; (right) theatre

construction systems

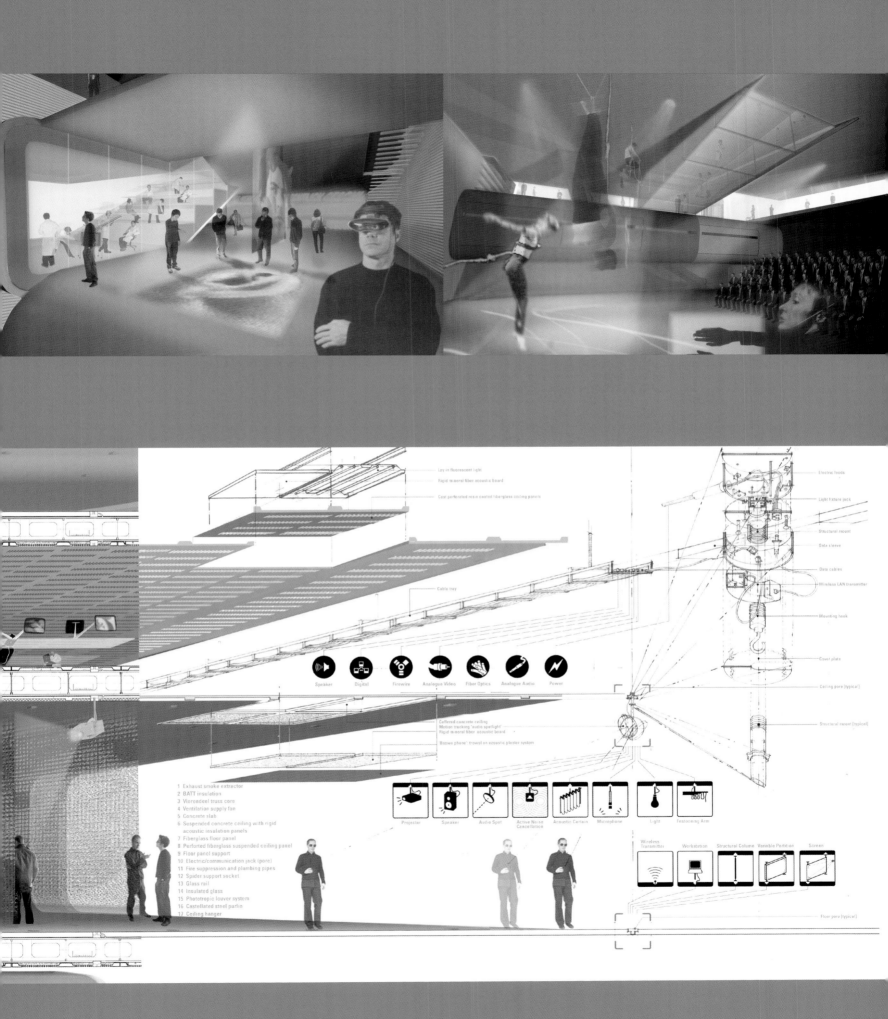

1 Exhaust smoke extractor
2 BATT insulation
3 Vierendeel truss core
4 Ventilation supply fan
5 Concrete slab
6 Suspended concrete ceiling with rigid
  acoustic isolation panels
7 Fiberglass floor panel
8 Perforated fiberglass suspended ceiling panel
9 Floor panel support
10 Electric/communication jack (pore)
11 Fire suppression and plumbing pipes
12 Spider support socket
13 Glass rail
14 Insulated glass
15 Phototropic louver system
16 Castellated steel purlin
17 Ceiling hanger

NOX

SoftOffice

SoftOffice is a structure where intensive movement and extensive movement are closely related. We all know, being humans, that our emotions, moods and feelings influence the way we move in space.

SoftOffice is a building where work and play are deeply interwoven, where children play and adults work. One half is reserved for very young children to play with interactive environments that are also present on the web. The other half functions as a so-called flexi-office where nobody has his or her own workplace. The office environment is made for both functional, formal conduct and for more informal creative conduct like writing, discussions and presentations. The scheme of this extensive movement always seemed skeletal, a mechanical framework of goals and tasks, not just in our lives in general, but especially in our work. To be able to control events we often resort to routines and habituation. But if behaviour and planning were nothing more than the blind repetition of

former actions nothing would ever happen, except maybe on the level of chance, but uncontrolled events make it impossible to organise and manage the work process. Although modern management theory still recognises that there is a necessary rigidity organising tasks around set goals, a certain relaxation of their implementation has become vital. While short- and long-term goals are crucial, because they form the hinges of planning strategies, they should not become so fixed that they start becoming unproductive and oppose innovation and creativity. This 'sideways orientation,' this flexibility is not just one of multitasking, but also a playing with the tasks themselves, a more fundamental sense of experimentation. Flexibility is in the first place, before anything else, one of the

mind, psychological and intensive. Next to time and people management the 'loose grip' on events and situations is also one of space and architecture because what is on the body's exterior can happen only when we have internalised it first, when we live it, experience it, and produce it day in day out in our actions.

In architecture this flexibility has always been associated with a variable usage of space, a multifunctionality that has subsequently resulted in an averaging of programme and an equalisation, even neutralisation of space (either through the hall or the generic office floor). This general openness always had the effect of generalising events and being unproductive, because this type of space was not engaged in the events themselves. In neutral spaces people always enter with

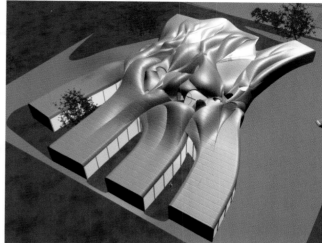

▲
SoftOfficeUK, Warwickshire

either preset notions of space that are not challenged by the architecture, or a generalised indifference that as a result becomes the main target of change for the management. The problem was not 'to open up space to more possibilities,' but the concept of the possible itself. The possible as a category is without any internal structure that can relate to variations; it does not produce variation by itself – it is without potential. The choice was always between determined functionalism or undetermined multifunctionalism. But potential is something different: "Potential means indeterminate yet capable of determination. ... The vague always tends to become determinate, simply because its vagueness does not determine it to be vague. ... It is not determinately nothing." (C.S. Peirce). Vagueness comes before the event, neutrality comes after. We have replaced the passive flexibility of neutrality with an active flexibility of vagueness. In opposition to neutrality, vagueness works with a differentiated field of vectors, of tendencies, that allow for clearly defined goals and habits and for yet undetermined

actions. It allows for both formal and informal conduct. However, this is not a clean and dry co-existence of two behavioural types as a mere addition or alternation, but more a multiplication, as one comes out of the other and shares the same continuum. To be able to switch between one and the other (in time) we need to materialise their in-between in space, opposing Mies's empty openness and replacing it with solid vagueness.

What becomes evident here is that the architecture of group behaviour with all its complex dynamics is directly related to the architecture of the building. A behaviour of continuous grouping and regrouping, of solidifying into certain configurations, then suddenly melting and regrouping into other fixed states. A behavioural vagueness paralleled by an architectural vagueness. If the skeletal structure of actions becomes as soft as cartilage and as complex as cancellous bone structure so does the architecture of the building. We should find ways where the intensive forces dealing with day-to-day decision making and coping

can actually become the formative forces of the architectural structure.

INTERMEZZO FLEXI-OFFICES

An analysis of flexi-offices reveals that there is a real, daily tension in the effectuation of their usage. This tension between the intended, traditional, static planning philosophies and the viable dynamic structure is actually the force that makes them productive. The surface area requirement of an office for 60 people in very different jobs (marketing, administration, online production, offline production, management, origination) would normally be at least 1000sq.m. Yet within the dynamics of an office culture, if one studies the occupancy rate of spaces incorporating time-space relationships, a very differentiated usage over time becomes apparent. The research for SoftOffice revealed three occupancy rates: 90%, 75% and 35%. The first group would contain people spending almost all their time behind their own desk; the second group were people who also spent a lot of time at other people's desks and at meetings. The third group travels around more and spends time in the car, restaurants, hotels, or at home.

This dynamic structure required an office area of 675sq.m, a reduction of 32% on traditional planning. But it is not just the quantifiable side of office space that has to change. The standard office landscape does not stimulate the desired extra communication and change of behaviour. In practice office space and furniture do not need to be designated for a particular person, nor strictly design-ed for a type of work but rather for a state of mind. Standard office spaces of general connectivity (flat floor, flat ceiling, general cable access) were set up next to more informal meeting spaces and very small capsules for individual work that requires concentration. The active programme is a continuum of expansion (communicative behavioural types) and contraction (the necessity to shut off, to discuss, meet, write, shout, either in small groups or alone). The passive programme, more a sub-programme, is one of cloakrooms, cleaning rooms, editing suites, etc.

INTERMEZZO CHILDREN'S SPACE

In contrast to the office space the children's space – the SCAPE – is a space of objects, a field or landscape where a substantial part of the movement is propelled by mock-ups from children's television programmes. While the adults in the office find a lateral freedom in a fundamentally longitudinally oriented system, the young children's movement in the SCAPE is gravitational and spiralling. They move 'around 'n' around' the objects. And they move from one thing to another, from one spiral to another spiral, without any overview: all tension is immediately released and rebuilt. As most of this is brought about by the iconography of mediated images, the architecture absorbs most of the spiralling in and out as an articulation of the floor surface only. This means the architecture does not need to follow the full move-ment of the spiral, especially not its rotational nature, just the fact that it is going in- or outward, which has a slight undulating effect on both floor and roof surface. The rest of the children's move-ment is produced by a combination of imagery and artificial lighting. Of these there are two categories: objects that are lit and objects that themselves radiate light. The lit objects are less interactive because a pure recognition of the tele-vision imagery is sufficient. For other areas a more interactive approach is needed, a zone where the building becomes alive and starts to play with the children. This area is called 'Glob,' a world designed by globally networked children. Glob is both present in the building and on a website.

Glob is a 'living organism' (some of its responses are calculated with genetic algorithms) that has the special ability to interact with children. Glob will grow, love and, of course, play. Glob creates an experiential environment for the children that affects their senses and their sense of humour. Together they will create drawings, music, stories and love.

INTENSIVE DESIGN TECHNIQUES

To map inward and outward going forces, to map contractive and expansive forces within one continuum a networked self-organising technique is required. An intensive technique means to inform a virtual system that during the processing of that information takes on an actual structure that is a registering of the infor-mation. The process has to take on a highly procedural form, like cooking; the instructions are not applied all at once, but one after the other, and timing becomes crucial. An extensive top-down technique would be satisfied with cutting differently sized holes out of sheet-like surfaces. The closed rooms needed for concentration would be subtracted from the surface of communication. In that case it would hardly be possible to create continuity between both states. And continuity is essential for tension between states. The expansive and contractive are not used as finalised properties but read

Experiments with material systems for calculating form. Each material machine restructures, or as Frei Otto says, "finds a form." Since they are agents, the materials have a certain flexibility and freedom to act. Machines used were sand, balloons, soap bubbles, glue, varnish and the wool-thread machines – as used for SoftOffice

▼

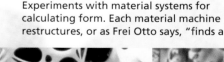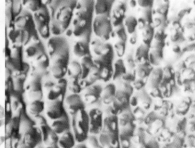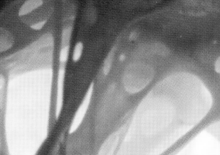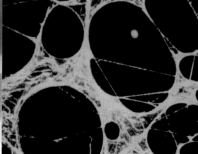

as tendencies, as working forces, as formative, not forms.

For this project a varnish technique and the wool-water technique were combined. The varnish technique is a surface-to-line-technique based on the fact that varnish, or lacquer, is highly viscous and can also later dry and store information.

The wool-water technique is a line-to-surface-technique where the lines are given beforehand in the form of wool threads, which are set up in a pattern where they are fixed to certain points, then given a certain amount of overlength. When the whole system is dipped into water and subsequently taken out, threads start to merge (thus using up the excess), and holes start to form next to surfaces of crossing threads.

Both techniques are fully systemic: all features are formed simultaneously. The holes are not taken out later but are formed with the various materialisations in the system. The system calculates everything at the same time, solid and void, during the same process, through thousands of minute iterations, where each positioning is dependent on the formation of another. Order and form are produced: they come about, they emerge during the process. It is soft constructivism, not a Russian mechanistic one. The constructive lines are not rigid H-beams but start as flexible rubber lines that meet up and at the end merge into a complex inflexibility. Thus analogue computing techniques are used not just to calculate structural form but also – on a higher level – organisational form.

THE RUBBER LACQUER MACHINE

The starting point is a non-volumetric whole where all elements are interconnected: a set of lines made up of rubber tubes (2mm in diameter) with an 8% overlength, each attached at certain points on a rigid wooden ring (450mm in diameter); seven points on the side of the children's space and four points on the side of the office space. From each point there is a rubber tube going to the opposite point at the other side of the ring, which makes a total of 28 lines. This system was doubled: two wooden rings each with 28 tubes, that not only connect one side to another but also one ring to another. This system was dipped into very liquid lacquer, analogous to the wool-water technique. But while the wool-water model is always flat, the two wooden rings can be separated during the hardening process. Instead of having holes and merging in a flat configuration, it is now possible to calculate the curvature of the rubber tubes and the intermediary curvature of the drying lacquer in a spatial configuration. The separation of the wooden rings during a three-hour procedure is analogous to the splitting of floor and ceiling. So, while calculating programmatic forces and mental states, structural forces are also being calculated. Complete vagueness: never fully column, never fully wall, never fully floor. The system negotiates everything with everything without resorting to equalisation. What now becomes most prominent in this system is that there is an expression of both rigidity and flexibility. The methodology permits the calculation of the in-between, a variation between the two states that are on opposite sides. While all flexibility is expressed in the middle of the system, the rigidity is produced close to the wooden rings, at the edge of the system. Type is at the edges, diagram in the middle. Full bottom-up in the middle, full top-down at the edges. Spatially, a spongy porous structure in the middle zone, clean separation of floor and ceiling at the edges (with columns in between). which means in the hall-like tendency of the structure, at the office side, four separate 'fingers' with gardens. Now the in-between becomes operative: it is not just a Cartesian choice, it is an actual sense of tension, a material state of in-between that is internalised in daily behaviour and functioning.

LARS SPUYBROEK

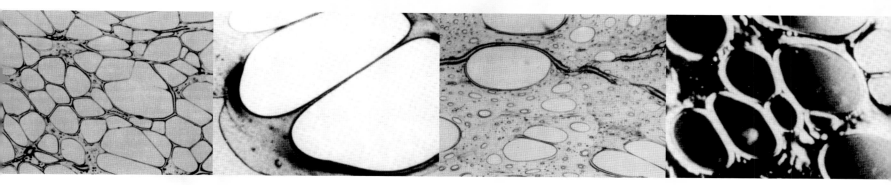

I arrived in New York by ship as a teenager, an immigrant, and like millions of others before me, my first sight was the Statue of Liberty and the amazing skyline of Manhattan. I have never forgotten that sight or what it stands for. This is what this project is all about.

When I first began this project, New Yorkers were divided as to whether to keep the site of the World Trade Centre empty or to fill the site completely and build upon it. I meditated many days on this seemingly impossible dichotomy. To acknowledge the terrible deaths which occurred on this site, while looking to the future with hope, seemed like two moments which could not be joined. I sought to find a solution which would bring these seemingly contradictory viewpoints into an unexpected unity. So, I went to look at the site, to stand within it, to see people walking around it, to feel its power and to listen to its voices. And this is what I heard, felt and saw.

The great slurry wall is the most dramatic element to survive the attack, an engineering wonder constructed on bedrock foundations and designed to hold back the Hudson River. The foundations withstood the unimaginable trauma of the destruction and stand as eloquent as the Constitution itself asserting the durability of Democracy and the value of individual life.

We have to be able to enter this ground while creating a quiet, meditative and spiritual space. We need to journey down, some 30ft into the Ground Zero Memorial site, past the slurry wall, a procession with deliberation.

But the foundation is not only the story of tragedy but also reveals the dimensions of life. The Path trains continue to traverse this ground now, as before, linking the past to the future. We need a Museum at the epicentre of Ground Zero, a museum of the event, of memory and hope. The Museum becomes the entrance, always accessible, leading us down into a space of reflection, of meditation, a space for the Memorial itself, which will be the result of an international competition.

Those who were lost have become heroes. To commemorate those lost lives, I created two large public places, the Park of Heroes and the Wedge of Light. Each year on September 11 between 8.46 am, when the first airplane hit and 10.28 am, when the second tower collapsed, the sun will shine without shadow, in perpetual tribute to altruism and courage.

More than four million of us came to see it, walked around it, peering through the construction wall, trying to understand the tragic vastness. So I designed two ramps, one from Liberty Street along the great slurry wall and one from Greenwich, behind the waterfall on the southern edge. Now we can see not only the Ground Zero Memorial site but the resurgence of life.

The exciting architecture of the new Lower Manhattan Rail Station with a concourse linking the Path trains, subways, hotels, a performing arts centre, office towers, underground malls, street level shops, restaurants and cafés creates an exhilarating affirmation of New York.

The sky will be home again to a towering spire 1776ft high, the Antenna Tower with gardens. Why gardens? Because gardens are a constant affirmation of life. A skyscraper rises above its predecessors, reasserting the pre-eminence of freedom and beauty, restoring the spiritual peak to the city, creating an icon that speaks of our vitality in the face of danger and our optimism in the aftermath of tragedy. Life victorious. *DL*

Daniel Libeskind

Memory Foundation

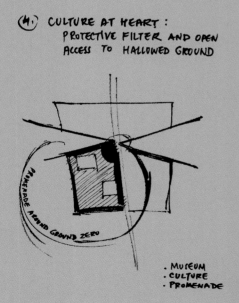

CULTURE AT HEART :
PROTECTIVE FILTER AND OPEN
ACCESS TO HALLOWED GROUND

PROMENADE AROUND GROUND ZERO

· MUSEUM
· CULTURE
· PROMENADE

Manhattan skyline ▶

◀ View West Street

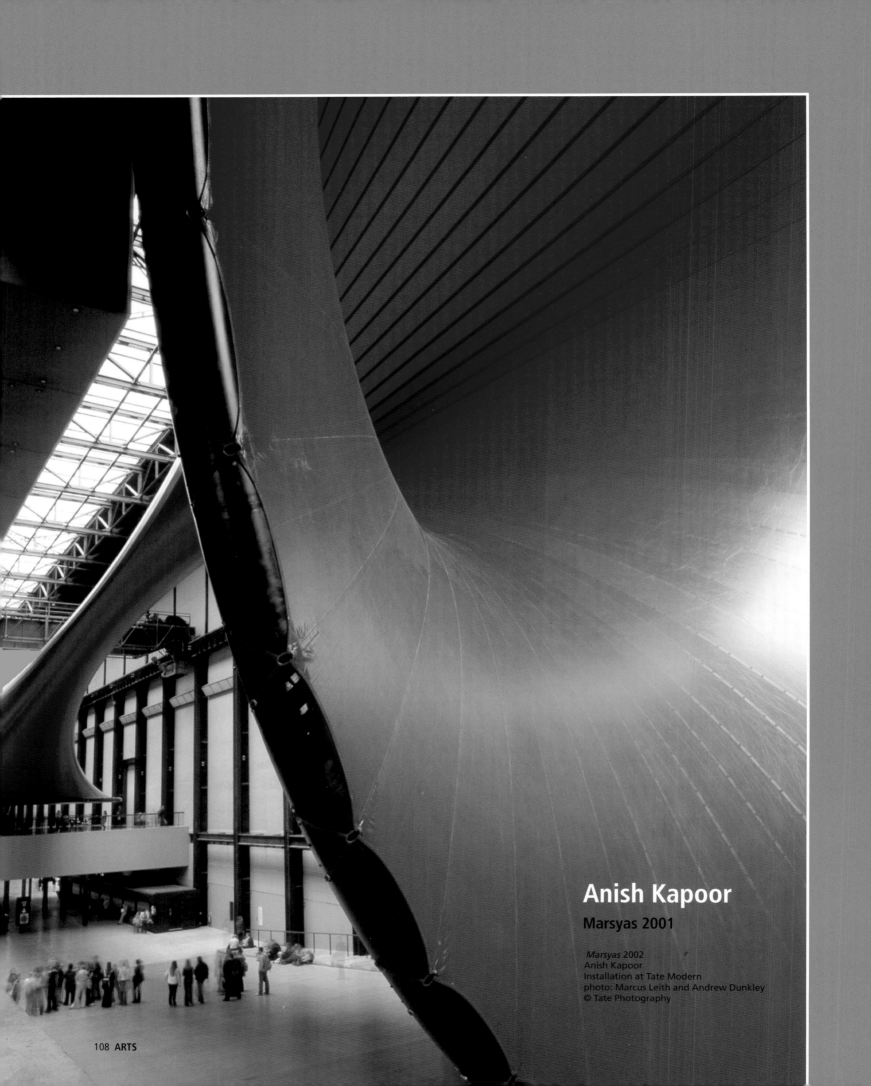

Anish Kapoor

Marsyas 2001

Marsyas 2002
Anish Kapoor
Installation at Tate Modern
photo: Marcus Leith and Andrew Dunkley
© Tate Photography

The Arts

"artists today don't believe in art. Ideas of art as embodying extraordinary creativity ... or occupying a higher place in human culture, are rapidly losing ground. It is becoming clear that art and artists are not necessarily special."

Jonathan Watkins, *Days Like These*, TATE GALLERY

(We very much doubt that the artists presented here would agree with this) *AP*

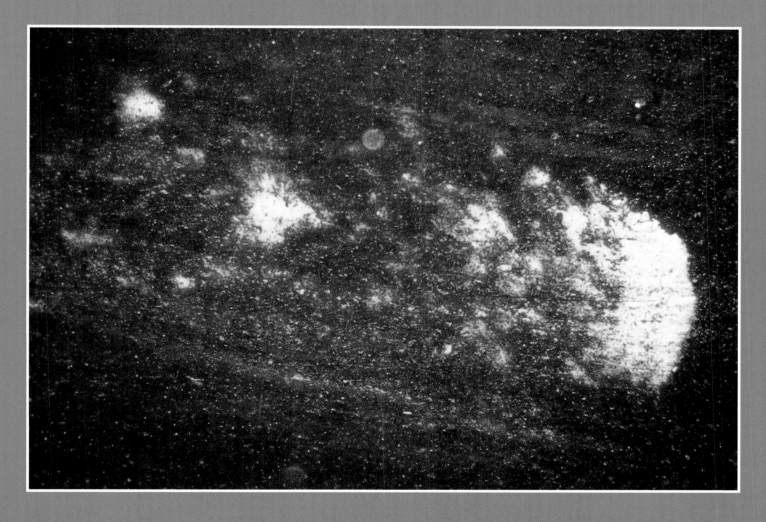

▲ *Einstein's Abstracts* 1999
Cornelia Parker
Photomicrograph (x 50) of the blackboard covered
with Einstein's equations from his lecture on the
Theory of Relativity, Oxford, 1931

Cornelia Parker

Einstein's Abstracts 1999

Pierre Huyghe
Les Grands Ensembles

◀ *Les Grands Ensembles*, 1994-2001.
Vistavision transferred to digital hard disk, 7:41
(loop). Music by Pan Sonic and Cédric Pigot
(random program). Edition of 5, 2 Artists's Proofs.
Courtesy the artist and Marian Goodman Gallery,
New York and Paris

Pierre Huyghe, winner of the Hugo Boss Prize 2002, has gained international prominence for works that explore the convergence of reality and fiction, memory and history. Incorporating film, video, sound, animation, sculpture, and architecture in his diverse works, the artist intervenes in familiar narrative structures to investigate the construction of collective and individual identities in relationship to various forms of cultural production. He is interested in both reading and making possible multiple, subjective reinterpretations of incidents and images that shape our realities. Through such retranslations, he offers a way for his characters and his viewers to take back control of their own images, their own stories.

The film installation *Les Grands Ensembles* (1994–2001) addresses alternative modes of representation and communication. A pair of bleak buildings, models based on 1970s' French housing projects, enact a subtle inanimate drama. Enveloped in fog, the uninhabited scene is both romantic and alienating. "These subsidized public projects ended up being an architectural and social failure," explains Huyghe. "They are a corruption of Le Corbusier's social and architectural Modernist theory." Though meant to be temporary, they are still here, much as we may try to ignore them. Huyghe brings the buildings into view and gives them agency. "Without beginning or ending," the two low-income towers dialogue in a strange Morse code given by the light of their respective windows, a blinking existence."

SUSAN CROSS

Chris Ofili
Afro Love and Unity

Chris Ofili has been selected to represent Britain at the Fiftieth International Venice Biennale of Art, which opens on 15th June 2003.

▶
Chris Ofili
Afro Love and Unity, 2002
Oil paint, acrylic paint, polyester resin, glitter,
map pins and elephant dung on linen with two
elephant dung supports 7ft x 5ft
Courtesy Artist/Victoria Miro Gallery

▲
Neue Nationalgalerie, Berlin
LED sign installation, 1999

Jewish Museum, Berlin,
Xenon projection,1999
▼

Jenny Holzer
Architectural Installations

Sometimes the messages are intensely clear, at others not overtly specific. They speak powerfully of human and social injustice and exploitation. Holzer's art seldom exists as self-contained language; it is a symbiotic collage of contextual elements in which language is enhanced by the site and the site energised by the language.

SIRI BLAKSTAD AND PETER PRAN

▲
Cremaster 3
Production photograph
The Chrysler Building, New York

Matthew Barney

The Cremaster Cycle

A five-part film cycle with sculptures, photographs, and drawings that describes the evolution of form through elaborate biochemical and psychosexual metaphors. Taking the cremaster muscle , which controls testicular contractions, as departure point they circulate around anatomical conditions of 'ascension' and 'descension' to metaphorically describe imaginary beings suspended in states of latency.

Imagine a biological and metabolic force converting into tangible form. And as that force transmogrifies and takes shape, it must follow one rule: it cannot subdivide into separate entities, even though it is compelled to do so at every turn. This is the process that governs Matthew Barney's *Cremaster* series. In his eccentrically erotic universe, nothing is construed as one thing or the other. Rigid dualistic categories – male/female, entropy/ order – give way to an enclosed system capable of self-mutation. Hybrid creatures revel in zones of genital indeterminacy, struggling to retain their polymorphous nature.

Barney manipulates a different theatrical genre in each film. In *Cremaster 1* – a fusion of Busby Berkeley-style dance routines and Leni Riefenstahl's choreo-graphic vision of Third Reich athletics – chorus girls form shifting outlines of reproductive organs on a football field, their movements determined from above by a starlet, who inhabits two Goodyear blimps simultaneously. *Cremaster 2* is a Gothic Western with strong psychobiographical undertones. *Cremaster 3*, the final instalment in the cycle is a distillation of the artist's major themes and signature aesthetic devices, filtered through an elaborate symbolic matrix involving Freemasonry, Celtic lore, and Art Deco design. Set in New York's Chrysler building, it includes detours to the Guggenheim Museum's Frank Lloyd Wright building, the harness track in Saratoga Springs, the Giant's Causeway in Northern Ireland and Fingal's Cave in the Scottish Hebrides.   *Nancy Spector*

Begehren (Desire)

Music Theatre by Beat Furrer
Stage design by Zaha Hadid

Today, innovative plans for opera demand the crossing of boundaries, new sound constellations, modified vocal characters and figures, and other expanses. In *Begehren* (Desire) Beat Furrer projects the Orpheus myth out of classical antiquity and into the present. Myth becomes wholly musical again and is performed in the territory of epic music theatre. Direction and choreography by Reinhild Hoffman. Stage design by Zaha Hadid.

◄

Production photographs. from left to right:
Cremaster 1; Cremaster 1, photo: Michael James
O'Brien; Cremaster 2 Production Photograph,
photo: Chris Winget

Melvin Charney
Un Dictionnaire

Looking at a system from the outside is revelatory, and provides fresh, incisive views. The unexpected events transmitted by wire-service news photographs – selected, classified, and collated by Charney to construct his *Dictionnaire* – to confront us with the shock of recognition that allows us to see architecture from outside its presentation as an isolated monument.

Fragmented, multi-layered, endlessly unique and uniquely repetitive, the news images have the same texture as the city. In its ability to move us *Un Dictionnaire* in its ideation, construction, and form, also proves the power of aesthetics in ethics.

Phyllis Lambert

►

Un Dictionnaire... Illuminations 2000
Melvin Charney
Triptych 30 x 20 cm
Collection NewArch

Stage design, photo: Hélène Binet
▼

Random Dance

Nemesis

Under its artistic director Wayne McGregor, Random Dance's work focuses on the exploration of dance and technology. Over the past six years it has collaborated with cutting edge, multidisciplinary artists to create award-winning technology based works that have placed the company at the forefront of the interface between dance and new technology. Random's extensive education programme is committed to developing work that explores the creative potential in the fusion of dance, the internet and digital technology.

Nemesis explores the relationship between body, screen and machine demonstrating an articulate dialogue between a rich choreographic language and a new performative relationship to a range of innovative media: animation, digital film, 3D architecture, electronic sound and virtual dancers. It is now exploring the possibilities of webcasting.

▲
Odette Hughes and Julian de Leon
in Random Dance's *Nemesis*
photo: Ravi Deepres

Odette Hughes in Random Dance's *Nemesis*
photo: Ravi Deepres
▼

Nicole Tran Ba Vang

To Be or Not To Be?

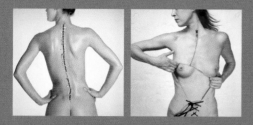

▲
Left: *Collection Croisière Spring/Summer 2002*
Right: *Spring/Summer Collection 2001*

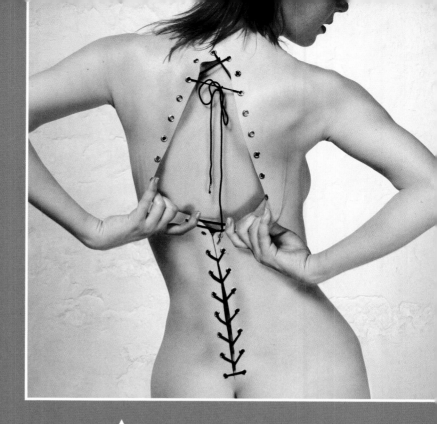

▲
Spring/Summer Collection 2001

Coutures Cellulaires 1999
▼

My work is defined by this play on words, my aim to probe the reality beyond appearance. Reality and appearance constitute a recurring question.

A revelation of the bipolarisation of the individual who, on the one hand, questions clothing beyond its function and, on the other, the body as screen and/or mirror.

Clothing merges with skin and, paradoxically, the body is unclothed when clothed in a covering of nudity.

Appearance has a powerful social function from which there is no escape.

It is an attempt to question what is by trying to break, to deconstruct what seems to be: it is when the gaze no longer has these markers that it goes beyond the image and it is inside this paradox – naked body and clothed in nakedness – that I insert myself.

Each year, a Spring/Summer and an Autumn/Winter collection based on the Collections of the fashion world reflect the constancy of this paradox.
Spring/Summer Collection 2001
The 'Post Punk Rock' trend of the season is evoked by 'nude clothes' fitted with safety pins, zips, etc. that pull the skin.

This series attempts to take away from appearance by 'tearing' it more violently. The idea of moulting is omnipresent.

One also finds the idea of the self trying to find itself, the body in pieces, held together by an extraneous hand....
Spring/Summer Collection 2002
The philosopher Epitectus raised the difficulty of being in tune with: what one is; what one would like to be; and the idea that others have of one. This series illustrates the confrontation of the individual with prevailing standards of beauty.

NTVB

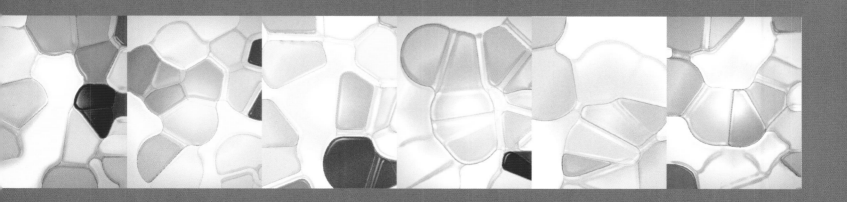

David Hockney's exhibition at Annely Juda's Gallery in London heralds an innovative period in his career: a series of striking watercolours. After experimenting with technology – from computer imaging to photography and from the photocopier to the fax machine – he drew inspiration here from the landscapes of the 'American Sublime' painters to produce a series of large-scale works entitled 'Paintings on Paper.' For these he used watercolour for the first time in his career, overcoming the technical problems of the medium for such large-scale works, extending in some cases to several sheets of paper, by putting on washes horizon-tally while drawing vertically so that he could see the lines.

The volumetric forms of these landscapes, reminiscent of the new shapes in architecture, had to be painted with speed and discipline. He decided to travel North to ensure longer periods of twilight when the colour of the landscape is not bleached but extremely rich and where in summer the sun never sets.

His own summing up of this new venture is that "there are losses and gains with any medium, but I thought the gains here far surpassed the losses."

▼ *Mountain and Cloud, Iceland* 2002, watercolour on paper (2 sheets) 45.5 x 122cm. Courtesy Annely Juda Fine Art

David Hockney

Painting on Paper

*"You've got to spend time to explore it.
I had the time and it's amazing."*

DH

on watercolour technique

Overleaf: *The Black Glacier* 2002, watercolour on paper (6 sheets) 91.5 x 183cm. Courtesy Annely Juda Fine Art

rip.dbox

Architecture in a media-saturated world

Night and Day, pre-release promotion
imagery for Sony Playstation 2

Attitude, the cast for the West End Musical
Closer to Heaven
▶

Images and concepts for a
piece on depression
▼

Rip.dbox is a collaboration between the New York based design studio dbox and London based photographer Rip. Encompassing everything from portraiture to conceptual design, the cross disciplinary nature of the coop marks a paradigm shift from the traditional arenas of architecture and photography towards a new visual medium, one that simultaneously explores the potential of spatial design, photography and the digital landscape. The collaboration specifically combines the practices of architecture and photography, extending the potential of both. Photography is used as a site to explore architectural design and architecture as a potential stage set for photographic shoots.

Fashion 1 (Metro) is a fashion editorial as well as a building commission for a New York restaurateur and his investor. The commissions, while separate, were based on a unique strategy. The space created required the participation of the reader of the magazine and the user of the final built work. For example, the bathroom spaces examine how multiple layers of different glass force different readings of the surface between the men's and women's restrooms. At certain 'safe' heights, the reflection in the mirror is replaced with the mirrored space beyond. In the fashion editorial, it is the photographic figure and her reflection that allow the distinctions in transparency to be read. The model's reflection in the mirror returns the viewer's gaze, accentuating the materiality of the surface. Underneath the basin, one is offered a voyeuristic view into the men's room. The legs of an occupant in the men's room appear to the left of the female model's legs, acting as further evidence of the materiality of the glass. The blurred motion of another occupant is segmented at three levels, 'mirroring' the female model's segmentation: opacity in the form of reflection at face level, translucency at torso level and transparency at leg level.

The initial architectural sketches created a framework for Rip's photography which in turn suggested a narrative that informed the design. This design process reverses the arbitrary superimposition of a scale figure into an architectural rendering. The figure 'scales' and influences the architecture as much as the architecture provides scale and influences the photography. As images and as a space, the work walks a line between architecture, commercial art, advertising and photography. It engages the viewer to ask questions about how the programme works and where the real begins and ends. It also invites the viewer to piece together the narrative from the evidence presented. Finally, as built space, it invites speculation about the position of architecture in our media-saturated world.

Stella McCartney
Mary McCartney Donald

"I'm obsessed with lingerie and lace, but I love structered things"

SM

◄

Mint-green vest and mesh skirt and vegetarian stilettos by Stella McCartney
jewellery: John Donald Jewellery, London EC2
location: Barbican residential, London, EC1
hand-tinted photo: Mary McCartney Donald

Mesh top with voluminous pink sleeves by Stella McCartney
jewellery: John Donald Jewellery, London EC2
location: Barbican residential, London, EC1
hand-tinted photo: Mary McCartney Donald

►

"....to wear a wedding dress means at least a kind of success. The unification and combination of men and women. That is what is called happiness..."

Yohji Yamamoto

THE BRIDEGROOM STRIPPED BARE

In July 2002 a host of fashion designers, models, stylists, celebrities and performers gathered at a West London studio to stage an ambitious and unprecedented fashion event. Taking the metamorphic potential of fashion imagery as their point of departure, and then following this through to its wildest extremes, photographer Nick Knight invited a global audience 'on set' to watch the preparation and execution of sixteen fantastical fashion stories broadcast live, via Webcams, on SHOWstudio. Ranging from transitions in gender, size, race or even species, each spectacular transformation was monitored from three perspectives, via the Webcam trained on the studio, via the camera broadcasting what transpired on stage and via the development of each 'shot' on the Polaroid board.

SHOWstudio

Nick Knight + Alexander McQueen
Transfomer

These three viewpoints have been captured to create a groundbreaking new project, which reveals the working processes at the heart of the contemporary fashion shoot for the first time. In two films drawn from the Webcam footage, watch the models arrive, the stylists work and the celebrities socialise as the sixteen fashion stories unfold. Video footage has been edited to show exactly what went on in front of Nick Knight's camera in four compelling short films. Animations of the final Polaroid images show the evolution of each evolving story and, when juxtaposed with the films, they demonstrate how the photographer makes his ultimate selection of what to omit or record in the final product.

At the end of a couture show, it is traditional to have a wedding dress. Mcqueen was the finale to *Transformer*.

A-POC

" In their uncut state they are simply a canvas, the wearer is handed a tool to make of it what they will and bring it to life."

Issey Miyake

A Piece Of Clothing

Issey Miyake & Dai Fujiwara

◄

One Piece, wool, nylon, polyester
A dress, born from a machine with one thread. A swirl of tapes is created, cut out from the cloth along its perforated lines.

►

One Piece, wool, nylon, polyester

Baguette. Just like the French bread, cut it wherever you like. Four items born from one shirt depending on where the lines of demarcation are cut ▶

◀ *Making Things* Exhibition, Tokyo, 2000
Huge bolts of fabric rolled like magic carpets, each holding scores of garments

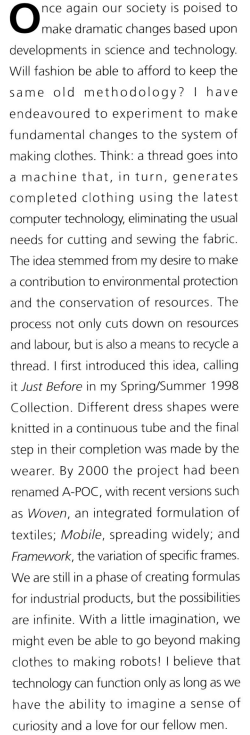

Once again our society is poised to make dramatic changes based upon developments in science and technology. Will fashion be able to afford to keep the same old methodology? I have endeavoured to experiment to make fundamental changes to the system of making clothes. Think: a thread goes into a machine that, in turn, generates completed clothing using the latest computer technology, eliminating the usual needs for cutting and sewing the fabric. The idea stemmed from my desire to make a contribution to environmental protection and the conservation of resources. The process not only cuts down on resources and labour, but is also a means to recycle a thread. I first introduced this idea, calling it *Just Before* in my Spring/Summer 1998 Collection. Different dress shapes were knitted in a continuous tube and the final step in their completion was made by the wearer. By 2000 the project had been renamed A-POC, with recent versions such as *Woven*, an integrated formulation of textiles; *Mobile*, spreading widely; and *Framework*, the variation of specific frames. We are still in a phase of creating formulas for industrial products, but the possibilities are infinite. With a little imagination, we might even be able to go beyond making clothes to making robots! I believe that technology can function only as long as we have the ability to imagine a sense of curiosity and a love for our fellow men.

Issey Miyake

A Piece of Cloth is a constantly evolving concept that will translate into different forms from this epoch to the next. These are all connected by an invisible thread both to the ancient days of their origin, as well as to the present metamorphosis, i.e. A-POC. The process of making things advances but never severs its ties with the knowledge of an age that preceded it.

It is still unknown how much influence will come from the innovative materials to be born from the latest nano- and bio-technology, but its origins were hinted at in materials found with buried ancient artefacts. When an excavated thread from a particular era is chemically analysed, sometimes molecules of sericin and fibroin are detected, identifying it as silk. According to documents, the silk fibre found in Maotai (Changsha Mawangadui) tomb was thinner than our present fibres. Silk fibre is made of polymers, meaning that it takes on a slender form. The longer the fibres, the faster the spinning speed can be; and, ultimately, production costs can be reduced.

There is little difference between ancient times and today in terms of the efforts and imagination required to move forward in terms of technology and production-efficiency. There is a series of astonishing innovations: the development of silkworm-feed, thread-making tech-nologies, genetic hybridisation, and even cloning. The power of the imagination has fuelled *A Piece of Cloth* throughout history.

Let us now think of machines.

Analysing A-POC clothing, one finds a set of dots. If the dots are considered as genes in a human body, each A-POC dress may consist of as many as 200 million 'genes.' And once the digital pattern of the dress is established, as many as needed can be commercially 'cloned.' And these genes or the 'crossing points' of the threads are where flows could occur.

The twentieth century was the 'epic epoch' in terms of making things in quantity and diversity with lowered costs, a result of continuous mass production. In prêt-à-porter, which is almost mass-produced haute couture, shapes and colours change every season. This is in opposition to, say, the designs of cars or household appliances, which use a continuous production method for the same product. When the prêt-à-porter season is over, a new one must be created in a flash, so it begins all over again. It is always fresh. In that sense, the global standards of present production systems of the personal computer or the car may be the beginning of their conversion to something analogous to the prêt-à-porter system. Standardisation is required for the reduction of production costs, while a diversification of designs is necessary to meet the wide range of customer demands. Prêt-à-porter was once an innovation, because it reduced production costs while diversifying designs.

Dai Fujiwara

少女都市

"....Today's Girls find that the only secure proof of their own existence is in their bodies... they flow and roam in and around the city."

Opening of the Japanese National Pavilion

City of Girls

Tokyo – An Alien Metropolis

Arata Isosaki

Portrait photography of present-day Girls in Japan by Hellen van Meene, a young Dutch photographer who found her models mostly wandering in city streets. On the basis of individual communication with them she created these portraits of the existence of Girls in Asia today. ▶

Let me first define the meaning of Girls as 'that splendid existence' which occurs before a young female is drawn into a system of gender-bias, and the separation of masculinity and femininity. The poet, William Wordsworth, once said of youth: '… Nothing can bring back the hour / Of splendour in the grass, of glory in the flower.' Yet, Girls today are 'déracinées' – a French word meaning rootless weeds. In the Japanese family system, the framework of a father-dominated structure disappeared long ago. Today's Girls find that the only secure proof of their own existence is in their bodies… they flow and roam in and around the city. There is no con-scious decision forming a division between what is inside and what is outside. Like life within an environment constantly under phosphorescent lighting, everything looks flat and indistinguishable and this creature Girl has no knowledge of how to deal with the dark. However, she is not isolated, as her thumb is in constant movement – in instant communication on a cellular phone with her friends.

Throughout history she has pursued the ideal of Pure Beauty. When she judges adults as ugly, she has an immediate physical response towards the object of disgust. The materialistic, media-oriented environments of the multi-layered city amplify her metaphysical reactions to that physical stimulus.

The entire psychological and even the physical existence of these Girls has become a sensory apparatus. And these sensors are at the core of the contemporary city. The way these Girls live may strike us as negative because of their combination of toughness and kitsch taste but I would like to discover in them the future of the 21st century City.

Looking back to that point when Girls' comics were born in the 1970s, we should probably have predicted the appearance of the kind of Girls we now see, who have such a tremendous impact on the cities of Japan. Amazingly, the faces and body language of the Girls appearing in the illustrated media at that time were largely dismissed as cheap stereotypes, while they were already evolving into new standards of social communication for Girls and Girls-to-be. Totally different from the female image of any previous age, this new Girl was developing into a printed heroine while also generating the impetus for the red carpet introduction of her virtual reality counterparts in the age of digital media.

It is remarkable that the character of the real Girls developed out of this artificial imagery and that Girls of matching body proportions derived from cartoon prototypes began filling the streets of Japanese cities with figures exhibiting nearly identical skin colour, eyes, voices, faces and make-up.

In Japanese, the word 'kawaii' is one that fits all circumstances and expresses the perceived charming qualities of dress, accessories, interior design and… well, everything. Literally meaning 'cute,' the word is most often used to indicate a trendy fetishism that implies a depth of caring – even love – for a material thing or media object.

When the majority of Girls show an interest in an item or product, it quickly emerges as a mainstream trend in the consumer marketplace. 'Loose socks' (thick cotton long socks which are worn loosely hanging between the knee and ankle), 'Tamagotchi' (the digital pet which must be fed and nurtured to prevent it from dying), and the newest

'Keitai' (cellular phones) are just a few of the many products that have been vitalised in the Japanese market by these Girls. It is not a question of taste: once something has been declared THEIR favourite, THEIR territory, its status as such is all that matters.

The city in such cases may not be too far removed from the urban images in the film *Blade Runner* where Rachael represents the artificially idealised, stylised android woman – manmade and provided with implanted memories of a non-existent childhood, as well as computer created snapshots of herself at six with parents she never really had, supporting and renewing the manufactured memories.

In the same way, each of us has private memories to help us establish our identities and grasp the reality of our own existence. Take these memories away and what is left? And what about the Girls of the new millennium… especially those who do not have fond memories of a real home and a vital urban existence? The single-minded determination when they choose even a trivial course of action may be the result of desperation and an insecurity that adults can never really fully fathom.

Girls say that they have to generate their own memories and establish memories of the present and of the future. The blank spaces created by the architects Sejima/Nishizawa provide a floating space in time where these Girls can begin to wander among their new reminiscences.

Do they dream of electric sheep? I wonder.*

NOTES: The term 'Shōjo Toshi' (City of Girls) first appeared in the title of a 'Jōkyo Gekijyou' (Red Tent Theatre Troupe) play by Jyuro Kara in 1969. *Do Androids Dream of Electric Sheep?* is a 1968 Sci-Fi novel by Philip K. Dick that provided source material for *Blade Runner*.

少女都市

Live Survive Protect
The Final Home

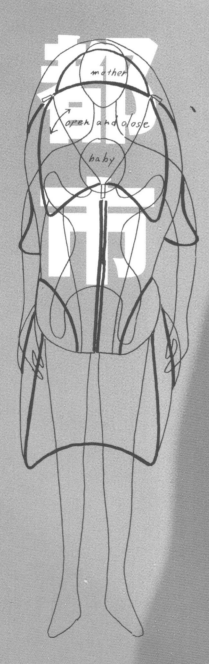

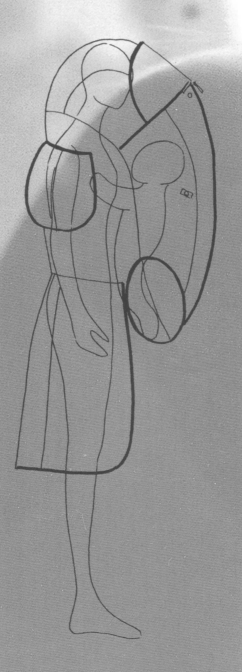

For some years now fashion designer, Kosuke Tsumura has been actively creating works on the theme of homelessness and nomadic life. *Mother* was developed under the *Final Home* umbrella. While the *Final Home* overcoat was born as the ultimate structure to protect the body in the disastrous situation of life in the city, *Mother* is a clothing structure or system designed to protect the young Girl mother and her offspring. It is a cocoon with a hood, embodying the strong will of the female of our species to protect her tiny children from the stereotypical, common-place, chatty, and inevitably noisy communication all around us in the city.

Kosuke Tsumura, *Mother*. photos, NewArch

Yoko Ono

A floating city
The second level world
Upstairs on the clouds
Mountains and rain roaring underneath
Like Venice, we have to commute by
boat through air currents to visit
each other's floating houses.
Cloud gardens to watch all day.

From The Soundless Music
(original text in Japanese) 1950

DOOR PIECE

Make a tiny door to get in and out
so that you have to bend and squeeze
each time you get in... this will
make you aware of your size and about
getting in and out.

1964 spring

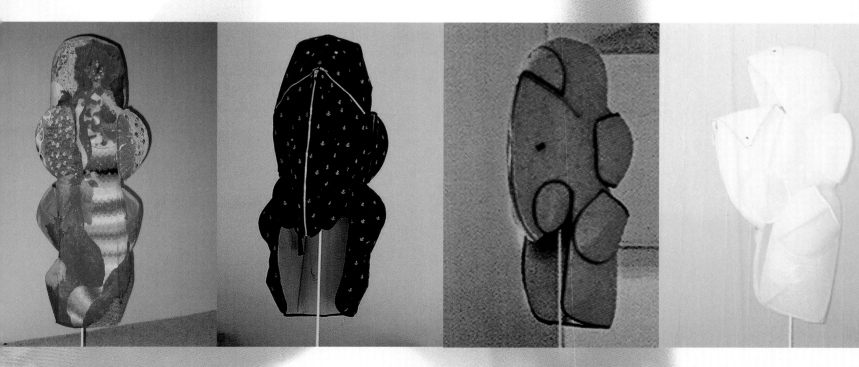

Design Experience

▲ Olian Spaces, Installation, Secession, Vienna 2002

The nextENTERprize
Audio Lounge

The characteristics of the audiolounge for the interviews of each team taking part in the exhibition *Trespassing* were developed by accident during an associative talk in the chatroom: making the user thirsty for audio / endless deep holes to crawl into and get lost in sound / something with no top and no bottom.

The finished audiolounge took the form of a murmuring object emitting different sounds through its holes as it was approached. Leaning into the holes visitors lost visual contact with their surroundings and were surrounded by the sound of the interviews conducted by the curators.

Andreas Thaler
Liquid Lounge

The Liquid Lounge can be described as a representation of the movement of water, as the freezing of a 'water moment': a droplet hits a smooth surface of water and causes waves in the form of concentric rings. These rings form the object's surfaces for sitting and walking. Video beamers are used to project water movements and 3D animations; the atmospheric changes simultaneously with the images; a sound installation consisting of digitally processed water noises runs in parallel.

Ross Lovegrove

Frozen Elasticity –

The Future Manufacture of Fluid Utopian Structures

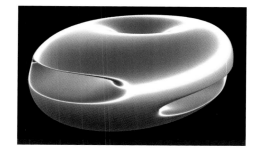

▲ Supernatural – fluid utopian structure

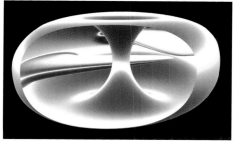

▼ Ty Nant water bottle, 2002

Will our future view of Architectural Utopia accept the rational debate that surrounds the way products are made, from cameras to water bottles, as perfectly replicated multiples, or will this be seen as limiting our creative instincts and challenging the restraining concept of urban conceptualisation or the creation of beauty as a singular architectural expression? Can we reconcile these opposing forces and combine them to achieve variable geometries: forms and surfaces derived from a material, technological and constructive logic that achieve the holistic integrity of unified structures and properties such as the lightness, transparency, translucency, opacity, impermeability, and thermal insulation required by habitable space.

The beauty of the virtual vision as expressed through contemporary computer imaging is not being translated into reality, thus leaving a frustrating void between emerging architectural visions and realities.

The revolution can begin once manufacturing methods permit flexibility in the way shape is made, linking more seamlessly the organic version of the mind to the machine, taking liquid materials such as polymers, expanding beaded foams, including glass and aluminium, and forming them in computerised pixelated moulds that expand and contract on three dimensions.

The process begins with the dream and lets the intelligence of the machine devise and construct the physical reality, incorporating visions of form and logic relating to the seamless evolution of natural/ artificial structures that the emerging minds of today wish to create as liquid organic or crystalline faceted structures. *RL*

▼ Liquid Lounge 3D animation. the visioneers.com

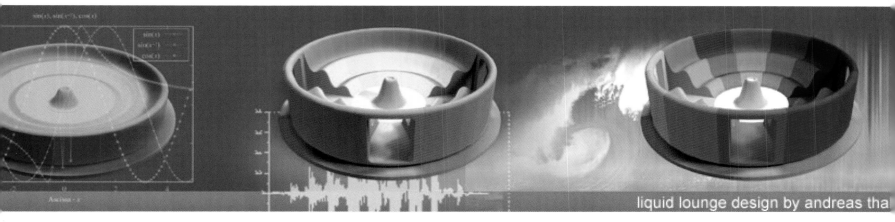

liquid lounge design by andreas tha

Zaha Hadid

Z-Scape Furniture
Glacier, Moraine, Stalactite and Stalagmite

Z-Scape is a compact ensemble of lounging furniture for public and private living rooms. The formal concept is derived from dynamic landscape formations. The different pieces are constituted as fragments determined by the overall mass and its diagonal veins. Along the veins the block splits offering large splinters for further erosive sculpting. Four pieces have emerged so far: stalactite, stalagmite, glacier, and moraine.

Within 5m by 2.5m, eleven pieces are melted together into a jigsaw puzzle, which can be opened up and recombined into other configurations. The lounging box chops off a condensed moment in a flow of interwoven soft and hard space. The soft space, moving up from the floor, is re-shaped into comfortable seating elements, while the hard space always has vertical flat surfaces on the top, as well as within its structure, giving rise to tables, desk and bar elements and a range of shelving.

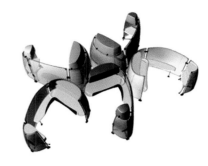

Asymptote
A3 Workstation

The A3 is a highly flexible and compelling new type of office system. The beautiful arabesque qualities of the cluster arrangements and layout configurations create a new 'officescape' that provides a desirable, human-scaled place to inhabit. The use of curvilinear geometry permits the creation of alcoves, impromptu gathering spots, breakout spaces, and meeting areas, all of which contribute to an active, imaginative, and engaged workplace.

Droog Design
Hybrid

Jan Hoogstad's high-rise buildings based on offshore constructions are hybrids comprising a durable core permitting a flexible interior and a mantle with a relatively short lifespan. Droog Design's proposals for the mantle, based on a concept developed by Jurgen Bey, Alias and Studio Open, use the interference of two linear patterns – the moiré effect – one inside and one on the mantle. Each user or function has its own colour. Together the colours form an ever-changing diamond pattern adjusted by foils.

DESIGN 141

I believe furniture should not be obstacles in life but raptures of experience. I try to develop furniture and objects as De-stressers – objects that bring enjoyment, not encumbrances, that simplify tasks, and increase our level of engagement and of beauty. Our lives are elevated when we experience beauty, comfort, luxury, performance, utility, seamlessly together.

KR

Organomica
rendering for
Johnson Community College, 2001

Karim Rashid

New experiences = more memories = longer life

I give birth to a multitude of things, both material and immaterial. I design products, objects, furniture, graphics, identity, space, clothes, cosmetics, lighting, environments, and I feel that design is everything we interface.

KR

Blobject
Fibreglass, 2001

MOMO 1000
Multi-bench seating
organic upholstered sofa, 2000
▼

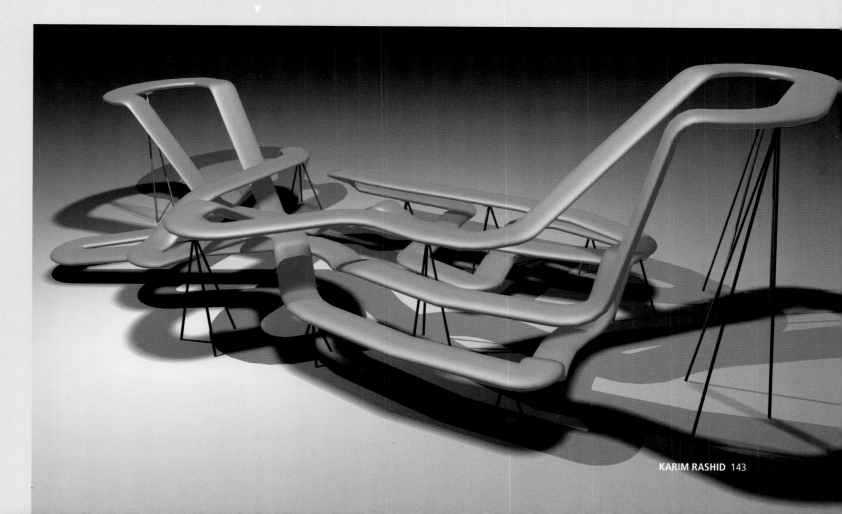

Alessi

City of Towers

Each architect was asked to design a tea and coffee service - a collection of objects that has played an emblematic, functional, ceremonial and exemplary role in the history of domestic commodities. It is an apt theme for a project which takes the visions of the world, idioms, materials, lights, colours, techniques and processes normally adopted by architects and applies them on a vastly reduced scale.

The first objective is to conduct a free-ranging survey into the future of domestic objects by endorsing and comparing a series of original visions generated when all constraints – practical and industrial – are removed. The second, focussed more precisely on Alessi, is to foster ideological, methodological, merchandisable and industrial renewal. In the 1970s, Alessi conducted a similar operation – Tea and Coffee Piazza – and the result was a marvellous story of micro-architecture for the table, of micro-town-planning for the apartment. The sense of architectural construction on the one hand and of domestic symbolism on the other was the keynote of each architect's design. This experiment radically changed the story of Alessi as an industrial manufacturer and contributed to a profound transformation of design worldwide.

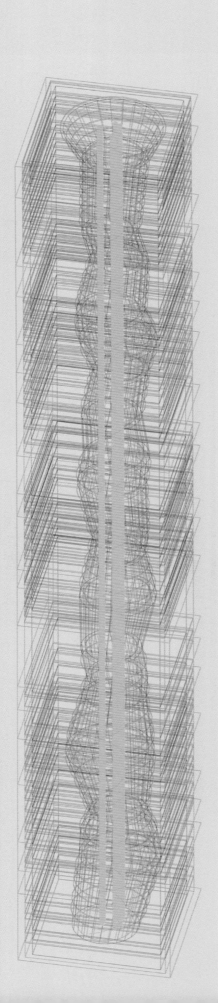

◀ Toyo Ito

◀ (far left from top) Greg Lynn FORM; UN Studio; Tom Kovac Architecture

Marcos Novak, *v4Dyzw*

LUXURY
PRIVATE GARDENS

edited by Haike Falkenberg

teNeues

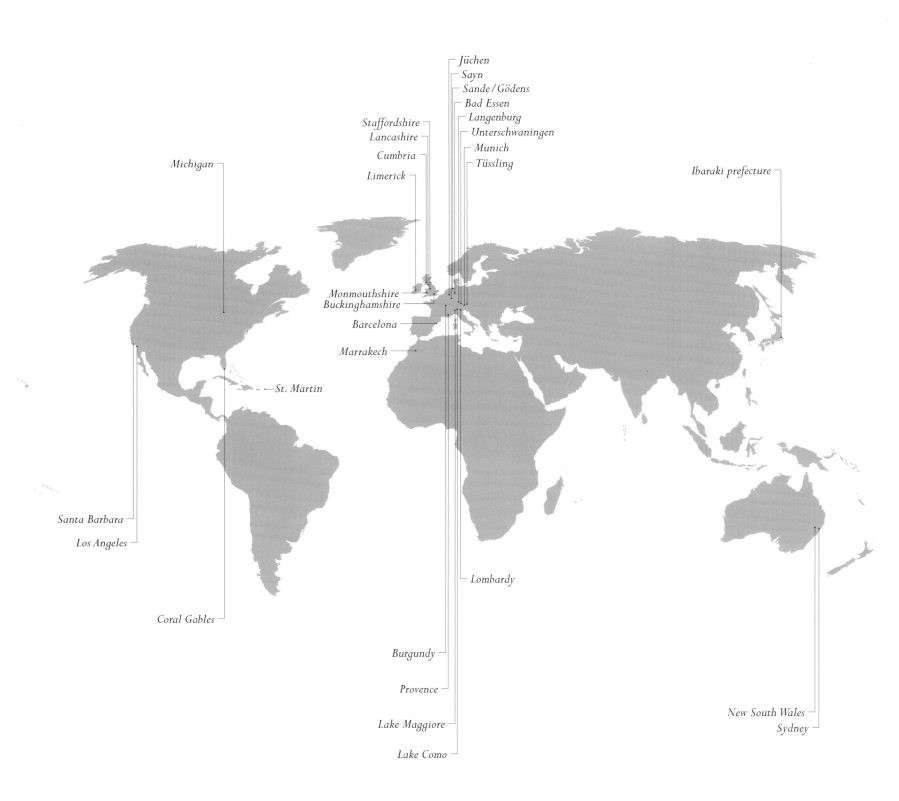

Jüchen
Sayn
Sande / Gödens
Bad Essen
Langenburg
Unterschwaningen
Munich
Tüssling

Staffordshire
Lancashire
Cumbria
Limerick

Michigan

Ibaraki prefecture

Monmouthshire
Buckinghamshire
Barcelona
Marrakech

St. Martin

Santa Barbara
Los Angeles

Lombardy

Coral Gables

Burgundy

Provence

New South Wales
Sydney

Lake Maggiore

Lake Como

Luxury Private Gardens

What is a luxury garden?

It is a *paradise* garden that gratifies all of the senses, such as—to chose a spectacular example—the gardens of the Alhambra in Granada, Spain.

And what distinguishes one luxury garden from the others? One word says it all: simplicity. When gardens like the one at Château de Courances in the Ile de France near Paris or the Odette Monteiro estate at Correias near Rio de Janeiro are stripped down to their bare essentials, they are like a well-cut couturier's gown—nothing but an utterly simple response to the unadorned landscape or the naked human body they are designed to fit. Russell Page, who was probably the greatest European garden designer of the 20th Century, once said: "About every great garden, there is an air of inevitability."

It stands to reason that most luxury gardens are designed for people with little or no concern about their cost. Such gardens tend to be built with an apparent complexity and on a scale that many people may initially find intimidating. However, a luxury garden can be within anyone's grasp. In pursuing this notion, it is important firstly to pause and consider the source of inspiration for luxury gardens.

As a landscape designer who works all over the world, from the flat countryside of the Ile de France to the Australian Outback, I believe that the first consideration must always be the innate qualities of the site. This applies whether the garden is large or small. It means that gardens in the Ile de France—composed of plangent, reflecting bodies of water such as ponds, swimming pools, canals or slow moving streams passively reflecting the sky and passing clouds above—will have that essential air of inevitability about them from the outset. On the other hand, there is the example of a garden in the Australian Outback that gives shade from the sun and protection from strong winds. While offering vistas to a distant but clearly defined horizon and recognizing an implausibly immense dome of Australian sky above, it will also address immutable truths as its starting point.

The small courtyard garden of a *riyadh* in the Medina of Marrakesh might seem to be a more difficult case. Yet, the starting point is also obvious here: It must be the sky, the quality of the natural light and the scale of the courtyard's enclosing walls. In addition, a leap of imagination might help by adding a pavilion—or a tent—on the roof above the courtyard. Such a pavilion might be designed to serve not only as the focal point for one of the courtyard's four sides, but also act as a vantage point for admiring the courtyard before looking at views of distant tall date palms and the Atlas Mountains silhouetted against the southern sky.

Each of these cases reveals that the sense of luxury arises when simple, inevitable notions are tailored to the site. And such simplicity should not be beyond anyone's budget, as long as the designer of the garden is disciplined and brave from the start. This means being single-minded, which is apparent in the dazzlingly electric blue used in the Majorelle garden of Marrakesh. Furthermore, it requires an awareness of the principles of landscape design. These include a sense of scale and the harmonious arrangement of masses and voids.

This book contains two gardens that I designed. The first is a parterre of succulent plants in Sydney's northern suburbs. In this garden the client carried out the construction and planting on his own, working under arc lights at night and on a strict budget. Yet, this is a luxury garden occupying space that had previously been set aside for a tennis court. Because succulent plants from countries such as Madagascar, South Africa and Mexico have nothing in common with the indigenous Australian bush on the parterre's northern side, I intentionally raised the garden above the native forest by means of retaining walls so they would be separated. In principle, this ploy is no different from Granada's Alhambra which is similarly divorced from the surrounding Andalusian hills by means of retaining walls. While such separation offers vistas of the indigenous surroundings, it also serves to emphasize both the differences and the similarities between man-made and natural landscapes. When the theme of the garden runs counter to its surroundings, the scheme will succeed only if the beholder is immediately aware of the garden designer's intention to separate the man-made landscape from the natural setting.

No matter what sumptuous appointments a garden may contain, a true luxury garden in my view should have a strongly unified and essentially simple design. The intentions of the garden designer should be clearcut and instantly apparent to the beholder on walking through the garden for the first time.

Andrew Pfeiffer

Was macht einen Luxusgarten aus?

Für mich ist es ein *Paradies*-Garten, der alle Sinne anspricht so wie – um ein spektakuläres Beispiel zu nennen – die Gärten der Alhambra in Granada, Spanien.

Und wodurch unterscheidet sich ein Luxusgarten von den anderen? Um es mit einem Wort auszudrücken: durch Einfachheit. Wenn man Gärten wie den des Schlosses Courances bei Paris oder das Odette Monteiro-Gut in Correias bei Rio de Janeiro auf das Wesentliche reduziert, zeigt sich nichts anderes als eine vollkommen schlichte Ergänzung der tatsächlichen Landschaft – so wie ein gut geschnittenes Haute-Couture-Kleid perfekt dem nackten Frauenkörper passt, für den es entworfen wurde. Russell Page, der wohl größte europäische Gartengestalter des 20. Jahrhunderts, sagte einmal: „Jeden großartigen Garten umgibt ein Flair des Unvermeidlichen."

Es verwundert nicht, dass die meisten Luxusgärten für Menschen angelegt werden, die sich um Geld nicht oder nur wenig kümmern müssen. Sie werden meist so gestaltet, dass sowohl ihre Größe als auch ihre augenfällige Komplexität viele Menschen einschüchtern. Meiner Meinung nach jedoch kann ein Luxusgarten für jedermann realisierbar sein. Um diesen Gedanken weiterzuspinnen, sollte man einen Moment innehalten und darüber nachsinnen, woher die Inspiration für einen luxuriösen Garten kommt.

Als Landschaftsarchitekt arbeite ich überall auf der Welt, vom flachen Land des Großraums Paris, der Ile de France, bis hin zum australischen Busch. Ich bin davon überzeugt, dass man zunächst die natürlichen Eigenschaften des Geländes berücksichtigen muss, wobei es auf die Größe des Gartens nicht ankommt. Das bedeutet, dass Gärten in der Ile de France mit beschaulichen Wasserflächen – in der Form von Weihern, Pools, Kanälen oder gemächlich strömenden Flüssen – die den darüber gespannten Himmel und die vorbeiziehenden Wolken widerspiegeln, von vornherein dieses Flair des Unvermeidlichen haben. Auf der anderen Seite ist auch ein Garten im australischen Busch, der Schatten spendet und vor starken Winden schützt – während er gleichzeitig Aussicht auf den entfernten, jedoch klar definierten Horizont bietet und den unbeschreiblich weiten Himmel Australiens unterstreicht – eine entsprechende Resonanz auf die hier geltenden unumstößlichen Gegebenheiten.

Auf den ersten Blick mag sich der Fall eines kleinen Hofgartens für ein Riad in der Medina von Marrakesch schwieriger gestalten. Aber auch hier ist der Ausgangspunkt offensichtlich: es muss zweifellos der Himmel sein, die Qualität des Lichts und die Ausmaße der den Hof umgebenden Mauern. Des Weiteren kann eine Prise Fantasie hilfreich sein und ein Pavillon – oder ein Zelt – wird auf das Dach oberhalb des Patios gesetzt. An solch einem Pavillon auf einer der vier Hofseiten kann sich nicht nur das Auge festhalten, sondern er kann auch als Aussichtspunkt dienen, um sowohl in den Hof unten als auch bis zu den in der Ferne liegenden hohen Dattelpalmen oder der Silhouette des Atlasgebirges zu blicken.

In jedem dieser Beispiele entspringt das Gefühl von Luxus den einfachen Visionen, die das Land zwangsläufig hervorruft. Eine derartige Simplizität sollte im Allgemeinen nicht außerhalb des Möglichen liegen. Vorraussetzung dazu ist erstens, dass der Gartengestalter diszipliniert und mutig ist; mutig im Sinne von unbeirrbar, wie es zum Beispiel die Wahl des strahlenden Blaus für den Majorelle Garten in Marrakesch zum Ausdruck bringt, und dass ihm zweitens die Prinzipien der Landschaftsgestaltung bewusst sind. Dazu gehören unter anderem die Proportionen sowie das harmonische Arrangement von Masse und Freiraum.

In diesem Buch werden zwei der von mir entworfenen Gärten vorgestellt. Einer ist ein Parterre aus Sukkulenten in einem Vorort nördlich von Sydney. Er ist ein gutes Beispiel für das zuvor Gesagte, denn sowohl Konstruktion als auch Bepflanzung hat der Kunde selbst vorgenommen, abends bei künstlicher Beleuchtung und mit einem begrenzten Budget. Trotzdem handelt es sich um einen Luxusgarten, an einer Stelle, wo ursprünglich ein Tennisplatz sein sollte. Da Sukkulente aus Madagaskar, Südafrika und Mexiko nichts mit dem australischen Buschland gemein haben, das im Norden an das Parterre grenzt, habe ich den Garten durch Stützmauern über den natürlichen Wald erhöht, um beide voneinander abzugrenzen. Dieser Kniff unterscheidet sich im Prinzip nicht stark von der Alhambra in Granada, die ähnlich durch Mauern von den Hügeln Andalusiens abgesetzt ist. Solche Separationen, die gleichzeitig Aussicht auf die heimische Landschaft bieten – dienen dazu, sowohl die Unterschiede als auch die Gemeinsamkeiten zwischen dem vom Menschen Gestalteten und der Natur hervorzuheben. Gärten, in denen das Gestaltete vom Natürlichen separiert werden soll, werden nur gelingen, wenn diese Absicht des Gestalters dem Betrachter auf den ersten Blick klar wird.

Ganz gleich welche luxuriösen Elemente ein Garten beinhalten mag, ein wahrer Luxusgarten sollte meiner Ansicht nach auf einem durch und durch einheitlichen und einfachen Design gründen. Und die Intentionen des Gartengestalters sollten so markant und offensichtlich sein, dass der Betrachter sie beim ersten Gang durch den Garten versteht.

Andrew Pfeiffer

Qu'est-ce qu'un jardin de luxe ?

C'est un jardin *paradisiaque* dans lequel tous les sens sont sollicités comme – pour choisir un exemple spectaculaire – les jardins de l'Alhambra à Grenade, en Espagne.

Et qu'est-ce qui différencie un jardin de luxe des autres ? En un mot : la simplicité. Des jardins comme celui du Château Courances en Ile-de-France, ou de la propriété Odette Monteiro, près de Rio de Janeiro, sont épurés jusqu'à l'essentiel, comme un vêtement de couturier bien coupé ; rien d'autre qu'une réponse extrêmement simple au paysage sans ornement ou au corps humain nu qu'il doit habiller. Russell Page, sans doute le plus grand créateur de jardin européen du XXème siècle, a déclaré un jour : « Dans presque tous les grands jardins, il y a un caractère inéluctable ».

La raison en est que la plupart des jardins de luxe sont conçus pour des personnes pour qui l'argent est peu ou rien. De tels jardins sont souvent construits à une échelle et un niveau de complexité apparente qui peuvent a priori en intimider beaucoup. Mais un jardin de luxe peut être à la portée de chacun. Pour continuer dans cette idée, il est important de s'arrêter un moment pour s'interroger sur les sources d'inspiration de ces jardins de luxe.

En tant que paysagiste travaillant dans le monde entier, de la campagne plate d'Ile-de-France au bush australien, je suis persuadé que la première considération doit toujours être les qualités innées du site, que le jardin soit grand ou petit. Cela signifie que les jardins d'Ile-de-France – composés d'éléments aquatiques mélancoliques, de bassins, de piscines, de canaux ou de ruisseaux lents reflétant passivement le ciel et les nuages qui passent – ont au premier coup d'œil ce caractère inéluctable essentiel. Et dans le bush australien, un jardin qui protège du soleil et des vents forts, tout en offrant une vue sur un horizon clairement défini et en soulignant l'immensité improbable de la voûte céleste australienne, a également comme origine une résonnance par rapport aux vérités immuables.

Le petit jardin de la cour d'un *ryad* dans la Médina de Marrakech pourrait paraître un cas plus difficile. Pourtant son point de départ est aussi évident : ce doit impérativement être le ciel, la qualité de la lumière naturelle et la dimension des murs d'enceinte eux-mêmes. De plus, avec un peu d'imagination, on peut ajouter un pavillon – ou une tente – sur le toit au-dessus de la cour. Un tel pavillon pourrait être conçu non seulement pour servir de point de convergence à l'un des quatre côtés de la cour, mais aussi de poste d'observation depuis lequel on peut admirer la cour avant d'observer les dattiers et la silhouette des monts Atlas au loin.

Chacun de ces cas révèle que l'impression de luxe naît quand des notions simples et inéluctables sont parfaitement adaptées au site. Et une telle simplicité ne devrait dépasser le budget d'aucun designer de jardin, à condition qu'il soit tout d'abord discipliné et courageux, c'est-à-dire déterminé, ce qui transparaît dans le bleu électrique flamboyant du jardin Majorelle à Marrakech. Ensuite, cela nécessite une connaissance des principes de l'aménagement paysager comme, entre autres, le sens des proportions et l'agencement harmonieux des pleins et des vides.

Ce livre présente notamment deux jardins de ma conception. L'un d'eux est un parterre de plantes grasses dans la banlieue nord de Sydney. Ce jardin est un cas à part parce que le client a entrepris lui-même la construction et la plantation, travaillant la nuit sous des arcs de lumière et avec un budget très serré. Néanmoins, c'est un jardin de luxe occupant un espace qui avait été conservé pour en faire un terrain de tennis. Parce que les plantes grasses provenant de pays comme Madagascar, l'Afrique du Sud et le Mexique n'ont rien en commun avec le bush australien qui s'étend sur la partie nord du parterre, j'ai volontairement élevé le jardin au-dessus de la forêt indigène par le biais de murs de soutènement pour les séparer l'un de l'autre. Ce stratagème n'est pas différent en principe de l'Alhambra qui est séparé de la même manière des collines andalouses environnantes. Même si cette séparation offre une vue sur le paysage, elle sert également à mettre en valeur à la fois les différences et les points communs entre l'artificiel et le naturel. Quand le thème du jardin va à l'encontre de son environnement, le projet peut être un succès seulement si le visiteur perçoit immédiatement l'intention du concepteur du jardin de séparer le paysage fabriqué par l'homme et le cadre naturel.

Quel que soit le faste des aménagements qu'il puisse contenir, pour moi, un jardin véritablement luxueux doit présenter un concept de création très simple et unifié. Les intentions du créateur du jardin doivent être nettes et instantanément lisibles pour le visiteur se promenant pour la première fois dans le jardin.

Andrew Pfeiffer

¿En qué consiste un jardín de lujo?

Para mí, es un jardín *paradisíaco* que apela a todos los sentidos. Un espectacular ejemplo lo constituirían los jardines de la Alhambra de Granada.

Y, ¿qué es lo que diferencia a un jardín de lujo del resto? Para expresarlo con una única palabra: la simplicidad. Cuando se llega a la esencia de jardines como los del Château Courances en las cercanías de París, o los de la finca Odette Monteiro en Correiras, cerca de Río de Janeiro, lo que se encuentra no es otra cosa que una simple respuesta al paisaje desnudo, como un buen vestido de alta costura que se adapta a la perfección al cuerpo desnudo de la mujer para la que fue concebido. Russell Page, posiblemente el paisajista europeo más importante del siglo XX, dijo una vez: "Todos los grandes jardines tienen cierto aire de inevitabilidad".

No sorprende pues que la mayoría de los jardines de lujo sean encargos de personas a las que el dinero les preocupa más bien poco. Dichos jardines suelen diseñarse con unas medidas y una complejidad aparente que en un primer momento puede llegar a intimidar a mucha gente. Sin embargo, en mi opinión, un jardín de lujo está al alcance de cualquiera. Abundando en esta idea, habría que detenerse a reflexionar y preguntarse de dónde procede la inspiración de uno de estos fastuosos jardines.

Como paisajista, trabajo por todo el mundo: desde las llanuras de la Ile de France a la zona selvática australiana. Estoy convencido de que lo primero a tener en cuenta son las características naturales del terreno, características que no van emparejadas con el tamaño del jardín. Esto significa que los jardines de la Ile de France, con sus estanques, piscinas, canales o sosegadas corrientes fluviales, formas todas ellas que invitan a la contemplación, que reflejan el cielo y las nubes que avanzan en lo alto, disfrutan desde un principio de ese aire de inevitabilidad. Por su parte, un jardín en los bosques australianos brinda tanto protección frente al sol y a los fuertes vientos como panorámicas al distante horizonte, definido nítidamente, remarcando la inmensidad indescriptible del cielo australiano. Este jardín acentúa igualmente las características inmutables del lugar desde un primer momento.

Un caso más complejo en primera instancia lo constituiría un pequeño jardín de un patio interior en una *riyadh* en la medina de Marrakech. No obstante, también en este caso el punto de partida es evidente: el cielo, la calidad de la luz natural y la magnitud de la muralla circundante. Asimismo, una pizca de imaginación ayudará a la hora de añadir un pabellón –o una tienda– en la azotea que queda sobre el patio, pabellón que no solo servirá como foco de atención visual desde uno de los cuatro costados del patio, sino que también hará las veces de atalaya desde la que observar el patio a sus pies y divisar en la lejanía las altas palmeras datileras o la silueta de la cordillera del Atlas.

En todos estos casos, la sensación de lujo proviene de sencillas concepciones determinadas por su entorno. Y esta simplicidad no tendría que estar reservada únicamente para unos pocos, siempre y cuando el diseñador del jardín sea en primer lugar disciplinado y osado; osadía entendida en el sentido de mantenerse imperturbable, como en el caso de la elección del azul eléctrico en el jardín Majorelle de Marrakech; y en segundo lugar, ser conocedor de los principios del paisajismo, principios tales como la proporción o la distribución armoniosa de volúmenes y espacios libres.

En esta obra aparecen dos de los jardines que he diseñado. Uno en un parterre de crasuláceas a las afueras de Sydney, un buen ejemplo de lo que se ha comentado más arriba, pues el mismo propietario se encargó tanto de la construcción como de la plantación, trabajando de noche con luz artificial y con un presupuesto limitado. A pesar de todo, es un verdadero jardín de lujo que ocupa el lugar que tenía que haber ocupado una pista de tenis. Dado que las plantas crasas de Madagascar, Sudáfrica y México no tienen nada en común con las oriundas de la selva australiana de la parte norte de este parterre, elevé el jardín con muros de contención superiores al bosque autóctono para diferenciar el uno del otro. En principio, esta argucia no difiere mucho de la Alhambra de Granada, que se disgrega de las colinas circundantes mediante muros de contención. Estas separaciones que, al mismo tiempo, ofrecen vistas panorámicas al paisaje autóctono, sirven para subrayar tanto las diferencias como las similitudes entre el resultado de la mano del hombre y la naturaleza. Casos como este, en el que el jardín se distancia de la naturaleza, solo son un éxito si la intención del paisajista es captada a la primera por el observador.

Son irrelevantes los elementos suntuosos contenidos en un jardín, pues un verdadero jardín de lujo ha de basarse en un diseño firmemente unificado y sencillo en su esencia. Las intenciones del diseñador de jardines han de ser evidentes y reconocibles de forma instantánea por aquel que camine la primera vez por el jardín.

Andrew Pfeiffer

Quali sono gli elementi di un giardino di lusso?

Per me è un giardino del *Paradiso*, che tocca tutti i sensi, come – per citare un esempio spettacolare – i giardini dell'Alhambra a Granada, in Spagna.

E da cosa si distingue un giardino di lusso da un altro? Per dirlo in una parola: attraverso la semplicità. Se riduciamo all'essenziale giardini come quello del castello Courances presso Parigi o la proprietà Odette Monteiro a Correias presso Rio de Janeiro, non appare null'altro che un'integrazione completamente semplice del paesaggio reale, così come un vestito di haute couture di ottimo taglio si adatta perfettamente al corpo nudo della donna per la quale è stato creato. Russell Page, probabilmente il più grande ideatore di giardini del XX secolo a livello europeo, un giorno ha detto: „Ogni giardino grandioso è circondato da un alone di inevitabilità."

Non sorprende che la maggior parte dei giardini di lusso vengano creati per persone che non si preoccupano di quanto spendono, o almeno se ne devono preoccupare poco. I giardini vengono per lo più allestiti in modo da intimidire molte persone per la loro grandezza e per la loro palese complessità. Eppure, secondo la mia opinione, un giardino di lusso può essere realizzato per chiunque. Per sviluppare questo pensiero, bisognerebbe fermarsi un momento e riflettere sulla fonte dell'ispirazione di un giardino di lusso.

In qualità di architetto paesaggistico sono attivo in tutto il mondo, dal territorio pianeggiante dell'area di Parigi, l'Ile de France, fino alla boscaglia australiana. Sono convinto che prima di tutto sia necessario considerare le caratteristiche naturali del terreno, e qui non è importante la misura del giardino. Questo significa che i giardini dell'Ile de France, con le loro tranquille superfici d'acqua – in forma di laghetti, piscine, canali o fiumi che scorrono lentamente –, che rispecchiano il cielo e le nuvole che passano, possiedono un alone d'inevitabilità. Dall'altro lato, c'è anche un giardino nella boscaglia australiana che dona ombra e protegge dai venti forti, offrendo al contempo la vista sull'orizzonte lontano ma ben definito e sottolineando il cielo incredibilmente vasto dell'Australia: una corrispondente risonanza delle caratteristiche proprie di questa regione.

A prima vista può sembrare più difficile allestire un piccolo giardino interno per un Riad nella Medina di Marrakech. Ma anche qui il punto di partenza è evidente: devono essere senza dubbio il cielo, la qualità della luce e le dimensioni delle mura che circondano il cortile. Inoltre, può essere d'aiuto un pizzico di fantasia, e un padiglione – o una tenda – viene posato sul tetto che sovrasta il patio. Su uno di questi padiglioni ai quattro lati del cortile interno lo sguardo non solo può soffermarsi, ma anche spaziare sia sul cortile in basso sia in lontananza sulle palme da dattero o sulla silhouette delle montagne dell'Atlante.

In ognuno di questi esempi, la sensazione del lusso scaturisce da visioni semplici inevitabilmente evocate dal paesaggio. In generale, una tale semplicità non dovrebbe trovarsi al di fuori del possibile. La premessa per ciò sono prima di tutto la disciplina e il coraggio del designer del giardino; coraggio, nel senso di determinazione, come viene per esempio espressa dal blu brillante scelto per il giardino Majorelle a Marrakech e, in secondo luogo, che gli siano chiari i principi della sistemazione del paesaggio. Di ciò fanno parte, tra l'altro, le proporzioni e l'allestimento armonico della massa e dello spazio.

In questo libro vengono presentati due dei giardini da me progettati. Uno è un parterre di piante grasse in un sobborgo a nord di Sydney. E' un buon esempio di quanto appena detto, perché sia la costruzione che la sistemazione delle piante sono state eseguite dal cliente stesso, la sera, con illuminazione artificiale e con un budget ridotto. Nonostante ciò, si tratta di un giardino di lusso, in un posto dove originariamente avrebbe dovuto esservi un campo da tennis. Dato che le piante grasse provenienti dal Madagascar, dal Sudafrica e dal Messico non hanno nulla a che vedere con la boscaglia australiana, che a nord confina con il parterre, ho innalzato il giardino al di sopra del bosco con dei muri di sostegno, allo scopo di delimitare l'uno dall'altro. Questo espediente non è molto diverso dall'Alhambra a Granada, che è separata tramite muri dalle colline dell'Andalusia. Queste separazioni, che al contempo offrono una vista sul paesaggio locale, servono a evidenziare sia le differenze che i punti in comune tra quanto ideato dall'uomo e quanto creato dalla natura. I giardini, nei quali l'ideato deve essere separato dal naturale, saranno riusciti solo se questa intenzione dell'ideatore è chiara all'osservatore già al primo sguardo.

Non importa quali elementi lussuosi possa contenere un giardino, un vero giardino di lusso a mio avviso dovrebbe basarsi su un design fortemente unitario ed essenzialmente semplice. Le intenzioni del designer di giardini dovrebbe essere nitido e riconoscibile istantaneamente dall'osservatore, mentre passeggia attraverso il giardino per la prima volta.

Andrew Pfeiffer

Taubman Garden

Michigan, USA

The apple trees from Ohio were actually brought in as mature specimens and planted in the garden with the aid of a crane. The lower vegetable garden parterre is located on one of the upper vegetable garden parterre's two main axes. Because frost can be expected until May, the beds are planted with tulip bulbs in the fall to give a spectacular flash of color in early May. The frost-sensitive vegetable plants and herbs are then bedded out later in the month. One focal point of this garden is a circular pond with a fountain.

Die Apfelbäume aus Ohio wurden als schon große Bäume mit Hilfe eines Krans verpflanzt. Das Parterre des unteren Gemüsegartens liegt auf einer der beiden Hauptachsen des oberen Gemüsegartenparterres. Da es noch bis Mai Frost geben kann, werden die Tulpenzwiebeln im Herbst gesetzt, damit sie im frühen Mai den Garten mit Farbe erfüllen. Die frostempfindlichen Gemüse und Kräuter werden dann etwas später im Monat gepflanzt. Einer der Blickpunkte des Gartens ist ein rundes Becken mit einer Fontäne.

Les pommiers ont été trouvés en Ohio à l'âge adulte et ont été transplantés dans le jardin à l'aide de grues. Le parterre inférieur du jardin potager est situé sur l'un des deux axes principaux du parterre supérieur du jardin potager. Comme on peut s'attendre à des gelées jusqu'en mai, des bulbes de tulipes ont été plantés en automne dans les parterres pour une explosion de couleurs spectaculaire début mai. Les plantes et herbes potagères sensibles au gel sont ensuite déracinées plus tard dans le mois. Un des points principaux de ce jardin est un bassin circulaire avec un jet d'eau.

Los manzanos, procedentes de Ohio, se transplantaron ya adultos con la ayuda de una grúa. El parterre del jardín inferior de hortalizas se apoya en uno de los dos ejes principales del parterre del jardín superior de hortalizas. Dado que las heladas son frecuentes hasta mayo, los bulbos de tulipán se plantan en otoño para que, llegado ese mes, el jardín se inunde de color. Hortalizas y hierbas, sensibles a las heladas, se plantan entrado ya el mes. Llama la atención el estanque circular con surtidor.

I meli provenienti dall'Ohio sono stati trapiantati nel giardino con l'aiuto di una gru. Il parterre dell'orto al livello inferiore si trova su una delle due assi principali del parterre dell'orto al livello superiore. Visto che le gelate possono verificarsi fino a maggio, in autunno vengono piantati bulbi di tulipano per dare un tocco di colore nei primi giorni di maggio. Le piante delle verdure e delle erbe sensibili al gelo vengono piantate più in là nel mese. Un punto focale di questo giardino è il laghetto rotondo con la fontana.

Much work went into devising imaginative combinations of plants.

Viel Arbeit wurde in die fantasievolle Zusammenstellung der Pflanzen gesteckt.

Il a fallu beaucoup de travail pour concevoir ces combinaisons créatives de plantes.

En la imaginativa configuración de las plantas se invirtió mucho trabajo.

Nelle composizioni delle piante, piene di fantasia, hanno comportato molto lavoro.

View from the upper vegetable garden parterre looking across the circular pond with its fountain and the terrace in front of the house. The main terrace in front of the house is paved with sawn New York bluestone into rectangles of various sizes.

Ein Blick aus dem Parterre des oberen Gemüsegartens über das runde Becken mit Fontäne zur Terrasse vor dem Haus. Die Hauptterrasse vor dem Haus ist mit Feldspat aus New York gepflastert, der in unterschiedlich große Rechtecke gesägt wurde.

La vue depuis le parterre supérieur du jardin potager mène au-delà du bassin circulaire et de la fontaine, vers la terrasse devant la maison. Cette terrasse principale est pavée de rectangles irréguliers de pierre bleue de New York.

Vistas desde el parterre del jardín superior de hortalizas al estanque con surtidor y a la terraza frente a la casa; el pavimento de esta terraza principal es de feldespato neoyorquino cortado en bloques rectangulares de distintos tamaños.

Vista dall'orto del livello superiore sul laghetto ornamentale circolare con la fontana, verso la terrazza di fronte alla casa. La terrazza principale di fronte alla casa è pavimentata con pietra blu di New York, in rettangoli sparsi di grandezza differente.

The lower vegetable garden beds are planted with pink tulips that reach their peak in mid-May. The box hedges are covered with burlap each fall to protect them from the extreme winter temperatures of Michigan. The labyrinthine patterns of the hedges look almost surreal when covered with snow.

Mitte Mai blühen in den Beeten des unteren Gemüsegartens die rosa Tulpen. Jeden Herbst werden die Buchs-baumhecken mit Leinen bedeckt, um sie vor den extremen Wintertemperaturen Michigans zu schützen. Das labyrinthartige Muster der Hecken erscheint schneebedeckt beinahe surreal.

Des tulipes roses, qui sont en pleine floraison à la mi-mai, ont également été plantées dans les parterres de la partie inférieure du jardin potager. Les haies de buis sont couverts de toile chaque automne pour les protéger des températures hivernales extrêmes du Michigan. Couvert de neige, les motifs labyrinthique des haies de buis prennent un aspect quasiment surréaliste.

A mediados de mayo florecen los tulipanes rosas en los planteles del jardín de hortalizas inferior. Los setos de boj se cubre con unas teles todos los otoños para protegerlos de las bajas temperaturas invernales de Michigan. Cubierto de nieve, el trazado laberíntico del seto adopta un aire un tanto surrealista.

Nelle aiuole dell'orto sul livello inferiore sono stati piantati anche tulipani rosa che raggiungono il loro mas-simo splendore a metà maggio. Ogni autunno le siepi di bosso vengono ricoperte con delle tele per proteggerle dalle estreme temperature invernali del Michigan. Il disegno del labirinto delle siepi innevate ha un aspetto quasi surreale.

Hope Ranch

Santa Barbara, California, USA

A multitude of very different gardens are arranged on the hilly property along a pergola overgrown with wisteria: A moon garden, a garden with predominantly fuzzy leaves, a Mediterranean corner, a mysterious spiral, a tropical garden and a rose garden as well as a gazebo in a sea of grass, waterfalls, a koi-carp pond with bridges and a meadow consisting solely of rain lilies (*Zephyrantes*). The wisteria path is planted completely with scented chamomile, because the owner wanted to be able to walk everywhere barefoot.

Eine Vielzahl sehr unterschiedlicher Gärten ordnet sich auf dem hügeligen Grundstück entlang eines glyzinienbewachsenen Laubenganges an: ein Mondgarten, ein Garten mit hauptsächlich krausen Blättern, eine Mittelmeerecke, eine geheimnisvolle Spirale, ein tropischer und ein Rosengarten sowie eine Laube in einem Meer aus Gras, Wasserfälle, ein Koi-Karpfenteich mit Brücken und eine Wiese ganz aus Zephirblumen, *Zephyrantes*. Der Glyziniengang ist vollständig mit duftender Kamille bepflanzt, da es Wunsch des Eigentümers war, überall barfuß gehen zu können.

Différents jardins très variés sont aménagés sur la propriété vallonnée, le long d'une pergola couverte de glycine : un jardin de lune, un jardin de feuilles duveteuses, un coin méditerranéen, une spirale mystérieuse, un jardin tropical et une roseraie, ainsi qu'une gloriette dans une mer d'herbes, des cascades, un étang à carpes koi avec des ponts et une prairie où poussent seulement des *zéphyrantes*. Le chemin couvert de glycine est aussi planté de camomille parfumée, le propriétaire souhaitant pouvoir marcher pieds nus partout.

Numerosos y variados jardines se jalonan en esta serpenteante parcela a lo largo de un camino flanqueado por glicinias que lleva a una glorieta: un jardín lunar, otro principalmente de hojas crespas, un rincón mediterráneo, una misteriosa espiral, un jardín tropical y otro de rosas, así como una glorieta en un mar de grama, cascadas, un estanque con carpas y peces koi con puentes y un prado con *Zephyrantes*. El sendero de glicinias está completamente cubierto de aromáticas camomila a petición del propietario, que deseaba caminar descalzo por todo el jardín.

Una molteplicità di giardini differenti tra loro sono disposti sul terreno collinare lungo un pergolato coperto di glicini: un giardino di luna, un giardino con foglie principalmente crespe, un angolo mediterraneo, una spirale misteriosa, un giardino tropicale e un roseto, oltre a un gazebo in un mare di erba, cascate, uno stagno con un vivaio di carpe koi attraversato da ponti e un prato pieno di fiori di zefiro, le *Zephyrantes*. Il pergolato di glicini è circondato completamente da camomilla profumata, visto che il proprietario desiderava che si potesse passeggiare ovunque a piedi nudi.

A seating corner protected from the rear invites visitors to hang out at the pond.

Am Teich lädt eine im Rücken geschützte Sitzecke zum Verweilen ein.

Cet espace protégé à l'arrière invite les visiteurs à s'asseoir un moment près de l'étang.

Unos bancos junto al estanque con respaldo protegido invitan a la contemplación.

Presso il laghetto è stato predisposto un angolo protetto per riposarsi.

The waterfalls designed with a multitude of rocks have a natural character. Skillfully arranged vertical elements such as the pavilion or even an individual tuft of grass serve to organize the relatively small garden and allow it to appear spacious.

Die mit vielen Felsen gestalteten Wasserfälle haben einen natürlichen Charakter. Geschickt angeordnete vertikale Elemente wie der Pavillon oder auch ein einzelnes Grasbüschel dienen der Gliederung und lassen den relativ kleinen Garten großzügig wirken.

Les cascades et leurs nombreux rochers ont un aspect naturel. Des éléments verticaux aménagés avec art, comme le pavillon ou même une simple touffe d'herbe, servent à organiser ce jardin relativement petit et lui permettent de paraître plus spacieux.

Las cascadas, compuestas por numerosas rocas, rezuman carácter natural. Ordenados de forma inteligente, los elementos verticales, como el pabellón o el manojo de hierbas, dividen el jardín, consiguiendo que parezca más amplio de lo que es.

Le cascate allestite con molte rocce hanno carattere naturale. Elementi verticali disposti abilmente, come il padiglione o anche un singolo ciuffo d'erba, servono a suddividere e fanno sembrare più vasto questo giardino relativamente piccolo.

Baroda Garden

Los Angeles, California, USA

The inspiration for this garden starts with the modern forms of the house and with the way the building sits on the site. The modernist vocabulary of geometric forms and a minimal plant palette set the stage for the approach to the house. The natural landscape down in the arroyo becomes intensified and engulfs the visitor with its vast scale.

Die modernen Linien des Wohnhauses sowie die Art und Weise seiner Ausrichtung auf dem Grundstück inspirierten den Garten. Der Eingangsbereich wird durch geometrische Formen und einige wenige Pflanzentypen charakterisiert. Zum Flussbett hin gewinnt die Landschaft an Intensität und schlägt den Besucher durch ihre schiere Größe in den Bann.

Les formes modernes de la maison et la manière dont le bâtiment s'intègre au site ont été la première source d'inspiration pour ce jardin. Un vocabulaire moderne des formes géométriques et une palette minimaliste de plantes mettent en scène l'approche vers la maison. En bas dans l'arroyo, le paysage naturel s'intensifie, engloutissant le visiteur dans son étendue démesurée.

Las líneas modernas de la vivienda y la manera en la que ésta se sitúa dentro de la parcela sirvieron de inspiración al jardín. Las formas geométricas y un reducido número de especies vegetales caracterizan la zona de entrada. El arroyo intensifica el paisaje natural, envolviendo al visitante en sus vastas dimensiones.

L'ispirazione per questo giardino è scaturita dalle forme moderne della casa e dal modo in cui l'edificio è costruito sul terreno. Forme geometriche e una piccola varietà di piante pongono le basi per l'area di accesso alla casa. Verso il letto del fiume il paesaggio naturale si intensifica, ammaliando il visitatore con la sua magnifica grandezza.

The natural setting contrasts with the modern architecture.

Die natürliche Umgebung kontrastiert mit der modernen Architektur.

Le cadre naturel contraste avec l'architecture moderne.

El entorno natural contrasta con la arquitectura moderna.

L'ambiente naturale contrasta con l'architettura moderna.

Several seating areas add reflective qualities throughout the garden. Behind the house, the modern garden merges into the surrounding natural setting.

Mehrere Sitzgelegenheiten geben dem Garten auch eine besinnliche Komponente. Hinter dem Haus verschmilzt die moderne Gartenanlage mit der natürlichen Umgebung.

Plusieurs sièges confèrent leurs qualités réflexives à tout le jardin. Derrière la maison, le jardin moderne se fond dans son environnement naturel.

Varios asientos aportan elementos para la meditación al jardín. El moderno jardín situado detrás de la casa se funde con el entorno natural.

Numerosi posti a sedere conferiscono una nota di romanticismo al giardino. Dietro alla casa, il giardino moderno si fonde con l'ambiente naturale circostante.

The long driveway to the house is lined with lawn, trees and art: a long sculpture by Brad Howe decorates the wall and the sculpture by Mark di Suvero is called "Square Root of Two."

Die lange Einfahrt ist von Rasen, Bäumen und Kunstwerken gesäumt: Eine lange Skulptur von Brad Howe schmückt die Wand, „Square Root of Two" heißt das Werk von Mark di Suvero.

La longue allée menant à la maison est bordée de pelouses, d'arbres et d'œuvres d'art : une longue sculpture de Brad Howe décore le mur, et on peut y contempler la sculpture de Mark di Suvero, intitulée « Square Root of Two ».

La calzada que lleva hasta la casa está bordeada por césped, árboles y obras de arte: una gran escultura de Brad Howe viste un muro; "Square Root of Two" es obra de Mark di Suvero.

La lunga strada d'accesso alla casa è bordata di prati, alberi e opere d'arte: una lunga scultura di Brad Howe adorna il muro, la scultura di Mark di Suvero è intitolata "Square Root of Two".

Baroda Garden *Los Angeles, California, USA* 33

Ward Garden

Coral Gables, Florida, USA

It's hard to imagine that this fantastic sub-tropical garden, which displays characteristics of the Florida scenery of the Everglades and Big Cypress, used to be a lawn. Extensive changes to the land and excavations revealed the oolithic substrate and allowed the raw surfaces of the rock outcrops to appear. The depressions, greatly diversified in their form and depth, became ponds and the water courses, whose shores are lined with native plants, create new micro-climates and habitats.

Es ist kaum vorstellbar, dass dieser fantastische sub-tropische Garten, der Charakteristika der Florida-Landschaften der Everglades und Big Cypress aufweist, zuvor eine Rasenfläche war. Umfangreiche Landveränderungen und Grabungen legten das oolithische Substrat frei und lassen die rauen Oberflächen der Felsen zu Tage treten. Die in Form und Tiefe sehr abwechslungsreichen Vertiefungen wurden zu Seen, und die Wasserläufe mit ihren mit einheimischen Pflanzen angelegten Uferzonen schaffen neue Mikroklimate und Lebensräume.

Il est difficile d'imaginer que ce fantastique jardin subtropical, caractéristique des paysages des Everglades et de Big Cypress en Floride, était auparavant une pelouse. De grands changements apportés au terrain et des excavations révèlent le substrat oolithique et permettent aux surfaces nues des affleurements rocheux d'apparaître. Les dépressions, qui sont extrêmement diversifiées dans leur forme et leur profondeur, deviennent des bassins. Les cours d'eau avec leurs berges abritant des plantes indigènes créent un microclimat et de nouveaux biotopes.

Cuesta imaginar que este fantástico jardín subtropical, característico de los paisajes de Florida, de sus marismas Everglades y del Big Cypress, fue antes una superficie con césped. Innumerables modificaciones del terreno y excavaciones dejaron al descubierto el sustrato oolítico, permitiendo salir a la luz a la superficie rugosa de las rocas. Las cavidades, de diversas formas y profundidades, se convirtieron en lagos. El curso del agua, con su ribera poblada de plantas autóctonas, ha generado nuevos microclimas y biotopos.

E' quasi incredibile che questo fantastico giardino subtropicale, che mostra le caratteristiche dei paesaggi della Florida delle Everglades e del Big Cypress, fosse in precedenza uno spazio erboso. Le radicali modifiche del terreno e gli scavi hanno liberato il substrato olistico e hanno portato alla luce le superfici grezze delle rocce. Gli avvallamenti molto vari in forma e profondità sono stati trasformati in laghi, e i corsi d'acqua, dalle sponde decorate con piante locali, creano un nuovo microclima e nuovi spazi vitali.

The rock outcrops vary in height from less than three feet to 20 feet.

Die Höhe der Felsen varriiert von knapp einem bis zu über sechs Meter.

La hauteur des affleurements rocheux varie d'à peine un mètre à plus de six mètres.

La altura de las rocas varía: desde las de escaso tamaño a las que superan los seis metros.

L'altezza della rupe varia da poco meno di un metro fino a più di sei metri.

It's surprising to learn that the dense vegetation and unusual garden design with concealed seating areas integrated into rock ledges borders on a number of residential buildings and a highway.

Die dichte Vegetation und ungewöhnliche Gartengestaltung mit auf Felsvorsprüngen versteckt eingefügten Sitzecken lässt nicht vermuten, dass das Grundstück an mehrere Wohnhäuser und eine Landstraße grenzt.

Il est surprenant d'apprendre qu'avec sa végétation dense et ses sièges intégrés aux saillies rocheuses, le jardin est tout proche de nombreux bâtiments résidentiels et d'une route très fréquentée.

La frondosa vegetación y la inusual configuración del jardín, con zonas de descanso ocultas tras los saltos de agua, no permite sospechar que el terreno linda con varias viviendas y una carretera.

La fitta vegetazione e l'allestimento insolito del giardino con angoli per sedersi nascosti nelle sporgenze rocciose, non lasciano presagire che il terreno confini con numerose abitazioni e una strada di campagna.

36   Ward Garden *Coral Gables, Florida, USA*

Villa Libellule

Terres Basses, St. Martin, Caribbean

Nestled in the soft, rolling hills of Terres Basses, this five-acre botanical wonderland is actually the result of a catastrophe. In 1995, the island of St. Martin was ravaged by Hurricane Luis. Afterwards, landscape artists Kevin Kirby and Michael Hopson transformed this fallow area into "Les Jardins de Libellule". The theme for Villa Libellule is a combination of Caribbean splendor with cacti, waves of bougainvillea and majestic palms shading quiet seating areas.

Dieses etwa 20.000 m² große botanische Wunderland schmiegt sich an die sanften Hügel von Terres Basses und entstand nach einer Katastrophe. Der Wirbelsturm Luis verwüstete die Insel St. Martin 1995. Das danach brach liegende Gelände verwandelten die Landschaftskünstler Kevin Kirby und Michael Hopson in die Libellen-Gärten. Ihr Motto für Villa Libellule war die Kombination karibischer Pracht mit Kakteen, Wellen von Bougainvillea und majestätischen Palmen, die Schatten für ruhige Sitzecken spenden.

Niché dans les collines aux pentes douces de Terres Basses, ce paradis botanique privé de 20.000 m² a été conçu suite à une catastrophe. L'ouragan Luis a ravagé Saint-Martin en 1995. Les artistes paysagers Kevin Kirby et Michael Hopson ont par la suite transformé cette zone en jachère en « Les Jardins de Libellule ». Le thème de la villa est la splendeur des états caribéens, avec des cactées, des océans de bougainvillées et des palmiers majestueux qui protègent les sièges du soleil.

Este "país de las maravillas" botánico de unos 20.000 m² se asienta en las suaves colinas de Terres Basses y se concibió tras una catástrofe. El huracán Luís arrasó la isla de St. Martin en 1995, dejando el terreno listo para los paisajistas Kevin Kirby y Michael Hopson, que crearon "Les Jardins de Libellule". En ellos se combina todo el esplendor caribeño mediante cactus, montones de buganvillas y majestuosas palmeras que dan sombra a las áreas de reposo.

Questa terra botanica delle meraviglie di circa 20.000 m², concepita dopo una catastrofe, si annida nelle dolci colline delle Terres Basses. L'uragano Luis ha devastato St. Martin nel 1995 e ha liberato il terreno per gli artisti paesaggistici Kevin Kirby e Michael Hopson, che hanno creato "Les Jardins de Libellule". Il tema di questo giardino è la combinazione di meraviglie caraibiche con cactus, ondate di buganvillea e palme maestose che donano ombra a tranquilli angoli dove sedersi.

The gardens are lulled by pagoda fountains and the rush of the Caribbean waves on the beach of Baie Rouge.

Sanft plätschernde Pagodenfontainen und das Rauschen der karibischen Wellen am Strand von Baie Rouge sind allgegenwärtig.

Les jardins sont bercés par les fontaines de la pagode et le silence des vagues caribéennes sur la plage de Baie Rouge.

El suave chapoteo de las fuentes de la pagoda y el rumor de las olas de la playa caribeña de Baie Rouge adormecen los jardines.

Ovunque vi sono fontane a pagoda e si ode il fruscio delle onde caraibiche sulla spiaggia Baie Rouge.

The yellow calyxes of the alamanda bush, the crimson panicles of flamboyant, also called "flame tree", are as much a part of the typical Caribbean flora as the elegant buds of the heliconia, hibiscus, ginger and the countless fanned and feathered palms with their variety of trunks.

Die gelben Blütenkelche des Alamandastrauches, die feuerroten Rispen des Flamboyant, auch Flammenbaum genannt, gehören genauso zur typischen karibischen Flora wie die eleganten Knospen der Helikonien, des Hibiskus, des Ingwers und die ungezählten gefächerten und gefiederten Palmen mit ihren unterschiedlichen Stämmen.

Les calices jaunes des buissons d'alamanda, et les panicules pourpres des flamboyants font tout aussi partie de la flore typique des Caraïbes que les boutons élégants des héliconias, des hibiscus, du gingembre et les innombrables palmiers brillants et duveteux et leurs troncs variés.

Los sépalos amarillos de la alamanda o las panículas en rojo vivo del árbol de fuego pertenecen a la flora típica del Caribe, así como los elegantes brotes de las heliconias, los hibiscos, el jengibre y las innumerables especies de palmeras con sus diferentes troncos.

I calici gialli del cespuglio di Alamanda, le pannocchie rosso fuoco del Flamboyant, detto anche albero delle fiamme, appartengono alla tipica flora caraibica esattamente come i boccioli eleganti delle eliconie, dell'ibisco e dello zenzero, oltre alle innumerevoli palme a ventaglio e a piume dai tronchi diversi.

At the foot of the hill, the wonderfully warm ocean and St. Martin's extensive possibilities are enticing, as are the neighboring islands of Anguilla and Saba in the distance. But it certainly isn't easy to leave this little paradise.

Am Fuße des Hügels lockt das herrlich warme Meer und das umfangreiche Angebot von St. Martin sowie in der Ferne die Nachbarinseln Anguilla und Saba, aber es fällt sicherlich nicht leicht, dieses kleine Paradies zu verlassen.

Au pied de la colline, l'océan merveilleusement chaud et les vastes possibilités offertes par Saint-Martin séduisent, tout comme les îles voisines d'Anguilla et de Saba au large. Mais il n'est pas facile de quitter ce petit paradis.

A los pies de la colina, las cálidas aguas del mar y la amplia oferta de St. Martin son de lo más tentador, tanto como las islas vecinas de Anguila y Saba; lo que es seguro es que costará bastante abandonar este paraíso.

Ai piedi della collina, il magnifico mare caldo e le mille attrattive di St. Martin attirano il visitatore insieme alle vicine isole di Anguilla e Saba: ma non è facile lasciare questo paradiso.

Adare Manor

Adare, Limerick, Ireland

The gigantic grounds belonging to Adare Manor include the spacious park, well-kept gardens, a formal French garden, wonderful old trees as well as the Maigue River, which is famous throughout Ireland for its trout. The formal garden with its geometric patterns shaped from box trees was designed by P. C. Hardwick around 1850. Another worthy sight is the majestic Lebanon cedar on the bank of the river. It is about 350 years old.

Auf dem riesigen Gelände, das zum Herrenhaus von Adare gehört, befinden sich neben dem weitläufigen Park gepflegte Gärten, ein formaler Französischer Garten, wunderbare alte Bäume sowie der Fluss Maigue, der in ganz Irland für seine Forellen berühmt ist. Der formale Garten mit den geometrischen, in Buchsbaum ausgeführten Mustern wurde um 1850 von P. C. Hardwick entworfen. Bemerkenswert ist auch die etwa 350 Jahre alte, majestätische, libanesische Zeder am Flussufer.

Le domaine immense qui appartient au Manoir Adare comprend le vaste parc, des jardins bien entretenus, un jardin à la française, de magnifiques vieux arbres et la rivière Maigue, réputée dans toute l'Irlande pour ses truites. Le jardin à la française avec ses topiaires de buis géométriques a été dessiné aux environs de 1850 par P. C. Hardwick. Un cèdre du Liban majestueux sur la berge de la rivière, âgé de 350 ans, vaut aussi le coup d'œil.

En el inmenso recinto perteneciente a la mansión de Adare, además de un extenso parque y cuidados jardines, encontramos un jardín formalista francés, magníficos árboles viejos y hasta el río Maigue, conocido en toda Irlanda por sus truchas. El diseño del jardín formalista, con sus setos de boj de líneas geométricas, fue obra de P. C. Hardwick allá por 1850. Cabe destacar igualmente el majestuoso cedro del Libano a orillas del río, de unos 350 años de antigüedad.

Sull'enorme terreno che appartiene alla casa padronale di Adare, accanto all'ampio parco, si trovano dei giardini curati, un giardino francese formale, fantastici alberi secolari e il fiume Maigue, che è famoso in tutta l'Irlanda per le sue trote. Il giardino formale con i disegni geometrici creati dal bosso è stato progettato intorno al 1850 da P. C. Hardwick. Degno di nota è anche il maestoso cedro libanese sulla sponda del fiume, vecchio di circa 350 anni.

Formal gardens are as much part of Adare Manor as forests and parks.

Formale Gärten gehören ebenso zu Adare Manor wie Wälder und Parkanlagen.

Les jardins à la française appartiennent au Adare Manor, tout comme les forêts et les parcs.

Los jardines formalistas son tan propios de Adare Manor como sus bosques y parques.

I giardini formali fanno parte di Adare Manor come i boschi e i parchi.

46   Adare Manor *Adare, Limerick, Ireland*

The mighty Lebanon cedar with its wide spreading branches inspires awe. Two-hundred-year-old beech trees, araucaria, cork oak, aspen and blossoming cherry trees are also part of the admirable park, captivating nature-lovers.

Die mächtige libanesische Zeder mit ihren weit auskragenden Ästen flößt Ehrfurcht ein. Zweihundertjährige Buchen, Araukarien, Korkeichen, Espen und blühende Kirschbäume gehören ebenfalls zu der bewundernswerten Anlage und bezaubern Naturliebhaber.

Le puissant cèdre du Liban avec ses larges branches étalées inspire le respect. Les hêtres bicentenaires, les araucaria, les chêne-liège, les trembles, et les cerisiers en fleurs font aussi partie de ce parc admirable et charment les amoureux de la nature.

El magnífico cedro del Líbano, con sus ramas extendidas, impone respeto. Hayas de doscientos años, araucarias, alcornoques, álamos y cerezos en flor pertenecen igualmente a este maravilloso lugar y fascinan al amante de la naturaleza.

L'imponente cedro libanese con i suoi rami molto sporgenti impone rispetto. Faggi bicentenari, araucarie, querce da sughero, pioppi tremoli e ciliegi in fiore fanno anch'essi parte del bellissimo complesso e ammaliano gli amanti della natura.

48   Adare Manor *Adare, Limerick, Ireland*

The French garden with its geometric patterns leads from the austerity of the imposing stone building into nature. A small number of colorful flowers add variety to the color range, which is dominated by green of all shades.

Der Französische Garten mit seinen geometrischen Mustern leitet von der Strenge des imposanten steinernen Gebäudes in die Natur über. Einige wenige bunte Blüten sorgen für Abwechslung in der Farbskala, die von Grün in allen Schattierungen beherrscht wird.

Le jardin à la française avec ses motifs géométriques crée un lien entre l'austérité de l'imposant bâtiment en pierre et la nature. Un petit nombre de fleurs colorées offrent une variété dans la gamme des couleurs, principalement dominée par les nuances de vert.

El jardín francés, de líneas geométricas, sirve de transición entre la sobriedad del imponente edificio de piedra y la naturaleza. Unas pocas flores de color dan vida a la paleta cromática, dominada por el verde en todas sus tonalidades.

Il giardino francese con i suoi disegni geometrici passa dal rigore dell'imponente edificio di pietra alla natura. Pochi fiori colorati creano un avvicendamento nella scala dei colori, che viene dominata dal verde in tutte le sue sfumature.

Holker Hall

Cumbria, United Kingdom

For generations, the family of the Lords of Cavendish have been beautifying their extremely well-tended estate on Morecambe Bay in the west of England. The large park and formal garden have mainly been designed in Victorian style. The family takes the view that gardens constantly change and continue to develop, making modifications essential. A good example of this is the labyrinth that artist Jim Buchanan recently laid out in precise harmony with the landscape.

Seit Generationen verschönert die Familie der Lords von Cavendish ihr außergewöhnlich gepflegtes Anwesen an der Morecambe Bucht im Westen Englands. Der große Park und der formale Garten sind hauptsächlich im viktorianischen Stil gestaltet. Die Familie vertritt die Auffassung, dass sich Gärten stetig verändern und weiterentwickeln, Neuerungen also unerlässlich sind. Ein gutes Beispiel dafür ist das Labyrinth, das der Künstler Jim Buchanan vor kurzem genau abgestimmt auf die Landschaft angelegt hat.

Depuis des générations, la famille des Lords de Cavendish embellit cette propriété extrêmement bien entretenue à Morecambe Bay, dans l'ouest de l'Angleterre. Le vaste parc et le jardin à la française ont été dessinés principalement dans le style victorien. La famille considère que comme les jardins changent constamment et continuent à se développer, il est essentiel de continuer à les modifier. Un bon exemple en est le labyrinthe que l'artiste Jim Buchanan a récemment aménagé en harmonie totale avec la nature.

Son muchas las generaciones de la familia de los lores de Cavendish que han embellecido su extraordinaria y cuidada propiedad en la bahía de Morecambe al oeste de Inglaterra. El gran parque y el jardín formalista son de estilo preponderantemente victoriano. En esta familia son de la opinión de que los jardines no dejan de cambiar y crecer: las reformas son indispensables. Un buen ejemplo es el laberinto que recientemente levantó el artista Jim Buchanan, totalmente integrado en el paisaje.

Da generazioni la famiglia dei lord di Cavendish abbelliscono la loro tenuta straordinariamente curata nell'insenatura di Morecambe, nell'Inghilterra occidentale. Il grande parco e il giardino formale sono allestiti principalmente in stile vittoriano. La famiglia è dell'opinione che i giardini cambiano e si sviluppano costantemente, rendendo indispensabili le innovazioni. Un buon esempio è il labirinto che è stato allestito dall'artista Jim Buchanan poco tempo fa, perfettamente adattato al paesaggio.

The morning fog makes the labyrinth at the middle of a wild-flower meadow appear untouched by time.

Im Morgennebel erscheint das inmitten der Wildblumenwiese gelegene Labyrinth der Zeit entrückt.

Le labyrinthe au milieu d'une prairie de fleurs sauvages semble au-delà du temps dans la brume du matin.

Con la bruma de la mañana, el laberinto, en medio de un prado de flores silvestres, parece venido de otra época.

Nella nebbia mattutina il labirinto che si trova in mezzo al prato di fiori selvaggi appare fuori tempo.

Jim Buchanan and Grania Cavendish *worked together on this labyrinth, whose form is based on the design of an Indian Hindu temple. Its asymmetrical center is slightly elevated and the twelve slate monoliths are reminiscent of the Cumbrian tradition of stone circles.*

Jim Buchanan und Grania Cavendish *arbeiteten zusammen an diesem Labyrinth, dessen Form auf den Entwurf eines indischen Hindu-Tempels zurückgeht. Der asymmetrische Mittelpunkt ist leicht erhöht und die zwölf Schiefermonolithe erinnern an die cumbrische Tradition der Steinkreise.*

Jim Buchanan et Grania Cavendish *ont travaillé ensemble sur ce labyrinthe, dont la forme est basée sur les plans d'un temple hindou en Inde. Le centre asymétrique est légèrement surélevé et les douze monolithes d'ardoise rappellent la tradition des cercles de pierre de Cumbrie.*

Jim Buchanan y Grania Cavendish *trabajaron juntos en este laberinto, cuya forma se inspira en el diseño de un templo hindú. El centro asimétrico está ligeramente elevado y los doce monolitos de pizarra recuerdan a la tradición de los crómlech de esta región de Cumbria.*

Jim Buchanan e Grania Cavendish *hanno collaborato alla realizzazione di questo labirinto, che si rifà nella forma a un tempio indù. Il centro asimmetrico è leggermente rialzato e i dodici monoliti di ardesia ricordano la tradizione cumbrica dei cerchi di pietra.*

Two of the garden's highlights are undoubtedly the sunken garden, seen here at dawn with its circle-shaped box tree hedges, and the sandstone cascade. It is lined with tree fern and rhododendron, running to the right and left of the path toward the pool with its fountain.

Zwei der Höhepunkte der Gartenanlage sind zweifellos der Senkgarten, hier in der Morgendämmerung, mit den kreisförmig geschnittenen Buchsbaumhecken sowie die Sandsteinkaskade. Sie wird von Baumfarn und Rhododendron gesäumt und läuft rechts und links des Weges auf das Wasserbecken mit der Fontäne zu.

Deux des joyaux du jardin sont sans aucun doute le jardin en contrebas, ici à l'aube avec ses haies de buis circulaires, et la cascade de grès. Ils sont bordés de fougères arborescentes et de rhododendrons, courant à droite et à gauche du sentier en direction du bassin et de sa fontaine.

Dos de los puntos de interés de este jardín son sin lugar a dudas el jardín hundido, aquí en una vista al alba con los setos podados en círculos, y la cascada de arenisca. Flanqueado por helechos de dicksonia y rododendro, conduce a izquierda y derecha del camino al estanque con surtidor.

I due punti culminanti del giardino sono senza dubbio il giardino ad avvallamenti, qui ritratto nel crepuscolo mattutino, con le siepi di bosso circolari e la cascata di arenaria, bordata di ciateacea e di rododendro, che percorre la strada a destra e a sinistra verso il bacino d'acqua con la fontana.

Gresgarth Hall
Lancashire, United Kingdom

For more than 25 years, Arabella Lennox-Boyd has committed herself to the design and further development of her country estate. Its diversity is reflected in the garden areas: The entrance court, the terrace gardens, lake and bog garden, a series of colorful theme gardens and flower borders framed by hedges, a large kitchen garden and even a meadow with a small forest. The estate looks like it came from a painting through the color play of the leaves and flowers.

Seit über 25 Jahren nimmt sich Arabella Lennox-Boyd der Gestaltung und Weiterentwicklung ihres großen Landsitzes an. Die Vielfältigkeit spiegelt sich in den verschiedenen Gartenbereichen wider: dem Eingangshof, den Terrassengärten, dem See und dem Moorgarten, einer Reihe durch Hecken eingefasster bunter Themengärten und Blumenrabatten, einem großen Küchengarten, bis hin zu einem Auenwäldchen. Durch das Farbspiel der Blätter und Blüten erscheint das Anwesen wie einem Gemälde entsprungen.

Depuis vingt-cinq ans, Arabella Lennox-Boyd participe à la rénovation et au développement du vaste domaine de sa maison de campagne. Sa diversité se reflète dans des espaces variés : la cour d'entrée, les jardins en terrasse, le lac et le jardin de marais, une série de jardins aux thèmes colorés et de bordures de fleurs encadrées de haies, un grand jardin potager et même une petite forêt sur la berge. La propriété seigneuriale semble sortir d'une peinture grâce au jeu de couleurs des feuilles et des fleurs.

Arabella Lennox-Boyd empleó más de 25 años en la nueva configuración y ampliación de los extensos terrenos pertenecientes a su casa de campo. La diversidad se refleja en las diferentes zonas: el patio de bienvenida, los jardines aterrazados, el lago y el jardín de pantano, una hilera de coloridos jardines temáticos y planteles de flores delimitados por setos, un jardín de cocina y hasta un bosquecillo junto a un prado. Gracias al juego de colores de hojas y flores, la vivienda parece salida de un cuadro.

Da più di 25 anni Arabella Lennox-Boyd si occupa del riallestimento e dello sviluppo del grande terreno intorno alla sua casa di campagna. La varietà si rispecchia nelle diverse aree: il cortile d'ingresso, i giardini terrazzati, il lago e il giardino del pantano, una serie di colorati giardini a tema circondati da siepi e le bordure di fiori, il grande orto fino al boschetto lungo il fiume. Attraverso il gioco di colori delle foglie e dei petali questo podere padronale sembra come uscire da un dipinto.

*A **Coalbrookdale cast-iron bench** is surrounded by roses: cerise pink 'Cardinal de Richelieu' in the foreground, with the pink 'Empress Josephine' and 'May Queen' on the wall.*

*Eine gusseiserne **Coalbrookdale Bank** wird von Rosen eingerahmt: Im Vordergrund die kirschrosa ‚Kardinal Richelieu', an der Wand die rosa ‚Kaiserin Josephine' und ‚Maikönigin'.*

*Un **banc en fonte de Coalbrookdale** est entouré de roses rouge cerise ‹ Cardinal de Richelieu › (premier plan), d' ‹ Empress Josephine › et de ‹ May Queen › roses sur le mur.*

*Un **banco 'coalbrookdale'** de hierro colado rodeado de rosas: en primer plano, las fucsias 'Cardenal Richelieu'; en la pared, las 'Emperatriz Josefina' y las 'Reina de Mayo'.*

*Una **panca Coalbrookdale** in ghisa è circondata dalle rose 'Cardinale Richelieu' (in primo piano), 'Imperatrice Josephine' e 'Regina di Maggio' (sul muro).*

Looking toward the house, this is a view between the double herbaceous borders in the morning sun. An ancient yew tree, covered by the bloom of rambling roses in early summer, completes the picture.

Ein Blick in der Morgensonne durch die doppelte Staudenrabatte zum Haus hin. Eine alte Eibe, die im Frühsommer von den Blüten der wuchernden Büschelrose überzogen wird, bildet den Schlusspunkt.

Vue sur la maison entre les doubles bordures de plantes herbacées, au soleil du matin. Un vieil if, couvert de roses rampantes en fleurs au début de l'été, complète le tableau.

Vista a la casa con la primera luz de la mañana entre la doble línea de hierbas. Un tejo maduro, cubierto en el inicio de la época estival por las rosas multiflora, cierra la panorámica.

La vista tra i doppi bordi erbacei, che guardano verso la casa, nel sole del mattino. Un antico albero di tasso, a inizio estate ricoperto dei petali delle rose rampicanti, chiude la vista.

View of the estate from the banks of the wild garden across the lake. A sea of Rosa 'Complicata' tumbles into the water, surrounded by long grasses and ox-eye daisies. Next to it, a view of the lake framed by lush foliage includes the vivacious, gray-green leaves of 'Hosta seboldiana elegans' and the willow-like leaves of 'Pyrus salicifolia Pendula'.

Das Haus hinter dem See vom Ufer des wilden Gartens aus gesehen. Eine Welle 'Complicata'-Rosen ergießt sich ins Wasser, umgeben von langen Gräsern und Wiesen-Margerite. Daneben eine Ansicht des Sees mit üppigem Blattwerk, unter anderem die schwungvollen, grau-grünen Blätter von 'Hosta seboldiana elegans' und das weidenähnliche Laub der Weidenblättrigen Birne 'Pyrus salicifolia Pendula'.

La maison vue de l'autre côté du lac depuis le jardin sauvage. Des roses ‹ Complicata › dégringolent dans l'eau, entourées de grandes herbes et de marguerites. À côté, une vue sur le lac encadré de feuillage luxuriant, notamment les feuilles épaisses, gris-vert, des ‹ Hosta seboldiana elegans ›, et les feuilles ressemblant à celles du saule du ‹ Pyrus salicifolia Pendula ›.

La vivienda desde el jardín silvestre en la ribera del lago al lado opuesto de la misma. Las rosas 'Complicata', rodeadas por hierbas de tallo alto y margaritas de prado, se adentran en el agua. Al costado, una panorámica del lago con abundante follaje, que incluye 'Hosta seboldiana elegans', con sus hojas de un verde grisáceo llenas de vida, y también 'Pyrus salicifolia Pendula', que asemejan un prado.

La casa vista al di là del lago dalla sponda del giardino selvaggio. Un'ondata di rose 'Complicata' si riversa nell'acqua, circondata da lunghi fili d'erba e da margherite. Accanto, la vista del lago incorniciato dal rigoglioso fogliame, come le foglie grigio-verdi dell' 'Hosta seboldiana elegans' e le foglie simili al salice della 'Pyrus salicifolia Pendula'.

The Trentham Estate

Trentham, Staffordshire, United Kingdom

In the lovely English countryside, you'll find Trentham Gardens with its Italian-inspired parterres de broderie and its somewhat less austere pleasure garden. The latter has recently been reawakened by the breathtakingly beautiful bed plantings designed by two world-famous garden designers—Tom Stuart-Smith and Piet Oudolf. Thousands of different herbaceous perennials and bulbs burst into true storms of color throughout the entire year.

Eingebettet in die liebliche englische Landschaft liegen diese Gärten mit den italienisch anmutenden Broderieparterres und dem etwas weniger strengen Lustgarten. Dieser ist erst vor kurzem durch atemberaubend schöne Beetbepflanzungen der beiden weltbekannten Gartengestalter Tom Stuart-Smith und Piet Oudolf zu neuem Leben erwacht. Tausende verschiedener Stauden und Zwiebeln entfachen das ganze Jahr wahre Farbstürme.

Ces jardins avec leurs parterres broderie d'inspiration italienne et les jardins de plaisir un peu moins austères sont nichés dans le ravissant paysage anglais. Ils ont été récemment remis en valeur par les plantations époustouflantes des deux designers à la renommée internationale Tom Stuart-Smith et Piet Oudolf. Des milliers de différentes espèces de plantes herbacées et de bulbes éclatent en vraies tempêtes de couleurs tout au long de l'année.

Enclavados en el encantador paisaje inglés encontramos estos jardines con sus parterres bordados con cierto aire italiano y un jardín de recreo no tan sobrio. Este último ha vuelto a cobrar vida gracias a los espléndidos planteles propuestos hace pocas fechas por los célebres paisajistas Tom Stuart-Smith y Piet Oudolf. Miles de matas y bulbos diferentes despliegan durante todo el año un vendaval de colores.

Questi giardini si trovano adagiati nel dolce paesaggio inglese, con il parterre della broderie di ispirazione italiana e il parco giardino, più giocoso. Quest'ultimo è rinato a nuova vita da poco, grazie alle splendide aiuole allestite dai due celebri ideatori di giardini Tom Stuart-Smith e Piet Oudolf. Migliaia di arbusti e bulbi diversi regalano vere e proprie tempeste di colori per tutta la durata dell'anno.

Whether it's fog, white frost or opposite light, this garden is always mesmerizing.

Ob im Nebel, mit Rauhreif oder im Gegenlicht, das Auge kann sich an diesem Garten kaum sattsehen.

Que ce soit dans le brouillard, couvert de givre blanc, ou en pleine lumière, ce jardin est toujours hypnotique.

Ya sea con bruma, escarcha o a contraluz, la vista no llega a saciarse en este jardín.

Che ci sia la nebbia, la brina o che ci si trovi in controluce, la vista di questo giardino non stanca mai.

Grand fountains and cleverly positioned vertical elements make Trentham Gardens stand out perfectly from the green foliage of the surrounding planting. The color play of the flowers is intentionally random and displays strong changes during the course of the seasons.

Wasserspiele und kalkuliert gesetzte, vertikale Elemente setzen die Gartenanlage vor der grünen Laubkulisse der Bepflanzung perfekt in Szene. Das Farbenspiel der Blüten ist absichtlich ungeordnet und zeigt im Laufe der Jahreszeiten starke Veränderungen.

Des jardins aquatiques et des éléments verticaux délibérément positionnés mettent en lumière les jardins devant la toile de fond verte des feuilles de la plantation. Le jeu de couleurs des fleurs est volontairement aléatoire et affiche de profondes variations au fil des saisons.

Juegos de agua y determinados elementos verticales ponen en escena a este jardín con el follaje de la plantación como telón de fondo. La mezcla cromática de las flores es ex profeso desordenada y experimenta grandes cambios a lo largo del año.

I giochi d'acqua e gli elementi verticali, posizionati in modo studiato, mettono perfettamente in risalto il complesso del giardino davanti allo scenario verde delle piantagione. Il gioco di colori è stato disposto intenzionalmente in modo disordinato e mostra dei forti cambiamenti nel corso delle stagioni.

Veddw House Garden

Devauden, Monmouthshire, United Kingdom

One of the enchanting features of this astonishingly diverse garden, which Anne Wareham and Charles Hawes have brought to life with endless devotion and untiring improvements, is its harmony with the surrounding landscape. Historical aspects also come into play. For example, the box tree parterre depicts a 19th century tithe map of the region while simultaneously enclosing all kinds of grasses.

Dieser erstaunlich vielfältige Garten, den Anne Wareham und Charles Hawes mit unendlicher Hingabe ins Leben gerufen haben und unermüdlich verbessern, bezaubert unter anderem durch die Harmonie mit der umgebenden Landschaft. Historische Aspekte spielen ebenfalls eine Rolle. So zeichnet beispielsweise das Buchsbaumparterre eine Zehntkarte der Region aus dem 19. Jahrhundert nach und rahmt zugleich verschiedenste Gräserarten ein.

Si ce jardin étonnamment divers, qu'Anne Wareham et Charles Hawes font vivre avec un dévouement infini et en l'améliorant sans relâche, enchante autant, c'est en partie en raison de son harmonie avec le paysage qui l'entoure. Les aspects historiques y jouent aussi un rôle. Par exemple, le parterre de buis représente une carte d'imposition de la région au XIXème siècle tout en encadrant des herbes très variées.

Este variado jardín es sorprendente. Anne Wareham y Charles Hawes, con inagotable dedicación, lo engendraron y no dejan de embellecerlo. Entre otras propiedades, fascina por la armonía con el paisaje circundante. Los aspectos históricos también desempeñan un papel primordial. Sirva de ejemplo el parterre de boj, que remeda un mapa del diezmo de la región del siglo XIX y que, paralelamente, cerca las especies de hierbas más diversas.

Questo giardino incredibilmente vario, al quale hanno dato nuova vita Anne Wareham e Charles Hawes con infinita dedizione, e al quale instancabilmente lavorano migliorandolo, affascina tra l'altro grazie all'armonia con il paesaggio circostante. Anche gli aspetti storici hanno il loro peso. Il parterre di alberi di bosso, per esempio, ridisegna una planimetria della regione del XIX secolo e al contempo incornicia i più vari tipi di erba.

The simple silhouette of the wooden buzzard underscores the lightness of the fireweed 'Chamerion angustifolium'.

Die schlichte Silhouette des hölzernen Bussards unterstreicht die Leichtigkeit des Waldweidenröschens, 'Chamerion angustifolium'.

La silhouette simple des buses de bois souligne la légèreté des lauriers de Saint-Antoine, ‹ Chamerion angustifolium ›.

La grácil silueta del ave de rapiña enfatiza la liviandad del epilobio 'Chamerion angustifolium'.

La semplice silhouette della poiana di legno sottolinea la leggerezza dell'epilobio a fiori piccoli, 'Chamerion angustifolium'.

The yew hedges behind the pool consciously imitate the gentle rolls of the hilly landscape around Monmouthshire. This section imparts meditative peace, its effect increased by a high wall of beautiful trees.

Ganz bewusst nehmen die Eibenhecken hinter dem Pool die Wellenbewegung der sanften Hügellandschaft des Monmouthshire auf. Dieser Abschnitt vermittelt meditative Ruhe, und die Wirkung wird durch die hohe Einrahmung mit den schönen Bäumen noch verstärkt.

Les haies d'ifs derrière la piscine imitent consciencieusement le mouvement de ressac du paysage doucement vallonné du Monmouthshire. Cette section transmet une paix méditative, et l'effet est accru par les magnifiques arbres qui forment un haut mur.

Los setos de tejo tras la piscina adoptan deliberadamente el ondulado vaivén del suave paisaje montañoso de Monmouthshire. Esta parte invita a la contemplación, efecto que se ve incrementado al estar enmarcada por unos esbeltos árboles a su alrededor.

Le siepi di tasso dietro alla piscina riprendono volutamente il movimento ondulato del dolce paesaggio collinare del Monmouthshire. Questa sezione trasmette tranquillità meditativa: l'effetto viene ulteriormente rafforzato dall'alta cornice dei magnifici alberi.

Every section has its own flair: In the vegetable garden, the arrangement of the cleverly supported box tree with the silvery shades of the decorative artichoke ('Cynara cardunculus') and the dark violet of the evergreen 'Heuchera micrantha Palace Purple' catch the eye while the light lilac orchid flowers contrast quite well with the gentle grasses.

Jeder Abschnitt hat sein eigenes Flair: im Gemüsegarten fällt der Blick auf das Arrangement des raffiniert gestutzten Buchsbaums mit dem silbrigem Ton der Zierartischocken, 'Cynara cardunculus', und dem dunklen Violett der immergrünen 'Heuchera micrantha Palace Purple', während sich die helllila Orchideenblüten vor saftigem Gras besonders gut abheben.

Chaque section a son propre style : dans le potager, l'agencement ingénieux des buis avec les teintes argentées des artichauts décoratifs (« Cynara cardunculus ») et le violet foncé de l' « Heuchera micrantha Palace Purple » à feuillage persistant attirent l'œil tandis que les orchidées lilas clair contrastent joliment avec l'herbe tendre.

Cada uno de los sectores tiene su propio encanto. En el jardín de hortalizas la vista se fija en el refinado acabado del boj truncado, con el tono plateado de la flor de cardo, 'Cynara cardunculus', y el violeta oscuro de la 'Heuchera micrantha Palace Purple', de hoja perenne, mientras que las orquídeas, en un lila claro, despuntan entre la suave grama.

Ogni sezione ha il suo fascino: nell'orto lo sguardo cade sulla combinazione del bosso potato in modo raffinato con la tonalità d'argento dei carciofi ornamentali, 'Cynara cardunculus', e il viola scuro della sempreverde 'Heuchera micrantha Palace Purple', mentre i fiori lilla chiaro delle orchidee risaltano magnificamente sull'erba succosa.

Veddw House Garden *Devauden, Monmouthshire, United Kingdom*   73

Chenies Manor

Chenies, Buckinghamshire, United Kingdom

This magnificent estate with its one-thousand year history is surrounded by a breathtaking garden varied twice a year with seasonal plantings by Alistair and Elizabeth MacLeod Matthews. In spring, the brilliant colors of more than 7,000 tulips intoxicate the viewer. Their carpets of flowers blend into the existing garden structure of herbaceous perennials, bushes, statues and paths. In the summer, the pink and red shades of dahlias harmonize with blue-violet petunias and the blue of sage in the sunken garden.

Das stattliche Anwesen mit tausendjähriger Geschichte wird von einem atemberaubenden Garten umgeben, der von Alistair and Elizabeth MacLeod Matthews zweimal im Jahr durch saisonale Pflanzungen variiert wird. Im Frühling berauschen die leuchtenden Farben der über 7.000 Tulpen den Betrachter, deren Blütenteppiche sich in die vorhandene Gartenstruktur der Stauden, Büsche, Statuen und Wege eingliedern. Im Sommer harmonieren im Senkgarten die Rosa- und Rottöne der Dahlien mit blau-violetten Petunien und dem Blau des Salbei.

Cette magnifique propriété à l'histoire millénaire est entourée par un jardin époustouflant qui change deux fois par an grâce aux plantations saisonnières d'Alistair et Elizabeth MacLeod Matthews. Au printemps, les couleurs brillantes de plus de 7.000 tulipes éblouissent le visiteur. Le tapis de fleurs est intégré à la structure de jardin existante comprenant des plantes herbacées, des buissons, statues et des sentiers. En été, les teintes roses et rouges des dahlias s'harmonisent avec le bleu-violet des pétunias et le bleu de la sauge dans le jardin en contrebas.

Esta magnífica propiedad, con una historia milenaria, está rodeada por un prodigioso jardín que, plantando especies de temporada, varía dos veces al año gracias a Alistair y Elizabeth MacLeod Matthews. En primavera, el visitante se embriaga con la luminosidad de más de 7.000 tulipanes, cuyo manto colorista se integra en la estructura del jardín formada por arbustos, matorrales, estatuas y senderos. En el jardín hundido, armonizan en verano las dalias en tonalidades rosas y rojas con las petunias violáceas y la salvia azulada.

Questa grande tenuta dalla storia millenaria è circondata da un giardino di bellezza straordinaria, che Alistair ed Elizabeth MacLeod Matthews variano due volte l'anno con piante stagionali. In primavera il visitatore viene rapito dai colori vivi degli oltre 7.000 tulipani i cui tappeti di fiori si inseriscono nella struttura del giardino fatta di piante perenni, cespugli, statue e viali. In estate, nel giardino ad avvallamenti, le tonalità di rosa e di rosso delle dalie armonizzano con le petunie blu-violette e il blu della salvia.

The sunken garden with the old manor in the background.

Der Senkgarten mit dem alten Herrenhaus im Hintergrund.

Le jardin en contrebas avec le vieux manoir à l'arrière-plan.

El jardín hundido con la antigua casa señorial al fondo.

Il giardino infossato con l'antico casale padronale sullo sfondo.

Chenies Manor *Chenies, Buckinghamshire, United Kingdom*

Chenies Manor is open to visitors, who enjoy exploring the many romantic corners of the garden. They can also broaden their knowledge at its summertime plant fair and purchase new plants to take home with them. On several occasions, even Queen Elizabeth I honored the estate with her visit.

Chenies Manor steht Besuchern offen, die gerne die vielen romantischen Ecken des Gartens erkunden oder auf der hauseigenen sommerlichen Pflanzenmesse ihre Kenntnisse erweitern und neue Pflanzen für zu Hause erstehen. Königin Elizabeth I. hat das Anwesen mehrmals mit ihrem Besuch beehrt.

Chenies Manor est ouvert aux visiteurs qui aiment découvrir les nombreux espaces romantiques du jardin. Ils peuvent étendre leur savoir lors de sa foire aux plantes d'été et acheter de nouvelles plantes pour les emporter chez eux. La reine Elizabeth I elle-même avait honoré à plusieurs reprises la propriété de sa visite.

Chenies Manor está abierta al público. El visitante descubre los numerosos rincones románticos de este jardín o amplía sus conocimientos en la feria floral que organiza la casa en verano, donde adquirir nuevas plantas para el hogar. La reina Isabel I ha honrado con varias visitas esta propiedad.

Chenies Manor è aperto ai visitatori che esplorano con piacere i molti angoli romantici del giardino o ampliano le loro conoscenze acquistando nuove piante alla fiera che si svolge qui ogni estate. La regina Elisabetta I ha già più volte onorato la tenuta con una sua visita.

The white garden is especially enchanting in the spring. The white 'Dreaming Girl' tulips in combination with the forget-me-nots look very elegant, indeed. In the summer, the pink-white, star-shaped blossoms of the fragrant decorative tobacco 'Nicotiana alata' glow above the darker petunias.

Der weiße Garten ist im Frühjahr besonders bezaubernd. Die weißen Tulpen „Dreaming Girl' in Kombination mit Vergissmeinnicht sehen ausgesprochen elegant aus. Im Sommer leuchten die rosa-weißen Sternblüten des duftenden Ziertabak, „Nicotiana alata', über den dunkleren Petunien.

Le jardin blanc est particulièrement séduisant au printemps. Les tulipes blanches ‹ Dreaming girls › associées aux myosotis semblent très élégantes. En été, les fleurs rose-blanc en forme d'étoile du tabac décoratif odorant ‹ Nicotiana alata › brillent au-dessus des pétunias plus sombres.

El jardín blanco es cautivador, especialmente en primavera. Los tulipanes blancos 'Dreaming Girl', combinados con las nomeolvides, le dan un toque de elegancia. En el estío, las flores blanquirrosas del aromático tabaco ornamental, 'Nicotiana alata', refulgen por encima de las petunias en tonos más oscuros.

Il giardino bianco è particolarmente affascinante in primavera. I tulipani bianchi 'Dreaming Girl', in combinazione con i nontiscordardime, hanno un aspetto particolarmente elegante. In estate i fiori a stella rosa-bianchi del profumato tabacco ornamentale, 'Nicotiana alata', risaltano tra le petunie più scure.

Chenies Manor *Chenies, Buckinghamshire, United Kingdom* 79

Gödens Castle

Sande/Gödens, Germany

Amid the marshy Frisian landscape lies the Baroque water castle of Gödens, erected in its current form in the year 1671. Surrounded by a spacious landscape park with mature trees, this country seat serves as an elegant backdrop for outings in the summer and for a Christmas market in the winter. Under the ownership of Counts von Wedel for generations, Gödens Castle with its splendid decoration is one of Northern Germany's most significant castles.

Inmitten der friesischen Marschlandschaft liegt das barocke Wasserschloss Gödens, das 1671 in seiner jetzigen Form gebaut worden ist. Umgeben von einem großzügigen Landschaftspark mit altem Baumbestand, stellt der Landsitz im Sommer elegante Kulisse einer Landpartie und im Winter eines Weihnachtsmarktes dar. Seit Generationen im Besitz der Grafen von Wedel, zählt Schloss Gödens mit seiner prachtvollen Ausstattung zu den bedeutendsten Schlössern Norddeutschlands.

Le *wasserburg* baroque de Gödens a été construit sous sa forme actuelle en 1671. Dans son décor frison féérique, le château est entouré d'un vaste parc paysager planté de vieux arbres. La gentilhommière sert de toile de fond élégante pour les excursions en été et le marché de Noël pendant l'hiver. Pendant des générations, le château de Gödens a été la propriété des Comtes von Wedel. Son splendide mobilier en fait un des châteaux les plus importants d'Allemagne.

En medio de las marismas de Frisia encontramos el castillo barroco de Gödens, construido con su fisonomía actual en 1671. Rodeado por un extenso parque paisajístico con la arboleda original, esta residencia es el marco estival perfecto para una jira en el campo y, en invierno, para un mercadillo de Navidad. Este castillo, perteneciente a los condes de Wedel desde hace generaciones, es uno de los más importantes del norte de Alemania gracias a su suntuosa decoración.

In mezzo al paesaggio della Marsch, in Frisia, si trova il castello barocco sull'acqua di Gödens, costruito nel 1671 nella sua attuale forma. Circondato da un vasto parco paesaggistico con alberi secolari, questa proprietà di campagna costituisce in estate uno scenario elegante per una scampagnata e, in inverno, per un mercatino di Natale. Da generazioni di proprietà dei conti von Wedel, il castello di Gödens, grazie al suo magnifico arredamento, è uno dei più importanti castelli della Germania del nord.

Simple elegance is the motto of the garden design.

Schlichte Eleganz ist das Motto der Gartengestaltung.

L'élégance simple est le leitmotiv de l'aménagement du jardin.

La fina elegancia marca la configuración del jardín.

La semplice eleganza è il motto dell'allestimento del giardino.

Long-stemmed roses in bright pink frame the castle without obstructing its view. Like most of the trees in the park, the wonderful lime tree lane is of time-honored age.

Hochstämmige Rosen in einem kräftigen Rosa umrahmen das Schloss, ohne den Blick zu verstellen. Der wunderbare Lindengang hat wie die meisten Bäume im Park ein stattliches Alter.

Des roses à haute tige d'un rose brillant entourent le château sans obstruer la vue. Comme la plupart des arbres du parc, la magnifique allée de tilleuls a atteint un âge respectable.

Rosas de tallo alto en un rosa intenso bordean el castillo sin distraer la mirada. El maravilloso paseo de tilos tiene, como la mayoría de árboles del parque, una edad considerable.

Rose ad alto fusto di color rosa acceso incorniciano il castello senza ostacolare la vista. La splendida passeggiata sotto i tigli ha, come la maggior parte degli alberi nel parco, una venerabile età.

Ippenburg Castle

Bad Essen – Osnabrück, Germany

The gates of Ippenburg Castle with its vast land and wonderful garden—based on the model of English cottage gardens—open to visitors a couple of times a year. This is especially true since the successful tradition of the Ippenburg Castle and Garden Festival was initiated in 1998. Baroness Viktoria von dem Bussche can thus present the splendor of the grounds and share her enthusiasm for nature and plants with both young and old.

Ein paar Mal im Jahr öffnen sich die Tore des Ippenburger Schlosses mit seinen großen Ländereien und dem wunderbaren, nach dem Vorbild englischer Cottagegärten gestalteten Garten für Besucher, insbesondere seit 1998 die erfolgreiche Tradition des Ippenburger Schloss- und Gartenfestivals ins Leben gerufen wurde. So kann Freifrau Viktoria von dem Bussche die Pracht der Anlage vorführen und Jung und Alt mit ihrer Begeisterung für Natur und Pflanzen anstecken.

Les portes du château d'Ippenburg avec son vaste domaine et son magnifique jardin – basé sur le modèle des jardins de cottage anglais – s'ouvrent pour les visiteurs quelques jours dans l'année. C'est particulièrement vrai depuis 1998 et l'instauration réussie du Festival du Château et du Jardin d'Ippenburg. La baronne Viktoria von dem Bussche aime montrer la splendeur de la propriété et partager son enthousiasme pour la nature et les plantes avec toutes les générations.

Un par de veces al año abre sus puertas el castillo de Ippenburg, con su extensa campiña y su maravilloso jardín, a imagen y semejanza de los jardines de las casas de campo inglesas. Lo visitan especialmente desde 1998, año en el que se instauró el tradicional festival del castillo y el jardín. La baronesa Viktoria von dem Bussche muestra entonces las maravillas del lugar y contagia a grandes y pequeños con su entusiasmo por la naturaleza.

Un paio di volte l'anno le porte del castello di Ippenburg, con i suoi ampi terreni e con il giardino allestito seguendo l'esempio di giardini da cottage inglesi, si aprono ai visitatori. In particolare, dal 1998 è stata inaugurata la fortunata tradizione del festival del castello e dei giardini di Ippenburg, dando modo alla baronessa Viktoria von dem Bussche di mostrare lo splendore del complesso e contagiare i giovani e gli adulti con il suo entusiasmo per la natura e le piante.

*The **'Ippenburg rose'**, named after the castle, in full bloom.*

Die nach dem Schloss benannte Rose 'Ippenburg Rose' in voller Blüte.

La rose nommée d'après le château, la ‹ Ippenburg Rose ›, en pleine floraison.

La rosa 'Ippenburg Rose', llamada así en honor al castillo, en plena floración.

La rosa 'Ippenburg Rose', che porta il nome del castello, in piena fioritura.

Whether under the old trees of the castle park or in the frequently redesigned garden, a multitude of romantic corners invite visitors for long walks.

Ob unter den alten Bäumen des Schlossparks oder im immer wieder neu gestalteten Garten locken eine Vielzahl romantischer Ecken zu ausgedehnten Spaziergängen.

Que ce soit sous les vieux arbres du parc du château ou dans le jardin fréquemment redessiné, une multitude de coins romantiques invitent les visiteurs à de longues promenades.

Ya sea bajo los antiquísimos árboles del parque o en el jardín siempre cambiante, son muchos los rincones románticos que inducen a dar un relajado paseo.

Sia sotto gli antichi alberi del parco del castello, sia nel giardino costantemente rinnovato con nuovi allestimenti, innumerevoli angoli romantici invitano a lunghe passeggiate.

The stately neo-Gothic castle structure with its more than 100 rooms is the center of the grounds, framed by tall chestnut trees on all sides. In the foreground, a small sundial stands at the center of the crossing.

Der prächtige neugotische Schlossbau mit seinen über 100 Zimmern ist der Mittelpunkt der Anlage, hohe Kastanien rahmen ihn ein. Im Vordergrund steht hier eine kleine Sonnenuhr in der Mitte der Wegkreuzung.

Le château seigneurial néo-gothique comptant plus de 100 chambres est le cœur du domaine, encadré de hauts châtaigniers de tous les côtés. Au premier plan, un petit cadran solaire se dresse à la croisée des chemins.

La espléndida construcción del castillo, en estilo neogótico, con sus más de 100 cámaras, es el centro de la propiedad. Grandes castaños la rodean. En un primer plano, un pequeño reloj de sol en el cruce de caminos.

Il magnifico edificio neogotico del castello con le sue oltre 100 camere e circondato da alti castagni, è il centro del complesso. In primo piano qui si trova, al centro dell'incrocio, una piccola meridiana.

Ippenburg Castle *Bad Essen — Osnabrück, Germany*   89

The majestic architecture, coupled with luxuriant roses, awakens memories of the Sleeping Beauty fairytale.

Die majestätische Architektur gepaart mit den üppigen Rosen ruft Erinnerungen an das Märchen von Dornröschen wach.

L'architecture majestueuse, mise en valeur par des rosiers luxuriants, évoque le conte de la Belle au Bois dormant.

La majestuosa arquitectura junto a las exuberancia de las rosas trae a la memoria recuerdos del cuento de La bella durmiente.

L'architettura maestosa e le rose rigogliose risvegliano il ricordo della favola della Bella Addormentata.

Low box tree hedges frame the effusively splendid flowers of the borders.

Niedrige Buchsbaumhecken fassen die überschwängliche Blütenpracht der Rabatten ein.

Des haies de buis basses encadrent les magnifiques fleurs touffues des bordures.

Unos setos de boj a escasa altura enmarcan el lirismo de los planteles en plena floración.

Le siepi di bosso incorniciano la magnificenza dei fiori delle aiuole.

Dyck Castle

Jüchen, Germany

The magnificent Dyck water castle can look back on a history of almost one-thousand years. The historical castle park was created as an extensive collection of plants modeled after an English landscape garden in the 18th century. Today, the whole estate, measuring 173 acres, presents a variety of new gardens ranging from modern landscape architecture, kitchen garden examples, playgrounds and climbing areas right up to botanical theme gardens.

Das herrliche Wasserschloss Dyck kann auf eine beinahe tausendjährige Geschichte blicken. Der historische Schlosspark wurde als umfangreiche Pflanzensammlung nach dem Vorbild eines englischen Landschaftsgartens im 18. Jahrhundert angelegt. Die heutige 70 ha große Gesamtanlage präsentiert eine Vielzahl neuer Gärten, die von moderner Landschaftsarchitektur über Hausgartenbeispiele, Spiel- und Kletterbereiche bis hin zu pflanzlichen Themengärten reichen.

Le magnifique château de Dyck, entouré d'eau, a une histoire quasiment millénaire. Le parc historique du château a été créé comme une vaste collection de plantes selon le modèle du jardin paysager anglais en vogue au XVIIIème siècle. Le domaine actuel de 70 hectares présente une variété de nouveaux jardins qui vont de l'architecture paysagère moderne aux modèles de jardins potagers, des zones de jeux et d'escalade et aux parterres de fleurs à thème.

Este majestuoso castillo con foso tiene a sus espaldas una historia de casi mil años. El histórico parque del castillo se ejecutó a modo de vasta colección de plantas siguiendo el ejemplo de un jardín paisajístico inglés del siglo XVIII. Hoy, con sus 70 hectáreas, cuenta con numerosos jardines nuevos, que abarcan desde la moderna arquitectura paisajista a los jardines temáticos por plantas, pasando por jardines particulares o temáticos, con zonas de juego o plantas enredaderas.

Il magnifico castello sull'acqua Dyck può vantarsi di una storia quasi millenaria. Il parco storico del castello è stato costruito come vasta collezione di piante seguendo l'esempio di un giardino paesaggistico inglese del XVIII secolo. L'intero complesso, attualmente di 70 ettari, presenta una molteplicità di nuovi giardini che spazia dall'architettura paesaggistica moderna a esempi di giardini privati, aree per giocare e per arrampicarsi, fino a giardini botanici a tema.

Many original details surprise and inspire the visitor.

Viele originelle Details überraschen und inspirieren den Besucher.

De nombreux détails originaux surprennent et inspirent le visiteur.

Muchos detalles originales sorprenden e inspiran al visitante.

Molti dettagli originali sorprendono e ispirano il visitatore.

As early as the 18th century, an extensive arboretum transformed the originally bare lowland around Dyck Castle into a diversely designed park that involved decades of work. It comprises many rare types of trees and bushes from the most diverse countries.

Ein weitläufiges Arboretum verwandelte bereits im 18. Jahrhundert nach jahrzehntelanger Arbeit die eigentlich unbewaldete Niederung um Schloss Dyck in einen abwechslungsreich gestalteten Park mit vielen seltenen Baum- und Straucharten aus verschiedensten Ländern.

Au XVIIIème siècle déjà, un riche arboretum avait nécessité plusieurs décennies de travail pour transformer les zones basses non-forestières autour du château de Dyck en un parc diversifié. De nombreuses espèces rares d'arbres et de buissons provenant de différents pays peuvent maintenant y être observées.

Tras décadas de trabajo, una extensa arboleda transformó allá por el siglo XVIII la llanura yerma en torno al castillo en un parque de lo más variado con especies infrecuente de árboles y arbustos de los países más diversos.

Un ampio arboreto ha trasformato già nel XVIII secolo, dopo un lavoro durato decenni, l'avvallamento disboscato intorno al castello Dyck in un parco diversificato con molte varietà rare di alberi e di cespugli dai paesi più diversi.

Dyck Castle *Jüchen, Germany*   95

Sayn Castle & Palace

Sayn, Germany

It was in 1987 when Princess Gabriela zu Sayn-Wittgenstein-Sayn had a butterfly garden built in the 22-acre English landscape park surrounding Sayn Castle & Palace. This butterfly garden blends wonderfully into the romantic ensemble. Tropical plants such as hibiscus, orchids, bananas, pineapple bushes and ferns delight the eye and are a habitat for countless colorful and exotic butterflies. The garden "Garten der Schmetterlinge Schloss Sayn" is open to visitors so that adults and children can (re)discover the fascinating world of butterflies.

Bereits 1987 ließ Fürstin Gabriela zu Sayn-Wittgenstein-Sayn in dem neun Hektar großen englischen Landschaftspark um Schloss und Burg Sayn einen Schmetterlingsgarten bauen, der sich hervorragend in das romantische Gartenensemble integriert. Tropische Pflanzen wie Hibiscus, Orchideen, Bananen, Ananasgewächse und Farne erfreuen das Auge und sind Lebensraum für unzählige farbenprächtige exotische Falter. Der „Garten der Schmetterlinge Schloss Sayn" steht Besuchern offen, denn Groß und Klein sollen die faszinierende Welt der Falter (wieder-) entdecken.

Dès 1987, la Princesse Gabriela zu Sayn-Wittgenstein-Sayn a fait construire un jardin aux papillons dans le jardin anglais paysager de neuf hectares autour de Sayn Castle & Palace. Il est merveilleusement intégré à l'ensemble du jardin romantique. Des plantes tropicales comme les hibiscus, les orchidées, les bananiers, les ananas et les fougères ravissent les yeux et sont le refuge d'innombrables papillons exotiques multicolores. Le jardin « Garten der Schmetterlinge Schloss Sayn » est ouvert aux visiteurs pour que les adultes et les enfants puissent (re)découvrir le monde fascinant des papillons.

En el parque paisajístico inglés de nueve hectáreas que rodea al castillo y al alcázar de Sayn, la duquesa Gabriela de Sayn-Wittgenstein-Sayn mandó construir en 1987 un jardín de mariposas que se integra a la perfección en el romántico conjunto ajardinado. Plantas tropicales como hibiscos, orquídeas, bananos, piñas y algún helecho alegran la vista y dan cobijo a incontables mariposas exóticas de vivos colores. El jardín "Garten der Schmetterlinge Schloss Sayn" se puede visitar. Niños y mayores descubrirán –de nuevo– el fascinante mundo de las mariposas.

Già nel 1987 la principessa Gabriela zu Sayn-Wittgenstein-Sayn fece costruire nel parco paesaggistico inglese di nove ettari, che circonda il castello e la fortezza di Sayn, un giardino di farfalle che si integra splendidamente nel complesso romantico del giardino. Piante tropicali come l'ibisco, le orchidee, le banane, l'ananas e le felci allietano l'occhio e sono lo spazio vitale di innumerevoli farfalle esotiche dai meravigliosi colori. Il giardino "Garten der Schmetterlinge Schloss Sayn" è aperto ai visitatori, perché grandi e piccini devono (ri-)scoprire il fantastico mondo delle farfalle.

The palace garden was designed in the mid-19th century by Karl-Friedrich Thelemann and created by Heinrich Siesmayer.

Der Schlosspark wurde Mitte des 19. Jahrhunderts von Karl-Friedrich Thelemann entworfen und von Heinrich Siesmayer angelegt.

Le parc du château a été dessiné au milieu du XIXème siècle par Karl-Friedrich Thelemann et créé par Heinrich Siesmayer.

El diseño del parque de este castillo, de mediados del siglo XIX, es obra de Karl-Friedrich Thelemann. Heinrich Siesmayer se encargó de su ejecución.

Il parco del castello è stato progettato alla metà del XIX secolo da Karl-Friedrich Thelemann e allestito da Heinrich Siesmayer.

Curving paths lead through the luxuriant tropical butterfly garden. Its seven bridges bear the names of the princely family's children and set important structural accents. Flora and fauna merge to create worthwhile compositions such as the White Tree Nymph 'Idea leuconoe' on the hibiscus flower.

Geschwungene Wege führen durch den üppigen tropischen Schmetterlingsgarten. Die sieben Brücken tragen die Namen der Kinder des Fürstenpaares und setzen wichtige strukturelle Akzente. Flora und Fauna bilden gemeinsam eine sehenswerte Komposition wie die Weiße Baumnymphe ‚Idea leuconoe' auf der Hibiskusblüte.

Des sentiers sinueux traversent le jardin des papillons, tropical et luxuriant. Les sept ponts portent les noms des enfants du couple princier et servent d'accents structurels. La flore et la faune fusionnent pour créer des compositions précieuses comme le papillon ‹ Idea leuconoe › sur une fleur d'hibiscus.

Sinuosos senderos cruzan el exuberante jardín tropical de las mariposas. Los siete puentes se bautizaron con los nombres de los hijos de los duques y refuerzan la estructura del jardín. Flora y fauna conforman una composición digna de admiración, como la mariposa 'Idea leuconoe' sobre una flor de hibisco.

Sentieri sinuosi intricate portano al rigoglioso giardino tropicale delle farfalle. I sette ponti portano il nome dei figli dei principi e pongono importanti accenti strutturali. La flora e la fauna creano nel loro insieme una composizione da non perdere, come l'‘Idea leuconoe', una farfalla sul fiore dell'ibisco.

Langenburg Castle

Langenburg, Germany

Langenburg Castle is located on a mountain ridge high above idyllic Jagts Valley in the Hohenloher Land. The Baroque garden has been maintained through the centuries by the princely Hohenlohe family. In 1993/94, it was restored based on old plans and rededicated. The large properties of the castle have been used sustainably for timber production, for example. Its garden provides the setting for the young tradition of "Fürstliche Gartentage", the castle's own garden fair, during which visitors can explore the grounds and talk to gardening experts.

Schloss Langenburg liegt auf einem Bergrücken hoch über dem idyllischen Jagtstal im Hohenloher Land. Der barocke Garten wurde über Jahrhunderte von der Fürstlichen Familie Hohenlohe erhalten und 1993/94 nach alten Plänen saniert und neu eingeweiht. Die großen Ländereien werden nachhaltig zum Beispiel zur Holzgewinnung genutzt. Der Garten ist Kulisse für die junge Tradition der Fürstlichen Gartentage, bei denen Besucher die Anlage erkunden und sich mit Gartenfachleuten austauschen können.

Le château de Langenburg est situé sur la crête d'une montagne au-dessus de la Vallée de Jagts dans le Land de Hohenlohe. Le jardin baroque a été préservé pendant des siècles par la famille princière de Hohenlohe. En 1993/94, il a été rénové selon les anciens plans et rouvert. Le vaste domaine est utilisé de manière durable, pour la production de bois par exemple. Le jardin est le cadre de la jeune tradition de la foire du jardin du château pendant laquelle les visiteurs peuvent découvrir le domaine et parler à des experts des jardins.

El castillo de Langenburg está situado en lo alto de una loma en el idílico valle de Jagtstal en la región de Hohenlohe. El jardín barroco ha sido conservado durante siglos por la principesca familia de Hohenlohe; en 1993/94 se restauró siguiendo los planos antiguos y se reinauguró. En la gran campiña se aplica la tala sostenible de árboles. El jardín es el marco de las Jornadas del jardín principesco, de reciente tradición, durante las cuales los visitantes intercambian impresiones con los responsables del jardín.

Il castello di Langenburg è situato sul dorso di una montagna che domina l'idilliaca valle Jagtstal, nell'Hohenlohe Land. Il giardino barocco è stato mantenuto per secoli dalla famiglia dei principi Hohenlohe e nel 1993/94 è stato risanato in base a vecchi progetti e nuovamente inaugurato. I grandi terreni vengono intensamente sfruttati, per esempio per la produzione di legname. Il giardino è lo scenario della recente tradizione denominata "Fürstliche Gartentage", durante la quale i visitatori possono esplorare il complesso e scambiare opinioni con esperti di giardini.

Cordon apples grow along the wall of the Baroque garden.

Entlang der Mauer des Barockgartens ziehen sich Spalieräpfel.

Les pommiers en contre-espalier poussent le long du mur du jardin baroque.

A lo largo del muro del jardín barroco se alinean los manzanos en espaldera.

Lungo il muro del giardino barocco vengono coltivati i meli a spalliera.

The little pavilion on the front side of the Baroque garden radiates in a new glow and the mighty keep behind it wears a green mantle of vine leaves in the summer. Atop the mountain ridge, the castle and garden offer wonderful views of the landscape below, which is especially striking when covered with snow.

Der kleine Pavillon an der Stirnseite des Barockgartens erstrahlt in neuem Glanz, und der mächtige Burgfried dahinter trägt im Sommer ein grünes Kleid aus Weinlaub. Schloss und Garten bieten vom Bergrücken hinab herrliche Ausblicke in die Landschaft, die schneebedeckt besonders apart wirkt.

En été, le petit pavillon à l'avant du jardin baroque prend un nouvel éclat et le puissant donjon derrière lui porte un manteau de feuilles de vignes. Le château et le jardin offrent une vue magnifique sur le paysage, particulièrement impressionnant recouvert de neige, en contrebas depuis la montagne.

El pequeño pabellón en la parte frontal del jardín barroco disfruta de un nuevo fulgor, y la imponente torreta a su espalda se cubre en verano de un manto verde de hojas de parra. Castillo y jardín gozan de majestuosas vistas desde la loma, y cuando está cubierto por la nieve, ofrece un espectáculo único.

Il piccolo padiglione sul lato frontale del giardino barocco si illumina di nuovo splendore e la maestosa torre del castello che vi si trova dietro si ricopre in estate di pampini verdi. Dal dorso della montagna verso valle, il castello e il giardino offrono una vista magnifica sul paesaggio, particolarmente affascinante quando è ricoperto di neve.

Dennenlohe Castle & Gardens

Unterschwaningen, Germany

Since 1990, Baron Süsskind has been spending almost every day in his garden. He has planted most of the plants and collected and laid out all of the rocks by himself. The very expansive grounds are arranged into three areas: The 25-acre rhododendron park, the continuously evolving landscape park—a patchwork of traditionally cultivated and wild landscapes—and the private garden of the castle. The ensemble has been awarded one of the twenty most beautiful parks in Germany.

Seit 1990 verbringt Baron Süsskind fast jeden Tag in seinem Garten, so sind fast alle Pflanzen von ihm selbst gepflanzt, alle Steine selbst gesammelt und gelegt. Das sehr weitläufige Gelände gliedert sich in drei Bereiche: den zehn Hektar großen Rhododendronpark, den ständig wachsenden Landschaftspark, ein Patchwork traditioneller Kultur- und Wildlandschaften, sowie den Privatgarten des Schlosses. Das Ensemble wurde als einer der zwanzig schönsten Parks Deutschlands ausgezeichnet.

Depuis 1990, le Baron Süsskind passe pratiquement chaque jour de sa vie dans son jardin. Il y a planté quasiment toutes les plantes, et aussi collecté et disposé toutes les pierres. Les terrains très vastes sont aménagés en trois zones : le parc de rhododendrons de dix hectares, le jardin paysager en constant développement qui est un patchwork de paysages traditionnels cultivés et sauvages, et le jardin privé du château. L'ensemble a été primé comme l'un des vingt plus beaux parcs d'Allemagne.

Desde 1990, el barón Süsskind pasa prácticamente todos los días en su jardín. Casi todas las plantas las ha plantado él mismo; y las piedras las ha escogido y dispuesto a su gusto. Este amplísimo terreno se divide en tres zonas: el parque de rododendros de diez hectáreas, el parque paisajístico que no deja de crecer, un tradicional mosaico de paisajes silvestres y cultivados y el jardín privado del castillo. Este conjunto fue galardonado como uno de los veinte parques más hermosos de Alemania.

Dal 1990 il barone Süsskind passa quasi ogni giorno nel suo giardino; quasi tutte le piante, quindi, sono state piantate da lui stesso, e tutte le pietre sono state da lui raccolte e posate. Il terreno, molto ampio, si suddivide in tre aree: il parco di rododendro di dieci ettari, il parco paesaggistico in costante crescita, un patchwork di paesaggi di cultura tradizionale e selvaggia, oltre al giardino privato del castello. Il complesso è stato premiato come uno dei più bei parchi della Germania.

Countless rhododendron flourish here in every available color.

Unzählige Rhododendren blühen hier in allen verfügbaren Farben.

D'innombrables rhododendrons fleurissent ici dans toutes les couleurs possibles.

Numerosos rododendros florecen en todos los colores posibles.

Innumerevoli rododendri fioriscono qui in tutti i colori possibili.

The wisteria bridge creates an elegant arch above the water, which has stepping stones and lotus flowers. The castle pond is so large that it has room for several islands.

Die Glyzinienbrücke spannt einen eleganten Bogen über das Wasser, in dem Trittsteine liegen und Lotus wächst. Der Schlossweiher ist so groß, dass mehrere Inseln Platz finden.

Le pont de glycine crée une arche élégante au-dessus de l'eau, avec ses pas japonais et ses fleurs de lotus. L'étang du château est si grand qu'il abrite plusieurs îles.

El puente de las glicinias describe un elegante arco sobre el agua, donde hay piedras pasaderas y crece el loto. El estanque de este castillo es tan grande que cuenta con varias islas.

Il ponte di glicini disegna un arco elegante sull'acqua in cui si trovano pietre calpestabili e fiori di loto. Il laghetto del castello è molto vasto e vi si trovano diverse isole.

A walk takes the visitor through the grounds, which have been designed with much knowledge and a loving hand. The path to the Japanese and Chinese streams follows the moon gate and the extraordinary metal bridge.

Ein Spaziergang führt den Besucher durch die mit großer Kenntnis und liebevoller Hand gestaltete Anlage. Entlang dem Mondtor sowie der außergewöhnlichen Metallbrücke gelangt er zum japanischen und chinesischen Bachlauf.

Une promenade mène le visiteur à travers le domaine, qui a été dessiné avec beaucoup de savoir et une main aimante. Le chemin vers les ruisseaux chinois et japonais suit la porte de lune et l'extraordinaire pont métallique.

Un paseo llevará al visitante por este parque creado con manos sabias y tiernas. Siguiendo la Puerta de la Luna y cruzando el curioso puente de metal, alcanzará el curso del arroyo japonés y chino.

La passeggiata porta il visitatore attraverso il giardino allestito con esperienza e amore. Lungo il portone della luna e lo straordinario ponte di metallo si giunge alla riva del ruscello giapponese e cinese.

Tüssling Castle

Tüssling, Germany

Tüssling Castle received its prominent face around 1590 as the four wings with their defiant corner turrets were constructed. Now it is one of the most beautiful and best-preserved castles of Bavaria. The current owner, Countess Stephanie Bruges von Pfuel, has been highly committed to giving the castle and its garden new splendor. The ensemble has developed the kind of well-arranged, bright beauty that allows both the building and the spacious park with its ancient, mature trees to stand out.

Sein markantes Gesicht bekam Schloss Tüssling um 1590 als die vier Flügel mit den trutzigen Ecktürmen errichtet wurden. Heute zählt es zu den schönsten und am besten erhaltenen Schlössern Bayerns. Die heutige Eigentümerin, Stephanie Gräfin Bruges von Pfuel, hat mit viel Engagement Schloss und Garten neuen Glanz verliehen. Das Ensemble entfaltet so eine gegliederte, helle Schönheit, die sowohl das Gebäude als auch die weitläufigen Parkanlagen mit dem alten Baumbestand zur Geltung kommen lassen.

Le château de Tüssling a reçu son aspect dominant aux environs de 1590 avec la construction des quatre ailes avec leurs tours d'angle altières. À présent, c'est l'un des plus beaux et des mieux préservés des châteaux de Bavière. Sa propriétaire actuelle, la comtesse Stephanie Bruges von Pfuel, s'est beaucoup investie pour donner à son château et au jardin une nouvelle splendeur. L'ensemble dégage une beauté brillante, bien aménagée, qui permet à la fois au bâtiment et au parc spacieux avec ses vieux arbres de se distinguer.

El Castillo de Tüssling ofrece esta fisonomía tan llamativa desde 1590, cuando las cuatro alas se unieron a las cuatro torres defensivas. Hoy es uno de los castillos bávaros más bellos y mejor conservados. La propietaria actual, Stephanie condesa de Bruges von Pfuel, le ha dado un nuevo fulgor a castillo y jardín. El conjunto despliega una belleza estructurada y clara, que destaca tanto el edificio como los extensos parques con sus arboledas primigenias.

L'aspetto massiccio è stato conferito a castello Tüssling intorno al 1590, quando furono costruite le quattro ali con le imponenti torri ad angolo. Oggi è uno dei castelli più belli e meglio conservati della Baviera. La proprietaria attuale, la contessa Stephanie di Bruges von Pfuel, ha donato con molto impegno un nuovo splendore al castello e al giardino. Il complesso manifesta così una bellezza articolata e luminosa, che valorizza sia l'edificio che l'ampia area del parco con il patrimonio arboreo secolare.

Romantic statues give a sense of lightness and elegance to the park.

Romantische Statuen verleihen dem Park Leichtigkeit und Eleganz.

Les statues romantiques confèrent une sensation de légèreté et d'élégance au parc.

Estatuas románticas confieren al parque liviandad y elegancia.

Le statue romantiche donano leggerezza ed eleganza al parco.

The distinctive central axis draws attention as easily toward the building as it does away from it into the park while the tender plants of the easy-care and long-blossoming borders are almost noticed just in passing—and yet, they are what actually creates that subtle lightness.

Der Blick wird entlang der markanten Mittelachse genauso leicht zum Gebäude hin wie von ihm weg in den Park geführt. Dabei wird die zarte Bepflanzung der pflegeleichten und langblühenden Rabatten nahezu nebenbei wahrgenommen — und doch wird erst durch sie die subtile Leichtigkeit hergestellt.

L'axe central caractéristique attire l'attention autant sur le bâtiment que sur le parc, et on remarqueà peine en passant les bordures faciles à entretenir et qui fleurissent une grande partie de l'année : pourtant, ce sont elles qui créent cette légèreté subtile.

La mirada avanza sin dificultad a lo largo del gran eje central y se dirige tanto al edificio como al parque que parte de él. Las delicadas especies vegetales siempre en flor de los parterres de fácil cuidado casi pasan desapercibidas, pero es precisamente a través de ellas como se crea esa liviandad tan sutil.

Lo sguardo viene condotto con leggerezza lungo l'mponente asse centrale sia verso l'edificio sia dall'edificio verso il parco. Le piante delicate delle aiuole facili da curare e di lunga fioritura vengono notate quasi incidentalmente — eppure sono proprio loro che creano questa sottile leggerezza!

The radiant green of the perfectly tended lawn as well as the vines pruned to equal height on the pillars, add the final touch to the inner courtyard lined by arcades, a gem of architectural Renaissance art.

Das strahlende Grün des perfekt gepflegten Rasens sowie die gleichmäßig in der Höhe gestutzten Ranken an den Säulen geben dem von Arkaden gesäumten Innenhof, einem Juwel architektonischer Renaissancekunst, den letzten Schliff.

Le vert lumineux de la pelouse parfaitement entretenue, ainsi que les plantes grimpantes qui sont taillées à hauteur égale sur les piliers, sont la touche finale de la cour intérieure soulignée par des arcades, un joyau de l'art architectural de la Renaissance.

El refulgente verde del cuidado césped junto a las enredaderas a la misma altura en torno a las columnas dan al patio interior con arcadas, una joya de la arquitectura renacentista, el último toque de distinción.

Il verde splendente del prato perfettamente curato e i viticci sulle colonne, potati nella parte superiore in modo regolare, danno l'ultimo tocco al cortile interno bordato di arcate, un gioiello di arte architettonica rinascimentale.

Villa Krantz

Munich, Germany

High-quality materials such as natural stone and bronze underscore the impressive concept and minimized design vocabulary in this garden, which emphasizes the neo-classical style of the villa without going overboard. The entrance area is lined by box trees and rhododendrons. To the right and left of the terrace, low box tree hedges border the colorful summer planting that changes every year. The ascending lawn with its water cascade of black granite and a border of light limestone are both unique and elegant.

Hochwertige Materialen wie Naturstein und Bronze unterstreichen das beeindruckende Konzept und die reduzierte Formensprache dieses Gartens, der den neuklassizistischen Stil der Villa betont, ohne zu übertreiben. Den Eingangsbereich säumen Buchsbaum und Rhododendron. Rechts und links der Terrasse fassen niedrige Buchshecken die farbenfrohe und jährlich wechselnde Sommerbepflanzung ein. Die ansteigende Rasenfläche mit der Wassertreppe aus schwarzem Granit und einem Saum aus hellem Kalkstein ist originell und edel zugleich.

Des matériaux de qualité comme la pierre naturelle et le bronze soulignent le concept impressionnant et le vocabulaire minimaliste de ce jardin, ce qui met en valeur le style néo-classique de la villa sans l'exagérer. L'entrée est bordée de buis et de rhododendrons. A gauche et à droite de la terrasse, les haies de buis suivent les plantations d'été colorées qui changent chaque année. La partie de pelouse ascendante avec ses escaliers d'eau en granit noir bordé de calcaire blanc est à la fois originale et élégante.

Materiales de gran calidad, tales como la piedra natural y el bronce, subrayan el impresionante concepto y el reducido lenguaje formal de este jardín, que remarca sin exagerar el estilo neoclásico de la mansión. La entrada está flanqueada por bojes y rododendros. A derecha e izquierda de la terraza, unos pequeños setos de boj rodean la flora estival, cambiante a lo largo del año y rica en colores. La superficie de césped en pendiente y la escalera de agua de granito negro ribeteada con caliza más clara resulta original y elegante al mismo tiempo.

Materiali pregiati come la pietra naturale e il bronzo sottolineano l'orginale progetto e il succinto linguaggio di forme di questo giardino, che evidenzia senza esagerazioni lo stile neoclassico della villa. L'area d'ingresso è bordata di bossi e rododendri. A destra e a sinistra del terrazzo, basse siepi di bosso abbracciano piante estive piene di colore che variano ogni anno. La superficie erbosa in salita con la scalinata d'acqua, fatta di pietra granito nero e un bordo di pietra calcarea chiara, è originale e preziosa al contempo.

Rocks and plants complement each other in a symphony of fresh green and cool water.

Stein und Pflanze ergänzen sich zu einer Sinfonie aus frischem Grün und kühlem Nass.

Les pierres et les plantes se complètent mutuellement dans une symphonie de vert tendre et d'eau fraîche.

Piedras y plantas conforman una sinfonía de fresco verdor y húmedo frescor.

Le pietre e le piante si completano in una sinfonia di freschezza fatta d'acqua e di verde.

The play of the green shades *enriches the design vocabulary of the spherically pruned box trees—or of the changing potted plants in their full bloom—of the hedge sofa growing in alignment and the three box tree, yew and beech hedges with their various leaf structures. The hedges are trimmed to graduating heights and form the boundary to the "wild nature" behind them.*

Das Spiel der Grüntöne *bereichert die Formensprache der kugelig geschnittenen Buchsbäume – bzw. der wechselnden Kübelpflanzen in voller Blüte –, des in der Flucht wachsenden Heckensofas und der drei Buchsbaum-, Eiben- und Buchenhecken mit ihren unterschiedlichen Blattstrukturen. Die Hecken sind in abgestufter Höhe geschnitten und bilden die Grenze zur „wilden Natur" dahinter.*

Le jeu de nuances vertes *enrichit le concept de création avec des buis taillés en boules (ou avec des plantes en pot en pleine floraison régulièrement changées) de la haie en forme de sofa qui déborde de l'alignement et trois haies de buis, d'if et de hêtre avec leurs feuilles aux formes variées. Les haies sont taillées à des hauteurs graduées et séparent le jardin de la « nature sauvage ».*

La combinación *de tonos verdes enriquece el lenguaje formal de los bojes podados con formas esféricas, así como de las plantas en flor de los maceteros, del sofá de seto alineado y de los tres setos de boj, tejo y haya con sus diversas estructuras foliares. Los setos están podados a diferentes alturas y constituyen la linde con la "naturaleza salvaje" a sus espaldas.*

Il gioco delle tonalità di verde *arricchisce il linguaggio delle forme degli alberi di bosso potati a sfera – o delle varie piante da vaso in fiore –, della siepe a forma di sofà che cresce allineao con le tre siepi di bosso, tasso e faggio con i loro differenti strutture del fogliame. Le siepi sono potate a gradini e costituiscono la delimitazione con la "natura selvaggia" dietro di esse.*

Val en Sel Manor & Gardens

Saint-Père-sous-Vézelay, Burgundy, France

Roses, mallow and hydrangea have a bewitching scent in this charming garden at the heart of Burgundy. The garden owner planted these plants and tends to them herself. Thanks to the rosemary bushes and lavender plants, the inner courtyard displays green foliage throughout the year. Old vines, roses and wisteria climb the walls of the building and harmonize the ensemble as a result. Next to the stream on one side of the garden, folding-chairs are ready for guests during the summer.

Rosen, Malven und Hortensien duften verführerisch in diesem charmanten Garten im Herzen des Burgund, den die Eigentümerin selbst anlegte und pflegt. Der Innenhof präsentiert dank der Rosmarinbüsche und Lavendelstauden das ganze Jahr über grünes Blattwerk. Alte Weinstöcke, Rosen und Glyzinien ranken sich an den Mauern der Gebäude empor und harmonisieren so das Ensemble. Neben dem Bachlauf an einer der Seiten des Gartens stehen im Sommer Liegestühle für die Gäste bereit.

Les roses, les mauves et les hortensias exhalent un parfum ensorcelant dans ce charmant jardin au cœur de la Bourgogne. La propriétaire l'a planté et l'entretient elle-même. Grâce aux buissons de romarin et de lavande, la cour intérieure affiche un feuillage vert tout au long de l'année. De vieilles vignes, des roses et de la glycine rampent sur les murs et harmonisent l'ensemble. Près du ruisseau, sur un côté du jardin, les chaises longues sont prêtes pour les invités pendant l'été.

Rosas, malvas y hortensias dejan sus seductores aromas en este delicioso jardín en el corazón de la Borgoña, jardín que la propia dueña cultiva y cuida. El patio interior cuenta con verdor todo el año gracias al romero y a la lavanda. Viejas cepas, rosas y glicinias trepan por los muros del edificio, otorgándole armonía al conjunto. Junto al arroyuelo, en uno de los lados del jardín, los invitados disfrutan de unas tumbonas en verano.

Il profumo delle rose, della malva e delle ortensie si spande in modo seducente in questo affascinante giardino nel cuore della Borgogna, ideato e curato dalla proprietaria stessa. Il cortile interno presenta foglie verdi per tutto l'arco dell'anno grazie ai cespugli di rosmarino e agli arbusti di lavanda. Glicini, rose e viti secolari si arrampicano sui muri dell'edificio creando un insieme armonico. Accanto al ruscello, su uno dei lati del giardino, in estate vengono predisposte delle sedie a sdraio per gli ospiti.

Val en Sel is located at the gates of the Morvan nature reserve.

Val en Sel liegt vor den Toren des Naturparks von Morvan.

Val en Sel est situé aux portes du Parc Naturel Régional du Morvan.

Val en Sel se sitúa a las puertas del Parque Natural de Morvan.

Val en Sel si trova davanti alle porte del parco naturale di Morvan.

126　Val en Sel Manor & Gardens　*Saint-Père-sous-Vézelay, Burgundy, France*

From spring to late fall, many different types of shapes and colors decorate the extra-wide borders of flowers that form large squares. The paths and the vine alley look especially charming because of the invitingly soft green of the mowed lawns.

Vom Frühling bis zum späten Herbst verzieren eine Vielzahl verschiedener Formen und Farben die besonders breiten Blumenrabatten, die große Vierecke zeichnen. Besonders lieblich wirken die Wege und der Rankengang durch das einladend weiche Grün des kurzgeschnittenen Rasens.

Du printemps à la fin de l'automne, des formes et des couleurs extrêmement variées décorent les immenses bordures de fleurs qui forment de grands carrés. Les sentiers et la pergola dégagent un charme particulier grâce au vert tendre accueillant des pelouses tondues.

Desde la primavera hasta finales del otoño, los amplios planteles florales, que conforman unos cuadrados de gran tamaño, están decorados con infinidad de formas y colores. Especialmente encantadoras son las sendas y el camino de trepado que cruza el suave césped cortado al mínimo.

Dalla primavera al tardo autunno, una molteplicità di diverse forme e colori decorano le larghe bordure di fiori che disegnano dei quadrati. Le vie e il viale con le piante rampicanti che si aprono attraverso il verde morbido e invitante del prato a erba bassa sono particolarmente attraenti.

Val en Sel Manor & Gardens *Saint-Père-sous-Vézelay, Burgundy, France* 127

Epoisses Castle

Epoisses, Burgundy, France

The history of Epoisses Castle dates back to the sixth century. In the Middle Ages, when the present garden area used to serve military purposes, it was expanded into a fortress and suffered major destruction during the French Revolution. Since that time, every generation of the Guitaut family has dedicated itself to the preservation and beautification of the estate. The park, which blossoms from Easter to All Saint's Day, is enchanting with its colorful borders and a tricolor garden in gold, green and silver.

Die Geschichte des Schlosses Epoisses geht bis auf das sechste Jahrhundert zurück. Im Mittelalter, als noch das Militär die heutige Gartenfläche nutzte, wurde es zur Festung ausgebaut und in der Französischen Revolution stark zerstört. Seitdem haben sich alle Generationen der Familie Guitaut der Erhaltung und Verschönerung des Anwesens gewidmet. Der von Ostern bis Allerheiligen in Blüte stehende Park bezaubert mit seinen bunten Rabatten und einem Trikolore-Garten in Gold, Grün und Silber.

L'histoire du château d'Epoisses remonte au sixième siècle. Au Moyen-âge, quand les militaires utilisaient encore l'espace du jardin actuel, il a été agrandi pour devenir une forteresse, et a aussi souffert d'une destruction majeure pendant la Révolution française. Depuis cette époque, chaque génération de la famille Guitaut s'est dévouée à la préservation et à l'embellissement de la propriété. Le parc, qui fleurit de Pâques à la Toussaint, enchante le visiteur avec ses bordures colorées et son jardin tricolore en or, vert et argent.

La historia del castillo de Epoisses se remonta al siglo VI. En la Edad Media, cuando la que es hoy superficie ajardinada estaba ocupada por el ejército, se transformó en una fortaleza, para luego sufrir graves daños durante la Revolución Francesa. Desde entonces, todas las generaciones de la familia Guitaut se han dedicado a su conservación y embellecimiento. El parque, en flor desde Pascua hasta Todos los santos, fascina por sus parterres coloristas y un jardín tricolor en oro, verde y plata.

La storia del castello Epoisses risale al sesto secolo. Nel Medioevo, quando era ancora la milizia a utilizzare l'area attuale del giardino, venne trasformata in una fortezza e durante la rivoluzione francese venne distrutta. Da allora tutte le generazioni della famiglia Guitaut si sono occupate del mantenimento e dell'abbellimento della tenuta. Il parco, che è in fiore per tutto il periodo da Pasqua a Ognissanti, affascina con le sue aiuole colorate e un giardino tricolore oro, verde e argento.

The 500 species of roses in the castle courtyard always attract attention.

Die 500 Rosenstämme im Schlosshof ziehen alle Blicke auf sich.

Les 500 rosiers dans la cour du château attirent toujours l'attention.

Los 500 rosales del patio del castillo atraen todas las miradas.

I 500 ceppi di rose nel cortile del castello attirano tutti gli sguardi.

As one enters the courtyard, time seems to stand still.

Sobald man den Hof betritt, scheint die Zeit stehen geblieben zu sein.

En entrant dans la cour intérieure, le temps semble se suspendre.

Tan pronto como se entra en el patio, el tiempo parece detenerse.

Appena si entra nel cortile, il tempo sembra fermarsi.

134 Epoisses Castle *Epoisses, Burgundy, France*

In contrast to the austerity of the castle with its moat (there used to be two) and the long, narrow rose beds in the castle courtyard, a cheerful mix of flowers thrives in the vegetable garden.

Im Gegensatz zur Strenge des Schlosses mit seinem ursprünglich doppelten Wassergraben und den langen schmalen Rosenbeeten im Schlosshof gedeiht im Gemüsegarten ein fröhlicher Blumenmix.

Contrastant avec l'austérité du château et son fossé unique (il y en avait auparavant deux), et les parterres de roses longs et étroits dans la cour du château, un joyeux mélange de fleurs éclot dans le jardin potager.

Como contrapunto a la sobriedad del castillo, con su doble foso y sus largos y finos planteles de rosas del patio del castillo, en el jardín de hortalizas los colores se mezclan alegremente.

Contrariamente al rigore del castello con il suo fossato originariamente doppio e le aiuole di rose lunghe e strette nel cortile, l'orto presenta un allegro miscuglio di fiori.

Epoisses Castle *Epoisses, Burgundy, France*   135

Galerie des Baumes

Jouques, Provence, France

A Provençal village housed the ruins of an 18th century castle that had never been completed and had lain dormant until a few years ago. It was then that a retired diplomat purchased a large portion of the grounds and had a Baroque garden *à la française* built on the overgrown terrace. Today, the remarkable old stairs are lined with selected African works of art that are objects of trade at "Galerie des Baumes" as if they had been designed for that purpose.

In einem provenzalischen Dorf lag die Ruine eines nie vollendeten Schlosses aus dem 18. Jahrhundert in einem tiefen Dornröschenschlaf. Vor wenigen Jahren erstand ein Diplomat im Ruhestand einen großen Teil der Anlage und ließ auf der verwilderten Terrasse einen Barockgarten *à la francaise* anlegen. Auf der imposanten alten Steintreppe präsentieren sich heute ausgesuchte afrikanische Kunstwerke, mit denen in der „Galerie des Baumes" gehandelt wird, als wäre sie dafür entworfen.

Les ruines d'un château du XVIIIème siècle jamais achevé dormaient profondément dans un village provençal comme la Belle au Bois dormant. Il y a quelques années, un diplomate à la retraite a acheté une large partie des terrains et a fait construire un jardin baroque à la française sur la grande terrasse fleurie. Des œuvres d'art africaines choisies, vendues par la « Galerie des Baumes », sont présentées sur l'impressionnant escalier de pierre comme s'il avait été conçu à cet effet.

En una aldea provenzal se encuentran las ruinas de un castillo del siglo XVIII nunca acabado, durmiendo el sueño de los justos. Hace pocos años, un diplomático retirado adquirió una parte considerable del inmueble y mandó crear un jardín barroco "a la francesa" en la terraza silvestre. En la imponente escalera de piedra se presentan hoy selectas obras de arte africano con las que se comercia en la "Galerie des Baumes", como si hubiera sido concebido precisamente para este fin.

In un villaggio provenzale, la rovina di un castello del XVIII secolo mai ultimato si trovava immerso nel sonno profondo della Bella Addormentata. Pochi anni fa un diplomatico in pensione acquistò gran parte del complesso e fece costruire un giardino barocco alla francese sul terrazzo incolto. Oggi, sull'imponente e antica scalinata in pietra fanno bella mostra di sé opere d'arte africane selezionate, con le quali si commercia nella "Galerie des Baumes", come se fosse stata progettata per questo.

One of the two magnificent cypresses that were preserved in the new design.

Eine der beiden prächtigen Zypressen, die bei der Neugestaltung erhalten werden konnten.

Un des deux magnifiques cyprès qui ont été préservés dans le nouveau plan.

Uno de los dos espléndidos cipreses que se pudieron conservar en el momento de la remodelación.

Uno dei due splendidi cipressi che è stato possibile mantenere durante la ristrutturazione.

Mature trees, *gravel, and lime sandstone highlight the African sculptures close to the main gate.*

Alte Bäume, *Kies und Kalksandstein setzen die afrikanischen Skulpturen nahe dem Haupttor in Szene.*

De vieux arbres, *du gravier et de la pierre silico-calcaire mettent en valeur les sculptures africaines près de la porte principale.*

Viejos arboles, *grava y arenisca constituyen el marco para las esculturas africanas junto a la entrada principal.*

Antichi alberi, *ghiaia e arenaria calcarea mettono in risalto le sculture africane vicino al portone principale.*

Galerie des Baumes *Jouques, Provence, France*   139

The tall box tree spheres replace the statues as eye-catchers in this enchanted Baroque garden. During the summer months, the violet of blossoming lavender gives its elegant, white-green palette of colors a new face. The newly added fountain fits in perfectly with the ensemble.

Die hochstämmigen Buchsbaumkugeln ersetzen die Statuen als Blickfänge in diesem zauberhaften Barockgarten. Seine elegante, weiß-grüne Farbpalette bekommt in den Sommermonaten durch das Violett von blühendem Lavendel ein neues Gesicht. Der neu hinzugefügte Brunnen passt sich perfekt in das Ensemble ein.

Les hautes sphères de buis remplacent les statues en tant que joyaux de ce jardin baroque enchanté. Sa palette élégante de couleurs allant du blanc au vert prend un nouveau visage pendant les mois d'été grâce au violet de la lavande en fleur. La fontaine récemment ajoutée s'accorde parfaitement à l'ensemble.

Las esferas de boj de largo tronco sustituyen a las estatuas a la hora de captar las miradas en este encantador jardín barroco. Su elegante paleta de colores blanquiverdes se renueva en los meses estivales con el violeta de la lavanda. La nueva fuente encaja a la perfección en el conjunto.

Le sfere di bosso ad alto fusto sostituiscono le statue nel loro ruolo di attrazione in questo incantevole giardino barocco, le cui eleganti sfumature bianco-verdi assumono nei mesi estivi un nuovo aspetto grazie al viola della lavanda in fiore. La fontana aggiunta recentemente si inserisce perfettamente nell'insieme.

The geometric division and the white paths allow the small garden to look spacious. The hillside location above the village provides sunshine throughout the day and wonderful views of the Provencal hills.

Die geometrische Aufteilung und weißen Wege lassen den kleinen Garten großzügig wirken. Die Hanglage oberhalb des Dorfes beschert ganztägigen Sonnenschein und wundervolle Ausblicke auf die provenzalische Hügellandschaft.

La division géométrique et les chemins blancs permettent au petit jardin de paraître plus grand. Son emplacement sur une colline au-dessus du village garantit l'ensoleillement tout au long de la journée, et offre une vue sur les collines provençales.

La división geométrica y los caminos en blanco consiguen que el jardín parezca más grande de lo que es en realidad. Su ubicación en pendiente hace que goce a diario de la luz del sol y de maravillosas vistas al paisaje de las colinas provenzales.

La suddivisione geometrica e le vie bianche fanno sembrare più vasto il piccolo giardino. La posizione in pendenza sopra al paese garantisce la luce del sole per tutto l'arco del giorno e una vista fantastica sul paesaggio collinare provenzale.

Villa near Carpentras

Provence, France

It is not obvious that this garden owned by a photographer was created just a few years ago. This effect was achieved by using old materials and regional techniques such as the dry stone walls as a border. The tree population of this former apricot plantation was enriched with old olive trees from Italy. The indigenous plants such as lavender, cistus, santolina and rosemary tolerate the very hot, dry summer and frosty winter.

Man sieht diesem Garten eines Fotografen nicht an, dass er erst vor wenigen Jahren angelegt wurde. Dies wurde durch den Einsatz alter Materialien und regionaler Techniken erzielt, wie beispielsweise Trockensteinmauern als Begrenzung. Der Baumbestand der ehemaligen Aprikosenplantage wurde um alte Olivenbäume aus Italien bereichert. Die heimischen Pflanzen, wie Lavendel, Zistus, Santolina sowie Rosmarin vertragen die sehr heißen trockenen Sommer und frostigen Winter.

Difficile de s'imaginer que ce jardin appartenant à un photographe a été aménagé il y a seulement quelques années. Cet effet a été obtenu en utilisant de vieux matériaux et des techniques régionales comme les murs de pierres sèches qui servent de clôture. Les abricotiers de l'ancien verger ont été enrichis de vieux oliviers importés d'Italie. Les plantes indigènes comme la lavande, le ciste, la santoline et le romarin tolèrent l'été très chaud et sec et l'hiver glacial.

En este jardín, cuyo propietario es fotógrafo, cuesta adivinar que su construcción se remonta unos pocos años. En ella se emplearon antiguos materiales y técnicas regionales, como por ejemplo muros de piedra en seco como deslinde. La masa arbórea perteneciente a la antigua plantación de albaricoques se vio enriquecida con viejos olivos italianos. Las plantas autóctonas, como espliego, jara, santolina y romero, soportan perfectamente la canícula estival y el rigor invernal.

Questo giardino di proprietà di un fotografo non sembra essere stato allestito solo pochi anni fa. Tale effetto è stato raggiunto grazie all'utilizzo di materiali antichi e tecniche regionali, come per esempio le mura di pietra secca come delimitazione. Il patrimonio arboreo dell'ex piantagione di albicocche è stato arricchito con ulivi secolari provenienti dall'Italia. Le piante locali, come la lavanda, il cisto, la santolina e il rosmarino resistono all'estate molto calda e secca e all'inverno gelido.

Mont Ventoux watches over the hilly landscape with its fruit plantations and vineyards.

Der Mont Ventoux wacht über die Hügellandschaft mit Obstplantagen und Weinreben.

Le Mont Ventoux domine le paysage vallonné planté de vergers et de vignes.

El monte Ventoux vela sobre el accidentado paisaje de plantaciones frutales y viñedos.

Il Mont Ventoux domina il paesaggio collinare con le piantagioni di frutta e le viti.

146   Villa near Carpentras *Provence, France*

The swimming pool has a dark-green bottom further intensifying its mirror effect. It is surrounded by a sea of lavender, while other parts of the garden—such as the seating corner shaded from the sun—have a completely different character.

Der Swimming Pool hat einen dunkelgrünen Boden, der den Spiegeleffekt noch verstärkt. Er ist von einem Meer Lavendel umgeben, während andere Teile des Gartens einen völlig anderen Charakter haben, wie die sonnengeschützte Sitzecke.

La piscine a un fond vert foncé qui en intensifie encore l'effet miroir. Elle est entourée d'une mer de lavande, mais d'autres parties du jardin — comme le lieu ombragé où l'on peut s'asseoir — ont un caractère totalement différent.

El fondo de la piscina es verde oscuro para intensificar el reflejo. Está rodeada por un manto de espliego, mientras que otras zonas del jardín tienen un carácter completamente diferente, como el porche a la sombra con mesa y sillas.

La piscina ha una pavimentazione verde scura che rafforza l'effetto a specchio. E' circondata da un mare di lavanda, mentre altre parti del giardino presentano un carattere completamente diverso, come l'angolo per riposarsi protetto dal sole.

Villa near Carpentras *Provence, France*   147

148   Villa near Carpentras *Provence, France*

Fountains and water designs gently splash in the herb garden bordered by low walls. It has neat herb beds and form-trimmed box trees. The newly planted fruit trees—cherries, figs and pears—will soon bear their first harvest.

Zart plätschern Brunnen und *Wasserspiele in dem mit Mäuerchen eingefassten Heilkräuter-Garten mit seinen adretten Kräuterbeeten und in Form geschnittenem Buchsbaum. Die neu gepflanzten Obstbäume – Kirschen, Feigen und Birnen – werden schon bald die ersten Früchte tragen.*

Les fontaines et les jardins d'eau éclaboussent avec douceur le jardin aromatique entouré de murets. Il dispose de carrés aromatiques bien délimités et de topiaires de buis. Les arbres fruitiers récemment plantés – cerisiers, figuiers et poiriers – porteront bientôt leurs premiers fruits.

Fuentes y juegos de agua tamborilean dulcemente en el jardín de primorosos parterres de hierbas medicinales acotado por un murete y bojes podados. Los árboles frutales recién plantados (cerezos, higueras y perales) pronto darán sus primeros frutos.

La fontana e i giochi d'acqua scorrono gorgogliando dolcemente nel giardino di piante officinali circondato da un muretto, con aiuole di erbe ben curate e con l'albero di bosso potato a forma. Gli alberi da frutto piantati di recente – ciliegi, fichi e peri – porteranno ben presto i primi frutti.

Villa near Carpentras *Provence, France* 149

Villa d'Este
Cernobbio, Lake Como, Italy

The lower garden portion of Villa d'Este dates back to the Renaissance. Especially noteworthy are the 500-year old sycamore trees and the mosaic of the Nympheum from the 16th century. Azaleas, camellias, oleander, rhododendron, hydrangia, roses and jasmine with all their pleasant flowers complement the shades of green of sculptured hedges and bamboo. Chestnut trees, magnolias, osmanthus, wisteria, palms, cypresses, holly and privet stand out among the diverse tree populations of the garden.

Der untere Gartenteil der Villa d'Este datiert aus der Renaissance. Besonders bemerkenswert sind die 500 Jahre alte Platane und das Mosaik des Nymphäum aus dem 16. Jahrhundert. Azaleen, Kamelien, Oleander, Rhododendren, Hortensien, Rosen und Jasmin ergänzen durch ihre gefälligen Blüten die Grüntöne der in Form geschnittenen Hecken und des Bambus. Im abwechslungsreichen Baumbestand sind Kastanien, Magnolien, Osmanthus, Glyzinien, Palmen, Zypressen, Stechpalmen und Liguster hervorzuheben.

La partie inférieure du jardin de la Villa d'Este remonte à la Renaissance. Les sycomores âgés de 500 ans et la mosaïque du nympheum du XVIème siècle sont particulièrement remarquables. Avec leurs jolies fleurs, les azalées, camélias, laurier-rose, rhododendrons, hortensias, roses et jasmins complètent les nuances de verts représentées par les haies taillées et le bambou. Les châtaigniers, les magnolias, les osmanthes, les glycines, les palmiers, les cyprès, le houx et les troènes se distinguent parmi la multitude d'arbres.

La parte inferior del jardín de Villa d'Este data del Renacimiento. Cabe destacar los plataneros que superan los 500 años de vida, o el mosaico del ninfeo del siglo XVI. Sus agradables flores –azaleas, camelias, adelfas, rododendros, hortensias, rosas y jazmines– completan los tonos verdes de los setos podados con formas y de bambú. Entre sus árboles y arbustos, cabe destacar castaños, magnolias, osmantus, glicinias, palmeras, cipreses, acebos y alheñas.

La parte inferiore del giardino di Villa d'Este risale ai tempi del Rinascimento. Sono particolarmente degni di nota i platani di 500 anni e il mosaico del ninfeo del XVI secolo. Azalee, camelie, oleandri, rododendri, ortensie, rose e gelsomino completano con i loro fiori leggiadri le tonalità di verde delle siepi potate a figura e del bambù. Il vario patrimonio arboreo comprende castagni, magnolie, osmanti, glicini, palme, cipressi, agrifogli e ligustri.

The garden benefits from the climate and charm of the privileged location on Lake Como.

Der Garten profitiert vom Klima und Charme der privilegierten Lage am Comer See.

Le jardin profite du climat et du charme de son emplacement privilégié sur le lac de Côme.

El jardín aprovecha el clima y el encanto de su emplazamiento privilegiado a orillas del lago Como.

Il giardino gode del clima e del fascino della posizione privilegiata sul lago di Como.

The tended parterres and the avenue leading from the Nympheum to the statues of Hercules and Lica are fabulous examples of the lovely Italian art of gardening. Proud cypresses line the double rows of stone-made pools.

Traumhafte Beispiele der lieblichen italienischen Gartenkunst sind die gepflegten Parterres und die Allee, die vom Nymphäum zu den Statuen von Herkules und Lica führt. Stolze Zypressen säumen die doppelreihigen steinernen Wasserbecken.

Les parterres soignés et l'avenue qui mène du nympheum aux statues d'Hercule et de Lica sont de fabuleux exemples de l'art délicat du jardin italien. De fiers cyprès suivent les doubles rangées de bassins de pierre.

Ejemplos de ensueño del delicioso arte italiano en el diseño de jardines son los cuidados parterres y la avenida, que lleva desde el ninfeo a las estatuas de Hércules y Lica. Abigarrados cipreses flanquean el canal de piedra en doble fila.

Esempi fantastici della soave arte italiana di creare giardini: il parterre e il viale alberato che conduce dal ninfeo alle statue di Ercole e Lica. I superbi cipressi circondano i bacini d'acqua di pietra a due file.

154   Villa d'Este *Cernobbio, Lake Como, Italy*

156   Villa d'Este *Cernobbio, Lake Como, Italy*

Polidora

Lake Maggiore, Italy

For a long time, this part of lakeshore of Lake Maggiore was all but inaccessible. As a result, the exotic conifers planted since 1900 by Vincenzo Sarto, the current owner's grandfather, have been able to thrive undisturbed. Visitors can now stay at the bed and breakfast while extensively exploring the mysterious beauty of the area. The impressive shore with its swamp cypresses and the collection of more than 1,000 specimens of azaleas are especially remarkable.

Dieser Seeuferabschnitt am Lago Maggiore war lange Zeit überhaupt nicht zugänglich. So gediehen die exotischen Nadelbäume, die seit 1900 von Vincenzo Sarto, dem Großvater des heutigen Eigentümers, angepflanzt wurden, völlig ungestört. Heute können Besucher in dem Bed & Breakfast absteigen und die geheimnisvolle Schönheit der Gegend ausführlich erkunden. Besonderes Interesse gilt dem beeindruckenden Sumpfzypressen-Strand und der Azaleensammlung mit über 1.000 Exemplaren.

Pendant longtemps, cette partie de la rive du lac Majeur n'a pas été accessible. Ainsi, les conifères exotiques plantés depuis 1900 par Vincenzo Sarto, le grand-père du propriétaire actuel, ont pu grandir tranquillement. Les visiteurs peuvent maintenant séjourner dans le Bed & Breakfast et découvrir toute sa beauté mystérieuse de la région. La plage de cyprès chauves et la collection de plus de 1.000 spécimens d'azalées sont particulièrement impressionnantes.

Durante mucho tiempo, el acceso a esta zona en la orilla del lago Maggiore estaba vedado. De ahí que las exóticas coníferas plantadas en 1900 por Vincenzo Sarto, abuelo del actual propietario, crecieran con toda tranquilidad. Actualmente se puede pernoctar en el bed & breakfast para descubrir su misteriosa belleza de la zona. Despierta gran interés el impresionante pantano con la playa de cipreses de pantano o la colección de azaleas con más de 1.000 ejemplares.

Questa porzione della sponda del lago Maggiore non è stata accessibile per molto tempo. Le conifere esotiche, che sono state piantate sin dal 1900 da Vincenzo Sarto, il nonno del proprietario attuale, hanno perciò potuto crescere indisturbate. Oggi i visitatori possono alloggiare nel bed & breakfast ed esplorarne a fondo la bellezza misteriosa della regione. Particolarmente interessante è la spiaggia di cipressi da palude e la collezione di azalee con oltre 1.000 esemplari.

The shore location of the garden is one of the things that makes it unique.

Die Tatsache, dass der Garten direkt am Seeufer liegt, gehört zu ihrer Einmaligkeit.

Grâce à son emplacement á la rive du lac, le jardin présente un caractère unique.

El hecho de que el jardín esté a orillas del lago es parte de su exclusividad.

Il fatto che il giardino si trovi direttamente sulla sponda del lago, lo rende unico.

For 20 years, GianLuca Sarto, the current owner, has been expanding his collection to include rare conifers, including 'Araucaria bidwillii', 'Aghatis australis', 'Cupressus cashmeriana', 'Cupressus funebris', 'Juniperus occidentalis' and 'Metasequoia glyptostroboides' as well as various types of pine trees.

GianLuca Sarto, der heutige Eigentümer, erweitert seit 20 Jahren die Sammlung um seltene Nadelbäume, unter anderen ‚Araucaria bidwillii‘, ‚Aghatis australis‘, ‚Cupressus cashmeriana‘, ‚Cupressus funebris‘, ‚Juniperus occidentalis‘, ‚Metasequoia glyptostroboides‘ sowie verschiedene Kiefernarten.

Depuis 20 ans, GianLuca Sarto, le propriétaire actuel, agrandit la collection de conifères rares. Elle comprend notamment des ‹ Araucaria bidwillii ›, ‹ Aghatis australis ›, ‹ Cupressus cashmeriana ›, ‹ Cupressus funebris ›, ‹ Juniperus occidentalis ›, ‹ Metasequoia glyptostroboides ›, ainsi que de nombreuses variétés de pins.

GianLuca Sarto, el actual propietario, lleva 20 años ampliando la colección con exóticas coníferas como las 'Araucaria bidwillii', 'Aghatis australis', 'Cupressus cashmeriana', 'Cupressus funebris', 'Juniperus occidentalis', 'Metasequoia glyptostroboides', así como diversas especies de pinos.

Gianluca Sarto, il proprietario attuale, da 20 anni amplia la collezione con conifere rare, tra le quali l'‘Araucaria bidwillii’, l'‘Aghatis australis’, il ‘Cupressus cashmeriana’, il ‘Cupressus funebris’, il ‘Juniperus occidentalis’, la ‘Metasequoia glyptostroboides’ e diverse tipologie di pini.

The stone walls lining the shore for more than half a mile have a story of their own. Gerolamo Pirinoli had them built in the late 19th century to keep the many workers on the eastern coast employed. The famous pink granite comes from Baveno, a small town on the opposite shore.

Ihre eigene Geschichte haben die fast einen Kilometer langen Steinwände, die das Ufer säumen. Gerolamo Pirinoli ließ sie im späten 19. Jahrhundert errichten, um vielen Arbeitern der Ostküste eine Anstellung zu geben. Der berühmte rosa Granit stammt aus Baveno, einer kleinen Stadt am gegenüberliegenden Ufer.

Les murs de pierre qui longent le rivage sur plus d'un kilomètre ont leur propre histoire. Gerolamo Pirinoli les a fait construire au tard XIXème siècle, donnant ainsi du travail aux nombreux ouvriers de la côte est. Le célèbre granit rose vient de Baveno, une petite ville sur la rive opposée.

Los muros de piedra que se extienden por la orilla casi un kilómetro tienen su propia historia. Gerolamo Pirinoli los levantó a finales del tarde siglo XIX para dar empleo a numerosos trabajadores de la costa oriental. El célebre granito rosa proviene de Baveno, una pequeña población de la orilla opuesta.

Le pareti di pietra che fiancheggiano la riva e che sono lunghe quasi un chilometro, hanno una loro storia. Gerolamo Pirinoli le fece costruire nel tardo XIX secolo per dare lavoro a molti operai della costa orientale. Il famoso granito rosa proviene da Baveno, una piccola città sulla sponda opposta.

Polidora *Lake Maggiore, Italy* 163

The **beautiful** old trunks of the swamp cypresses ('Taxodium distichum'), which have formed cypress knees to hold themselves securely in the water, are reflected in iridescent gold on the surface of the water. In the fall, the trees burst into brilliant red that glows far across the lake.

Die wunderschönen alten Stämme der Sumpfzypressen (‚Taxodium distichum'), die zum festen Halt im Wasser sogenannte Atemknie gebildet haben, spiegeln sich goldgelb schillernd auf der Wasseroberfläche. Im Herbst entflammen die Bäume in leuchtendem Rot, das weit über den See leuchtet.

Les magnifiques vieux troncs des cyprès chauves (« Taxodium distichum »), qui ont formé des excroissances pour pouvoir tenir dans l'eau, ont un reflet doré iridescent sur la surface de l'eau. En automne, les arbres éclatent d'un rouge brillant qui luit bien au-delà du lac.

Los maravillosos troncos viejos de estos cipreses de pantano ('Taxodium distichum') han desarrollado protuberancias leñosas para sujetarse en el agua y respirar. Sus reflejos dorados centellean en la superficie. En otoño, los árboles se encienden con un rojo intenso que refulge por todo el lago.

I magnifici tronchi secolari dei cipressi da palude ('Taxodium distichum'), che hanno creato un forte appiglio grazie alle radici che fuoriescono dall'acqua, si specchiano con scintillanti colori dorati sulla superficie dell'acqua. In autunno gli alberi si infiammano di un colore rosso vivo che brilla ben oltre il lago.

Villa Rusconi-Clerici

Lake Maggiore, Italy

Even at Lake Maggiore, a park like that of Villa Rusconi-Clerici with its location directly on the lake is a rare sight: The garden, which was extended to Lake Maggiore in 1875 and recently restored in an exemplary manner, has a special character because of the proud villa on the hill and the organic layout of the paths. Antique stone sculptures are effective eye-catchers. Its greatest botanical treasures include large numbers of camellia and rhododendron, some of which are as tall as trees, and age-old magnolias.

Selbst am Lago Maggiore hat ein Park wie der der Villa Rusconi-Clerici mit ihrer direkten Seelage Seltenheitswert: Der 1875 bis zum Lago Maggiore hin erweiterte und in den letzten Jahren vorbildlich restaurierte Garten ist durch die auf der Anhöhe thronende Villa und die organisch verlaufenden Wege geprägt. Antike Stein-Skulpturen bilden wirkungsvolle Blickfänge. Zu den größten botanischen Schätzen zählt der ausgedehnte Bestand teils baumhoher Kamelien und Rhododendren sowie uralte Magnolien.

Même sur le lac Majeur, le parc de la Villa Rusconi-Clerici, avec son emplacement donnant directement sur le lac, est rare : le jardin, qui a été agrandi en 1875 pour atteindre le lac Majeur, et récemment restauré d'une manière exemplaire, a un caractère très particulier grâce à la fière villa sur la colline et à l'agencement organique des chemins. Les sculptures de pierre antiques attirent tous les regards. Ses plus grands trésors botaniques comprennent un grand nombre de camélias et de rhododendrons, dont certains sont aussi grands que des arbres, et les vieux magnolias.

Hasta en el lago Maggiore, un parque como el de la Villa Rusconi-Clerici posee algo muy singular: el embarcadero. Este jardín, ampliado en 1875 hasta la orilla del lago y cuyas recientes renovaciones han sido ejemplares, se distingue por su residencia en lo alto de una loma y por los senderos que corren de forma orgánica. Antiguas esculturas de piedra capturan las miradas. Entre los tesoros botánicos, cuenta con camelias y rododendros de la altura de un árbol y antiquísimas magnolias.

Perfino sul lago Maggiore un parco come quello di Villa Rusconi-Clerici è una rarità, a causa della sua posizione sul lago: il giardino, ampliato nel 1875 fino al lago Maggiore e restaurato in modo esemplare negli ultimi anni, è caratterizzato dalla villa troneggiante sull'altura e da sentieri che scorrono organicamente. Le antiche sculture di pietra creano degli accenti ad effetto. L'ampio patrimonio forestale, fatto in parte di camelie e rododendri alti come alberi e di magnolie secolari, fa parte dei maggiori tesori botanici esistenti.

Artfully curved, surrounded by 'Convallaria', and highlighted by antique sculptures, the paths lead from the lake to the villa. The main plants are fan palms, rhododendron and camellias.

Kunstvoll geschwungene, mit ‚Convallaria' umpflanzte und von antiken Skulpturen betonte Wege führen vom See zur Villa. Leitpflanzen sind Fächerpalmen, Rhododendren und Kamelien.

Bordés de ‹ Convallaria › et mis en valeur par des sculptures antiques, les chemins aux courbes artistiques mènent du lac à la villa. Les plantes principales sont les palmiers nains, les rhododendrons et les camélias.

Ampliado con aire artístico, el sendero destaca por sus nuevas plantaciones de convalaria y antiguas esculturas. Palmeras de abanicos, rododendros y camelias marcan el camino.

Le vie, che si snodano ad arte, circondate da convallaria e arricchite da antiche sculture, portano dal lago alla villa. Le piante principali sono le palme a ventaglio, i rododendri e le camelie.

From the jetty *at the house, the family goes on trips to the villages on the lake and to the small island nearby. Hydrangea, camellias, roses and antique pots on the small garden walls form a flowering border.*

Vom hauseigenen Bootssteg *unternimmt die Familie Ausflüge zur nahe gelegenen kleinen Insel und zu den Orten am See. Hortensien, Kamelien, Rosen und antike Gefäße auf dem Gartenmäuerchen bilden einen blühenden Saum.*

Depuis le débarcadère *privé de la maison, la famille part en excursion vers les petites îles et villes à proximité du lac. Les hortensias, les camélias, les roses et les pots antiques sur les murs petits du jardin forment une bordure florissante.*

Desde el embarcadero *de la casa, la familia realiza excursiones a una pequeña isla y a otros poblados a orillas del lago. Hortensias, camelias, rosas y viejos recipientes del murete del jardín crean una cenefa en flor.*

Dal pontile *proprio della casa la famiglia intraprende gite verso la piccola isola nelle vicinanze e verso gli altri luoghi del lago. Le ortensie, le camelie, le rose e i vasi antichi sul muretto del giardino creano una bordura fiorita.*

Frontal view of the villa with its centrally located parterres. To the left and to the right, the view is limited and guided by camellia and rhododendron bushes. Roses and palms create the effective foreground for the three-arch loggia and the winter garden has a green mantle of climbing roses.

Frontalansicht der Villa mit zentral angelegten Parterres. Die Kamelien- und Rhododendrenbüsche zur Linken und zur Rechten begrenzen und lenken den Blick. Rosen und Palmen bilden den wirkungsvollen Vordergrund für die dreibogige Loggia, und der Wintergarten besitzt ein grünes Kleid aus Kletterrosen.

Vue de face de la villa avec ses parterres au centre. Les buissons de camélias et de rhododendrons forment une bordure à gauche et à droite, guidant la vue. Les rosiers et les palmiers créent une toile de fond remarquable pour la loggia à trois arches, et le jardin d'hiver a revêtu un manteau vert de rosiers grimpants.

Panorámica frontal de la villa con el parterre central. Los arbustos de camelias y rododendros a izquierda y derecha delimitan y guían la mirada. Rosas y palmeras conforman el impactante primer plano del porche con tres arcos. El jardín de invierno dispone de un vestido verde de rosas trepadoras.

Vista frontale della villa con il pianterreno posizionato al centro. I cespugli di camelie e di rododendri sulla sinistra e sulla destra confinano e attirano lo sguardo. Le rose e le palme creano un primo piano d'effetto per la loggia a tre arcate, mentre il giardino d'inverno possiede un manto verde di rose rampicanti.

Vertical Garden

Lombardy, Italy

The design of this castle garden is defined by its hillside location. During a complex makeover, its divided sections were rearranged and interlinked so that the owner can now make unhindered use of the entire garden. The current layout of three vertically ascending levels pays homage to the original design. Walking through the garden, a visitor will recognize the intimacy of the various green spaces as well as their contact with the surrounding urban structure.

Die Gestaltung dieses Schlossgartens wird durch die Hügellage bestimmt. Bei der komplexen Neuanlage wurden die zerstückelten Räume neu geordnet und miteinander verknüpft, sodass der Eigentümer nun den gesamten Garten mühelos nutzen kann. Die heutige Aufteilung in drei vertikal aufsteigenden Ebenen respektiert die ursprüngliche Anlage. Ein Spaziergang erschließt dem Besucher die Intimität der verschiedenen Grünräume sowie ihre Berührungspunkte mit der umgebenden urbanen Struktur.

La conception du jardin de ce château a été déterminée par sa situation à flanc de colline. Dans cette nouvelle installation complexe, les parcelles divisées sont réaménagées et reliées ensemble pour que le propriétaire puisse facilement utiliser le jardin entier. La disposition actuelle verticale sur trois niveaux montre un respect pour le design originel. Une promenade révèle au visiteur l'intimité des divers espaces verts, ainsi que leur point de contact avec la structure urbaine environnante.

La configuración del jardín de este castillo viene determinada por su emplazamiento sobre una colina. En el complejo anexo de nueva construcción se reordenaron los espacios divididos y se vincularon para que el propietario pudiera disfrutar de todo el jardín. La actual división en tres planos verticales ascendentes respeta la disposición original. Con un paseo, el visitante será capaz de descubrir la intimidad de los espacios verdes y los puntos de contacto con la estructura urbana circundante.

L'allestimento di questo giardino del castello è determinato dalla posizione collinare. Nel nuovo complesso gli spazi spezzettati sono stati riordinati e collegati fra loro, in modo che il proprietario possa utilizzare l'intero giardino senza problemi. L'attuale suddivisione su tre livelli risalenti verticalmente rispetta il complesso originario. Una passeggiata rivela al visitatore l'intimità dei diversi spazi verdi e i loro punti di incontro con la struttura urbana circostante.

New outlooks present themselves time and again, such as here through the slender cypresses in the upper portion of the garden.

Immer wieder präsentieren sich neue Ausblicke, wie hier durch die schlanken Zypressen im oberen Teil des Gartens.

De nouvelles vues sont sans cesse offertes, comme ici à travers les cyprès élégants dans la partie supérieure du jardin.

No dejan de descubrirse nuevas perspectivas, como esta a través de los esbeltos cipreses en la parte superior del jardín.

Si presentano sempre nuove vedute, così come qui attraverso i cipressi slanciati nella parte superiore del giardino.

The old castle and its garden once again form a unit. A small number of added decorative elements along with form-trimmed bushes and hedges differentiate the various sections and set accents.

Das alte Schloss und der Garten bilden wieder eine Einheit. Wenige hinzugefügte Dekorationselemente und die in Form geschnittenen Sträucher und Hecken differenzieren die verschiedenen Räume und setzen Akzente.

Le vieux château et le jardin sont unis une fois encore. Un petit nombre d'éléments décoratifs, ainsi que des buissons et des haies taillés dans diverses formes, différencient les espaces et donnent le ton.

El antiguo castillo y el jardín vuelven a constituir una unidad. Pocos elementos decorativos añadidos y los arbustos y setos podados con diversas formas distinguen los diversos espacios y marcan las diferencias.

L'antico castello e il giardino compongono di nuovo un tutt'uno. Alcuni elementi decorativi aggiunti e i cespugli e le siepi potati a sagoma differenziano i diversi spazi e conferiscono un tono di originalità.

Landscape Park

Lombardy, Italy

Designed by Duca Uberto Visconti di Modrone and revised in 1907 with the aid of architect Emilio Alemagna, this estate had been left to itself for many years. Now a lot of devotion has gone into putting new life into its wonderful garden architecture. At the same time, functional aspects have been integrated, such as retaining and filtration basins for rainwater or a greenhouse for the citrus trees to survive during the winter.

Während langer Jahre war diese von Duca Uberto Visconti di Modrone entworfene und 1907 zusammen mit dem Architekten Emilio Alemagna überarbeitete Anlage sich selbst überlassen. Mit viel Hingabe wurde die wundervolle Gartenarchitektur nun zu neuem Leben erweckt. Gleichzeitig wurden funktionelle Aspekte wie Auffang- und Reinigungsbecken für Regenwasser oder ein Gewächshaus zur Überwinterung der Zitrusbäume integriert.

Ce parc, conçu par Duca Uberto Visconti di Modrone et refait en 1907 en association avec l'architecte Emilio Alemagna, a été livré à lui-même pendant de nombreuses années. La merveilleuse architecture du jardin a maintenant repris une nouvelle vie grâce à beaucoup de dévouement. Dans le même temps, des aspects fonctionnels ont été intégrés : par exemple, le réservoir de collecte et de filtration des eaux de pluie ou la serre pour l'hibernation des agrumes.

Durante muchos años, esta finca diseñada por Duca Uberto Visconti di Modrone y que, junto al arquitecto Emilio Alemagna, fue retocada en 1907, estuvo abandonada. Con total dedicación se consiguió volver a insuflar vida a esta maravillosa arquitectura paisajística. Simultáneamente, se integraron aspectos funcionales como aljibes de recogida y depuración de aguas pluviales o un invernadero de invierno para los cítricos.

Questo complesso, progettato dal Duca Uberto Visconti di Modrone e rielaborato nel 1907 insieme all'architetto Emilio Alemagna, fu abbandonato a se stesso per molti anni. Con molta dedizione la magnifica architettura del giardino è ora rinata a nuova vita. Al contempo sono stati integrati degli aspetti funzionali come il bacino di raccolta e di depurazione dell'acqua piovana o la serra per lo svernamento dei limoni.

The ambience of dawn makes the garden seem downright mythical.

In der Morgenstimmung wirkt der Garten besonders verwunschen.

Le jardin paraît particulièrement charmant dans l'ambiance du matin.

A primeras horas, el jardín da la sensación de estar encantado.

Alle prime luci del mattino il giardino sembra incantato.

The view of the parterre framed by the brick-flooring pattern and the changing color play of the leaves is simply beautiful.

Die Aussicht auf das vom Muster der Pflasterung gerahmte Parterre und das wechselnde Farbspiel des Laubs ist schlichtweg wunderschön.

La vue sur le parterre encadré d'un motif de briques et le jeu de couleurs changeantes des feuilles est simplement magnifique.

Las vistas sobre el parterre enmarcado por el adoquinado con formas geométricas y el cambiante juego cromático del follaje son sencillamente magníficas.

La vista sul parterre incorniciato dal disegno del lastricato e il gioco di colori cangianti delle foglie è semplicemente meraviglioso.

178   Landscape Park *Lombardy, Italy*

The carefully employed modern elements, such as those for lighting or seating, blend in with the traditional garden architecture. The waterfall and other water designs as well as the tree-lined paths radiate in a new glow after the renovation.

Die mit Bedacht eingesetzten modernen Elemente, beispielsweise für die Beleuchtung oder als Sitzgelegenheiten, verschmelzen mit der traditionellen Gartenarchitektur. Der Wasserfall und weitere Wasserspiele sowie die baumbestandenen Wege erstrahlen nach der Renovierung in neuem Glanz.

Les éléments modernes employés avec soin, comme l'éclairage ou les sièges, se mêlent à l'architecture traditionnelle du jardin. La cascade et les autres designs d'eau, ainsi que les sentiers bordés d'arbres, ont acquis un nouveau rayonnement après la rénovation.

Los elementos modernos incluidos deliberadamente, como por ejemplo la iluminación o los diversos asientos, se funden con la arquitectura paisajista tradicional. La cascada y otros divertimentos acuáticos, así como los senderos flanqueados por árboles, vuelven a brillar con nuevo fulgor tras la remodelación.

Gli elementi moderni utilizzati in modo ragionato, per esempio per l'illuminazione o come posti per accomodarsi, si fondono con l'architettura tradizionale del giardino. La cascata e altri giochi d'acqua, oltre alle vie fiancheggiate di alberi, irradiano nuovo splendore dopo la ristrutturazione.

House 2

Barcelona, Spain

This 43,056 square-feet garden was redesigned along with the renovation of the residential house. In the upper area, stone walls support the steep hillside property. Its heterogenous vegetation was reduced to selected species and colors that blossom throughout the year. *Teucrium fruticans*, whose little gray leaves form a lovely contrast with the light marble and dark green of the garden, grows in a long bed as a visual shield on the redesigned terrace in front of the living room.

Dieser 4.000 m² große Garten wurde nach der Renovierung des Wohnhauses ebenfalls neu angelegt. Im oberen Bereich stützen Steinmauern das abschüssige Gelände. Die heterogene Vegetation wurde auf ausgesuchte Spezies und Farben reduziert, die das ganze Jahr über Blüten tragen. In der neuangelegten Terrasse vor dem Wohnzimmer wächst in einem langen Beet *Teucrium fruticans* als Sichtschutz, dessen kleine graue Blätter einen schönen Kontrast zu dem hellen Marmor und dem dunklen Grün des Gartens bilden.

Ce jardin de 4.000 m² a été conçu récemment après la rénovation de la maison résidentielle. Dans la partie supérieure, des murs de pierre soutiennent le flanc abrupt de la propriété. La végétation hétéroclite a été réduite à des couleurs et des espèces choisies qui fleurissent toute l'année. Les *Teucrium fruticans*, dont les petites feuilles grises forment un contraste ravissant avec le marbre clair et le vert sombre du jardin, poussent dans une longue butte comme un bouclier visuel pour la terrasse récemment aménagée devant la salle de séjour.

Tras reformar la vivienda, este jardín de 4.000 m² se sometió igualmente a una remodelación. En la zona superior, unos muretes de piedra contienen el escarpado terreno. La heterogénea vegetación se redujo a una selección de especies y colores que florecen todo el año. En las nuevas terrazas ante la sala de estar, en un parterre lineal crece el *Teucrium fruticans* como divisor visual; sus pequeñas hojas grises contrastan con el mármol en tonos claros y el intenso verdor del jardín.

Dopo la ristrutturazione dell'abitazione, è stato ricostruito anche questo giardino di 4.000 m². Nell'area superiore, mura di pietra sorreggono il terreno scosceso. La vegetazione eterogenea è stata ridotta a specie e colori selezionati, che fioriscono per tutto l'arco dell'anno. Sul terrazzo allestito ex novo davanti al salone, in una lunga aiuola, cresce il *Teucrium fruticans*, che serve alla protezione da sguardi indiscreti, e che con le sue piccole foglie grigie crea un bel contrasto con il marmo chiaro e il verde scuro del giardino.

Impressive mature trees lend character to the garden: Stone pines, cypresses, palms and a one-hundred-year-old olive tree.

Imposante alte Bäume verleihen dem Garten Charakter: Pinien, Zypressen, Palmen und ein hundertjähriger Olivenbaum.

De vieux arbres imposants donnent du caractère au jardin : des pins, des cyprès, des palmiers et un olivier centenaire.

Unos imponentes árboles antiquísimos imprimen carácter al jardín: pinos, cipreses, palmeras y un olivo centenario.

Imponenti alberi secolari donano carattere al giardino: pini, cipressi, palme e un ulivo centenario.

184   House 2 *Barcelona, Spain*

The swimming pool, unchangeable in its shape and location, received a protective separation from the path with a splendid olive tree, bushes and stones. Thanks to the hillside location, the treetops contrast nicely with the blue sky and reveal various views of the city.

Das Schwimmbad, das in Form und Lage nicht verändert werden konnte, bekam zum Weg hin eine schutzbietende Abtrennung mit dem prächtigen Olivenbaum, Büschen und Steinen. Dank der Hügellage heben sich die Baumkronen gut vor dem strahlend blauen Himmel ab, und man hat verschiedene Ausblicke auf die Stadt.

La piscine, dont la forme et l'emplacement ne peuvent être changés, est séparée et protégée du sentier par des oliviers, des buissons et des pierres. Grâce à l'emplacement sur le flanc d'une colline, les frondaisons contrastent joliment avec le ciel bleu et mettent en valeur plusieurs vues de la ville.

La piscina, cuya forma y ubicación no se pudo modificar, se convirtió en una división protectora con respecto al magnífico olivo, los arbustos y las rocas. Gracias a lo abrupto del terreno, las copas de los árboles despuntan hacia el azul del cielo y se goza de diferentes panorámicas sobre la ciudad.

La piscina, della quale non si è potuta modificare la forma, né la posizione, è stata arricchita verso la via con un divisorio protettivo costituito dal magnifico ulivo, cespugli e pietre. Grazie alla posizione collinare, le corone degli alberi si distaccano completamente dal cielo blu radioso, e si hanno diversi panorami sulla città.

Jardin Majorelle

Marrakech, Morocco

The former studio of artist Jacques Majorelle, which served him as both a source of inspiration and retreat, now accomodates the collection of Islamic art of Pierre Bergé and Yves Saint Laurent. The floral diversity is based on the founder's passion for collecting and includes significant arrays of cacti, palms, bamboo, flowering plants in pots as well as water plants. In the middle of the hustle and bustle of the city, this garden is a little paradise for people and animals.

Das ehemalige Atelier des Künstlers Jacques Majorelle, das ihm Inspirationsquelle und Rückzugsort zugleich war, beherbergt heute die Sammlung islamischer Kunst von Pierre Bergé und Yves Saint Laurent. Die florale Vielfalt rührt von der Sammelleidenschaft des Gründers her und umfasst bedeutende Bestände an Kakteen, Palmen, Bambus, Blühpflanzen in Töpfen sowie Wasserpflanzen. Inmitten des Stadttrubels ist der Garten ein kleines Paradies für Mensch und Tier.

L'ancien atelier de l'artiste Jacques Majorelle, pour lui à la fois source d'inspiration et refuge, abrite maintenant la collection d'art islamique de Pierre Bergé et Yves Saint-Laurent. La diversité florale est basée sur la passion de collectionneur de son créateur et comprend un nombre considérable de cactées, palmiers, bambous et plantes fleuries en pots, ainsi que des plantes aquatiques. Au milieu du tohu-bohu de la ville, le jardin est un petit paradis pour les hommes et les animaux.

El antiguo atelier del artista Jacques Majorelle, que le sirvió de fuente de inspiración y retiro, alberga en la actualidad una colección de arte islámico de Pierre Bergé e Yves Saint Laurent. La diversidad floral le viene de la pasión por coleccionar de su fundador y comprende significativos ejemplares de cactus, palmeras, bambúes, plantas en flor en macetas, así como vegetación de estanque. Entre el bullicio de la ciudad, este jardín representa un pequeño paraíso para hombres y animales.

L'ex atelier dell'artista Jacques Majorelle, che gli fungeva da fonte d'ispirazione e al contempo da luogo di ritiro, ospita oggi la collezione di arte islamica di Pierre Bergé e Yves Saint Laurent. La molteplicità floreale scaturisce dalla passione per il collezionismo del fondatore e comprende una quantità significativa di cactus, palme, bambù, piante da fiore in vasi e piante d'acqua. Nel mezzo del trambusto cittadino, il giardino rappresenta un piccolo paradiso per l'uomo e per gli animali.

The color of the house is called "Majorelle Blue" as it fascinatingly shimmers through all the green.

Der Farbton des Hauses heißt „Majorelle Blau" und schimmert faszinierend durch das Grün.

La couleur caractéristique de la maison est appelée « Bleu Majorelle » et brille à travers tout le jardin.

El color de la casa se denomina "azul majorelle" y brilla de forma fascinante en contraste con el verde.

Il colore della casa è detto „blu Majorelle" e spicca in modo affascinante attraverso il verde.

While the cacti are snug in the red soil, the water surfaces were consciously placed as a counterpoint to the desert-like landscape.

Während sich die Kakteen in der roten Erde überaus wohlfühlen, wurden die Wasserflächen bewusst als Kontrapunkt zur wüstenartigen Landschaft gesetzt.

Alors que les cactées s'accordent parfaitement au sol rouge, les surfaces aquatiques sont utilisées comme contrepoint au paysage désertique.

Mientras que los cactus se sienten como en casa en la tierra roja, los estanques representan un contrapunto deliberado al paisaje de cariz desértico.

Mentre i cactus si trovano a loro agio nella terra rossa, le superfici d'acqua sono state posizionate volutamente come contrappunto al paesaggio desertico.

A walk through the palm forest is reminiscent of an oasis. The impressive collection includes specimens from the entire Mediterranean area, the Canary Islands, East Africa, Mesopotamia and even California.

Ein Spaziergang durch den Palmenwald erinnert an eine Oase. Die beeindruckende Sammlung umfasst Exemplare aus dem gesamten Mittelmeerraum, von den kanarischen Inseln, aus Ostafrika, Mesopotamien und sogar Kalifornien.

Une promenade à travers la palmeraie évoque une oasis. La collection impressionnante comprend des spécimens de toute la zone méditerranéenne, des îles Canaries, d'Afrique de l'Est, de Mésopotamie et même de Californie.

Un paseo por el bosque de palmeras recuerda a un oasis. La impresionante colección incluye ejemplares de toda la región mediterránea, de las Islas Canarias, de África oriental, de Mesopotamia e, incluso, de California.

Una passeggiata attraverso il bosco di palme ricorda un'oasi. L'impressionante collezione comprende esemplari provenienti dall'intera area mediterranea, dalle isole Canarie, dall'Africa orientale, dalla Mesopotamia e addirittura dalla California.

Jardin Majorelle *Marrakech, Morocco* 191

Rembel Garden

Sydney, Australia

Andrew Pfeiffer has the owner's resourcefulness to thank for the fulfillment of a long-cherished dream to design a formal garden with nothing but cacti and succulents. The garden walls with their yellow paint highlight the atmosphere inside that seems charged with a special kind of energy. Water is used symbolically to emphasize its scarcity. The shape of the second parterre—made completely of endemic plants—is inspired by certain contemporary dot paintings of the Australian aborigines.

Dem Einfallsreichtum des Eigentümers verdankte Andrew Pfeiffer die Erfüllung eines lange gehegten Wunsches, nämlich einen formalen Garten nur mit Kakteen und Sukkulenten zu gestalten. Die gelb gestrichenen Gartenmauern betonen die besondere energiegeladene Atmosphäre. Wasser wird symbolisch eingesetzt, um hervorzuheben, wie selten es ist. Die Form des zweiten Parterre ganz aus einheimischen Pflanzen wurde inspiriert durch die zeitgenössische Kunstrichtung der „dot paintings" der australischen Ureinwohner.

Andrew Pfeiffer peut remercier l'ingéniosité du propriétaire pour l'accomplissement d'un souhait longtemps nourri : concevoir un jardin traditionnel en utilisant seulement des cactées et des plantes grasses. Les murs du jardin avec leur peinture jaune mettent en valeur l'atmosphère spécialement chargée en énergie. L'eau est utilisée symboliquement pour souligner sa rareté. La forme du second parterre, composé uniquement de plantes indigènes, est inspirée par un style d'art contemporain à partir des peintures pointillistes des aborigènes australiens.

Andrew Pfeiffer ha de agradecer a la imaginación del propietario el cumplimiento de un deseo anhelado durante mucho tiempo: un jardín formalista compuesto únicamente de cactus y crasuláceas. El muro del jardín, en amarillo, subraya un ambiente ya de por sí muy cargado de energía. La utilización del agua se hace de forma simbólica para realzar su rareza. La forma del segundo parterre, todo él con plantas autóctonas, ha sido inspirada por las pautas de una escuela artística contemporánea: el "punteado" típico de los aborígenes australianos.

Grazie all'ingegnosità del proprietario, Andrew Pfeiffer ha potuto realizzare un desiderio che aveva da molto tempo: la realizzazione di un giardino formale fatto solo di cactus e piante grasse. Le mura del giardino, dipinte di giallo, sottolineano la particolare atmosfera carica di energia. L'acqua viene inserita in modo simbolico, per mettere in risalto la sua scarsità. La forma del secondo parterre, fatto completamente di piante locali, si ispira al „dot paintings", una tendenza artistica contemporanea degli aborigeni australiani.

The garden designer has succeeded in reinterpreting a traditional formal garden with cacti and succulents in reddish sand substrate.

Mit Kakteen und Sukkulenten in rötlichem Sandsubstrat ist dem Gartengestalter die Neuinterpretation eines traditionellen formalen Gartens gelungen.

Le créateur du jardin a réussi la réinterprétation d'un jardin traditionnel à la française avec des cactées et des plantes grasses dans un substrat de sable rougeâtre.

Cactus y crasuláceas sobre un sustrato arenoso en rojo simbolizan la reinterpretación de un jardín formalista tradicional por parte del paisajista.

Con i cactus e le piante grasse sul substrato di sabbia rossa, l'ideatore di questo complesso è riuscito a reinterpretare un giardino formale tradizionale.

194   Rembel Garden *Sydney, Australia*

The fascination in the variety of shapes and the wealth of plants bursting with health delight the eye, even if you're less than enthusiastic about thorny plants.

Die Faszination der Formenvielfalt und die Reichhaltigkeit der vor Gesundheit strotzenden Pflanzen entzücken das Auge, auch wenn sich vielleicht nicht jedermann für Stachelpflanzen begeistert.

La variété de formes et la richesse des plantes luxuriantes ravissent la vue, même pour ceux qui ne s'intéressent pas forcément aux plantes à piquants.

La fascinación de la diversidad de formas y la riqueza de plantas realmente sanas embelesan la vista, si bien las cactáceas no son del agrado de todo el mundo.

Il fascino della molteplicità di forme e la ricchezza delle piante che scoppiano di salute deliziano la vista, anche se forse non tutti si entusiasmano per le piante con le spine.

Rembel Garden *Sydney, Australia*   195

The fact that cacti and endemic plants require little water makes them predestined for the extreme climate of Australia. In the evening sun, their colorful aspects retreat into the background as the graphic effects of their striking silhouettes take centerstage.

Dass die Kakteen und einheimischen Pflanzen wenig Wasser benötigen, prädestiniert diese Pflanzen für das extreme Klima Australiens. In der Abendsonne treten die farblichen Aspekte in den Hintergrund und die grafische Wirkung der prägnanten Silhouetten in den Vordergrund.

Comme les cactées et les plantes indigènes nécessitent peu d'eau, ces plantes sont faites pour le climat extrême de l'Australie. Dans le ciel du soir, les couleurs passent au second plan et l'effet graphique des silhouettes surprenantes entre en scène.

Puesto que cactos y plantas autóctonas requieren poca agua, estas plantas están predestinadas al extremo clima australiano. Al caer la tarde, al fondo pincelan los toques de color, mientras que en un primer plano destacan sus precisas siluetas.

La particolarità che i cactus e le piante locali abbiano bisogno di poca acqua, li rende particolarmente adatti al clima estremo dell'Australia. Nel sole del tramonto gli aspetti colorati passano in secondo piano, mettendo in risalto l'effetto grafico delle caratteristiche silhouette.

Rembel Garden *Sydney, Australia* 197

The parterre covers the ground like gigantic rolled-out canvas. Concentrating on indigenous plants that also grow in the adjacent bush and require hardly any water creates an extraordinary feeling of harmony with nature.

Wie eine riesige auf dem Boden ausgebreitete Leinwand überzieht das Parterre das Gelände. Durch die Beschränkung auf einheimische Pflanzen, die auch wild in dem angrenzenden Buschland wachsen und keine Bewässerung benötigen, entsteht ein außerordentliches Gefühl des Einklangs und der Harmonie mit der Natur.

Le parterre couvre le terrain comme une gigantesque toile qui aurait été déroulée. Le fait de se limiter aux plantes indigènes, qui poussent aussi dans le bush voisin et ne nécessitent pas d'eau, crée une extraordinaire sensation d'harmonie avec la nature.

Como un gigantesco lienzo extendido sobre el suelo, el parterre cubre el terreno. Al haberse limitado a plantas autóctonas, que crecen igualmente de forma silvestre en la floresta contiguo y no requieren de riego, se genera una sensación extraordinaria de unidad y armonía con la naturaleza.

Il parterre attraversa il terreno come un enorme schermo dispiegato sul pavimento. Grazie alla limitazione a piante locali, che crescono anche nel terreno cespuglioso limitrofo e che non necessitano di annaffiamento, si crea una sensazione straordinaria di accordo e armonia con la natura.

Garangula Garden

New South Wales, Australia

The owner of this typical farmstead from the 19th century let the garden designer have a free hand. As a result, the vast property was divided into a number of spaces so that the swimming pool, tennis court and terraces each have their own areas. But the garden is far from being designed with a compass alone. Instead, it comprises a series of visual metaphors that beholders can connect with each other any way they want.

Die Eigentümer dieses typischen Gehöfts aus dem 19. Jahrhundert ließen dem Gartengestalter freie Hand. Daraufhin wurde das weitläufige Gelände in mehrere Räume unterteilt, sodass Swimming Pool, Tennisplatz und Terrassen ihre jeweils eigenen Bereiche haben. Aber der Garten ist weit davon entfernt, mit dem Zirkel entworfen zu sein. Eher findet man hier eine Reihe visueller Metaphern, die vom Betrachter wahlweise in Zusammenhang gesetzt werden.

Le propriétaire de cette ferme typique du XIXème siècle a laissé le champ libre au paysagiste. Ainsi, la propriété a été divisée en de nombreuses zones pour que la piscine, le court de tennis et les terrasses aient chacun leur espace propre. Mais le jardin est loin d'être dessiné à l'équerre. Il propose plutôt une série de métaphores visuelles que l'observateur peut choisir de relier entre elles.

Los propietarios de esta quinta del siglo XIX le dieron carta blanca al paisajista. Acto seguido, el amplio terreno se dividió en varios espacios, para que la piscina, la pista de tenis y las terrazas dispusieran de sus propias áreas. Sin embargo, el diseño del jardín no sigue precisamente las líneas ortodoxas. Lo que aquí se puede encontrar es más bien una serie de metáforas visuales que el observador podrá interrelacionar a discreción.

I proprietari di questa tipica fattoria del XIX secolo hanno lasciato mano libera all'ideatore del giardino. L'ampio terreno è stato suddiviso in più spazi, in modo che la piscina, il campo da tennis e le terrazze potessero ognuna avere il proprio ambiente. Ma il giardino è tutt'altro che disegnato con il compasso. Piuttosto, è possibile trovarvi una serie di metafore visuali che vengono messe in relazione in base alla scelta di chi osserva.

The astonishing spatial diversity reveals itself step by step.

Die erstaunliche Raumvielfalt erschließt sich Schritt für Schritt.

L'étonnante diversité spatiale se dévoile pas à pas.

La sorprendente diversidad de espacios se descubre paso a paso.

L'impressionante molteplicità viene rivelata passo dopo passo.

Eye-catchers at the swimming pool are the fog tower that can also be illuminated to heighten the atmosphere, as well as the water opening connecting it with the pool. Right next to it, the thick hedge reveals the beginning of a path.

Hingucker am Schwimmbad sind der Nebelturm, der zur Steigerung der Atmosphäre auch noch beleuchtet werden kann, sowie die Wasserspalte, die ihn mit dem Becken verbindet. Gleich daneben blitzt ein Weganfang durch die dichte Hecke.

Les principaux attraits de la piscine sont la tour de brouillard qui peut aussi être illuminée pour plus d'atmosphère, ainsi que le ruisseau qui la relie à la piscine. Juste à côté, le début du chemin brille à travers l'épaisse haie.

Lo más destacado de la zona de la piscina es la torre de niebla que, para crear más atmósfera, puede iluminarse, al igual que la grieta de agua que la comunica con la piscina. Junto a ella, comienza un sendero que atraviesa un espeso seto.

Punti che attraggono l'attenzione sulla piscina sono la torre pluviale, che per aumentare l'atmosfera può anche essere illuminata, e la fenditura d'acqua che la collega con la piscina. Subito accanto si intravede l'inizio di una strada attraverso la fitta siepe.

Plants and paths *can really play with one's imagination, frequently surprising, yet forming a harmonized whole. The entire garden has a very playful, poetic flair.*

Pflanzen und Wege *schaffen magische Installationen, die häufig überraschen und dennoch ein abgestimmtes Ganzes bilden. Die gesamte Anlage hat ein sehr spielerisches, poetisches Flair.*

Les plantes et les sentiers *créent des installations magiques et souvent surprenantes, formant cependant un tout harmonieux. Le jardin dans son ensemble a un côté très ludique et poétique.*

Plantas y senderos *crean instalaciones mágicas que suelen sorprender, pero que simultáneamente consiguen conformar un todo unificado. Todo el jardín tiene cierto aire lúdico-poético.*

Le piante e le vie creano *degli insediamenti magici che spesso sorprendono e al contempo costituiscono un insieme armonioso. L'intero complesso ha una nota molto giocosa e poetica.*

Garangula Garden *New South Wales, Australia* 205

There are but few strict geometrical elements that raise the tension between man-made creations and the natural landscape behind them. Various art objects at selected places are prominently displayed in this garden.

Wenige strenge geometrische Elemente erhöhen die Spannung zwischen dem vom Menschen Geschaffenen und der dahinter sichtbaren natürlichen Landschaft. An ausgewählten Stellen kommen verschiedene Kunstobjekte in diesem Garten besonders zur Geltung.

Quelques éléments géométriques stricts font naître une tension entre ce que les hommes ont créé et le décor naturel. Des objets d'art variés s'affichent à leur avantage dans des lieux privilégiés de ce jardin.

Unos pocos elementos geométricos sobrios elevan la tensión entre los paisajes creados por el hombre y la naturaleza que se ve a sus espaldas. Emplazados en puntos muy concretos del parque, destacan sobremanera diversas obras de arte.

Alcuni elementi rigidi e geometrici aumentano la tensione tra quanto creato dall'uomo e il paesaggio naturale visibile sullo sfondo. In determinati punti di questo giardino vengono messi in risalto diversi oggetti d'arte.

Suifo-So
Ibaraki prefecture, Japan

The garden and guesthouse are inseparably connected with each other in this design, because one could not exist without the other. Their location on the shore of Lake Kasumigaura was decisive for the integration of water: Impressive ponds at various levels interact with each other. The slope of the area results in three large waterfalls. This dignified garden design is an outstanding example of traditional Japanese culture.

Bei diesem Entwurf sind Garten und Gästehaus untrennbar miteinander verbunden, der eine könnte nicht ohne das andere sein. Die Lage am Ufer des Kasumigaurasees war ausschlaggebend für die Integration von Wasser: Die beeindruckenden Teiche auf unterschiedlichen Niveaus interagieren miteinander und dank des Gefälles gibt es allein drei große Wasserfälle. Dieser würdevoll gestaltete Garten ist ein herausragendes Beispiel der traditionellen japanischen Kultur.

Le jardin et la maison d'hôtes sont reliés inséparablement dans ce design car l'un ne pourrait exister sans l'autre. L'emplacement sur la berge du Lac Kasumigaura a été décisif pour l'intégration de l'eau : des étangs impressionnants sur différents niveaux interagissent entre eux. Grâce à la pente, trois grandes cascades sont créées. Ce jardin plein de dignité est un exemple exceptionnel de culture traditionnelle japonaise.

Este diseño vincula de forma inseparable al jardín con la residencia: el uno no tiene sentido sin la otra. Su emplazamiento, a orillas del lago Kasumigaura, fue determinante para la integración del agua. Los impresionantes estanques a diferentes alturas interactúan unos con otros. La existencia de estos desniveles da lugar a tres cascadas. Este jardín de majestuosa concepción es un extraordinario ejemplo de la cultura tradicional japonesa.

In questo progetto il giardino e la casa per gli ospiti sono collegati inseparabilmente tra loro, l'uno non potrebbe esistere senza l'altra. La posizione sulla sponda del lago Kasumigaura è stata decisiva per l'integrazione dell'acqua: gli incantevoli laghetti sui diversi livelli interagiscono tra di loro e, grazie alle pendenze, vengono a formarsi tre grandi cascate. Questo giardino allestito in modo dignitoso è uno straordinario esempio della cultura tradizionale giapponese.

The garden is a paradox of gentle, dynamic beauty.

Der Garten ist ein Paradox sanft-dynamischer Schönheit.

Le jardin est un paradoxe de beauté à la fois douce et dynamique.

El jardín constituye una paradoja de belleza sutil y dinámica.

Il giardino è un gioco di contrasti dalla bellezza delicata e dinamica.

Every single room was designed to offer a view of a certain "garden scene". To create this effect, the position of the windows and the different levels have been coordinated on the inside and outside. The natural hues highlight this harmony.

Jeder einzelne Raum wurde so entwickelt, dass er Ausblick auf eine bestimmte „Gartenszene" bietet. Dazu wurden unter anderem die Lage der Fenster sowie die Höhenstufen innen und außen aufeinander abgestimmt. Die natürlichen Farbtöne unterstreichen diese Harmonie.

Chaque pièce a été pensée de manière à offrir une vue sur une « scène de jardin » particulière. Pour créer cet effet, la position des fenêtres et les différents niveaux ont été coordonnés à l'intérieur et à l'extérieur. Les tons naturels mettent en valeur cette harmonie.

Cada uno de sus rincones se creó de manera que ofreciera panorámicas a un determinado "cuadro del jardín". Para ello, se coordinó la disposición de las ventanas y la altura de los peldaños interiores y exteriores. Las tonalidades naturales subrayan esa armonía.

Ogni singolo spazio è stato sviluppato in modo da offrire la vista su una determinata "scena del giardino". Per questo sono state fatte concordare tra di loro la posizione delle finestre e dei diversi livelli all'interno e all'esterno. Le tonalità dei colori naturali sottolineano questa armonia.

Suifo-So *Ibaraki prefecture, Japan* 213

The focus is on water. *Sometimes it is still and projects the reflection of the water rings on the ceiling when the sun shines. In other places, it rushes through and over the stones and rocks so that its spray sprinkles the plants.*

Wasser steht im Mittelpunkt. *Manchmal ist es unbewegt und projiziert bei Sonnenschein die Reflexe der Wasserringe an die Zimmerdecke. An anderer Stelle rauscht es durch und über Steine und Felsen, sodass Gischt- tropfen die Pflanzen benetzen.*

L'accent est mis sur l'eau. *Parfois elle est tranquille et quand le soleil brille, elle projette la réflexion des ronds dans l'eau au plafond. Ailleurs, elle court à travers et au-dessus des pierres et des rochers pour que les embruns arrosent les plantes.*

El agua es el principal protagonista. *En ocasiones, cuando está inmóvil y recibe la luz del sol, proyecta los reflejos de sus anillos en los techos de las cámaras. En otros puntos, se bate de forma estruendosa entre rocas y piedras, rociando las plantas.*

L'acqua è l'elemento principale. *A volte è immobile e, quando c'è il sole, proietta i riflessi dei suoi anelli sul soffitto della stanza. In un altro punto, scroscia attraverso pietre e rocce, così che gli schizzi dell'acqua bagnano le piante.*

The visitor to the garden is drawn to the beauty of the four seasons, as well as Japanese esthetics. This place awakens sensitivity and directs attention to the little things that are so easily overlooked in everyday life.

Der Besucher kann sich hier der Schönheit der vier Jahreszeiten sowie der japanischen Ästhetik nicht entziehen. Dieser Ort weckt die Sensibilität, und lenkt die Aufmerksamkeit auf die kleinen Dinge des Lebens, die im Alltag so leicht verschüttet werden.

Le visiteur du jardin est attiré par la beauté des quatre saisons, ainsi que par l'esthétique japonaise. Cet endroit éveille les sens et dirige l'attention vers les petites choses qu'on néglige facilement dans la vie de tous les jours.

En este jardín, al visitante no le serán ajenas la belleza de las cuatro estaciones ni la estética japonesa. A uno se le despierta la sensibilidad y se presta más atención a las pequeñas cosas de la vida, que se relegan con tanta facilidad en el día a día.

Qui il visitatore non si può sottrarre alla bellezza delle quattro stagioni e dell'estetica giapponese. Questo luogo risveglia la sensibilità e sposta l'attenzione sulle piccole cose della vita, così facilmente travolte dalla quotidianità.

216 Suifo-So *Ibaraki prefecture, Japan*

Index

Tüssling

Tüssling Castle
Location: Tüssling, Germany
Web: www.schloss-tuessling.de
Garden location: Tüssling, Germany
Garden website: www.garten-schloss-tuessling.de

Munich

Villa Krantz
Garden designer: Rainer Schmidt Landscape Architects
Location: Munich, Germany
Web: www.rainerschmidt.com
Garden location: Munich, Germany

France

Saint-Père-sous-Vézelay

Val en Sel Manor & Gardens
Garden designer: Dominique Armengaud-Carrez
Location: Saint-Père-sous-Vézelay, Burgundy, France
Web: http://valensel.vezelay.free.fr
Garden location: Saint-Père-sous-Vézelay, Burgundy, France
Garden website: http://valensel.vezelay.free.fr

Epoisses

Epoisses Castle
Garden location: Epoisses, Burgundy, France
Garden website: www.epoisses.com

Jouques

Galerie des Baumes
Garden designer: Jacques Casalini
Location: Velaux, France
Web: www.createurjardin.ift.fr
Garden location: Jouques, Provence, France
Garden contact: www.galeriedesbaumes.fr

Provence

Villa near Carpentras
Garden designer: Anthony Paul MSGD
Location: Surrey, United Kingdom
Web: www.anthonypaullandscapedesign.com
Garden location: Provence, France

Italy

Cernobbio

Villa d'Este
Garden location: Cernobbio, Lake Como, Italy
Garden website: www.villadeste.it

Lake Maggiore

Polidora
Garden designer: Sarto family since 1900
Location: Lake Maggiore, Italy
Web: www.polidora.com
Garden location: Lake Maggiore, Italy
Garden website: www.polidora.com

Lake Maggiore

Villa Rusconi-Clerici
Garden location: Lake Maggiore, Italy
Garden website: www.villarusconiclerici.it

Lombardy

Vertical Garden
Garden designer: Patrizia Pozzi
Location: Milan, Italy
Web: www.patriziapozzi.it
Structual project: Lorenzo Cobianchi
Garden location: Lombardy, Italy

Lombardy

Landscape Park
Garden designer: Patrizia Pozzi
Location: Milan, Italy
Web: www.patriziapozzi.it
Scenography project: Mario Garbuglia
Garden location: Lombardy, Italy

Spain

Barcelona

House 2
Garden designer: Magda Sunyer
Location: Barcelona, Spain
Garden location: Barcelona, Spain

Morocco

Marrakech

Jardin Majorelle
Garden designer: initially by Jacques Majorelle (deceased), restored by Pierre Bergé and Yves Saint Laurent
Garden location: Marrakech, Morocco
Garden website: www.jardinmajorelle.com

Australia

Sydney

Rembel Garden
Garden designer: Andrew Pfeiffer
Location: Sydney, Australia
Web: www.andrewpfeiffer.net
Garden location: Sydney, Australia

New South Wales

Garangula Garden
Garden designer: Vladimir Sitta (Terragram)
Location: Surry Hills, Australia
Web: www.terragram.com.au
Garden location: New South Wales, Australia

Japan

Ibaraki prefecture

Suifo-So
Garden designer: Shunmyo Masuno
Location: Yokohama, Japan
Web: www.kenkhoji.jp/s
Garden location: Ibaraki prefecture, Japan

Photo Credits

Produced by fusion publishing gmbh, stuttgart . los angeles

Editorial team:

Haike Falkenberg (Editor & garden texts)

Andrew Pfeiffer (Introduction)

Hanna Martin, Anne-Kathrin Meier (Editorial coordination)

Katharina Feuer (Layout)

Alphagriese Fachübersetzungen, Düsseldorf (Translations)

Jan Hausberg, Martin Herterich (Imaging & prepress)

Dr. Suzanne Kirkbright, Artes Translations, UK (Copy editing)

Published by teNeues Publishing Group

teNeues Verlag GmbH + Co. KG
Am Selder 37, 47906 Kempen, Germany
Tel.: 0049-(0)2152-916-0, Fax: 0049-(0)2152-916-111
E-mail: books@teneues.de
Press department: arehn@teneues.de
Tel.: 0049-(0)2152-916-202

teNeues Publishing Company
16 West 22nd Street, New York, NY 10010, USA
Tel.: 001-212-627-9090, Fax: 001-212-627-9511

teNeues Publishing UK Ltd.
P.O. Box 402, West Byfleet, KT14 7ZF, Great Britain
Tel.: 0044-1932-403509, Fax: 0044-1932-403514

teNeues France S.A.R.L.
93, rue Bannier, 45000 Orléans, France
Tel.: 0033-2-38541071, Fax: 0033-2-38625340

www.teneues.com

© 2008 teNeues Verlag GmbH + Co. KG, Kempen

ISBN: 978-3-8327-9226-8

Printed in Italy